THE
ICEMAN

THE
ICEMAN

THE RISE AND FALL OF A CRIME LORD

JIM WILSON
AND
RUSSELL FINDLAY

BIRLINN

First published in 2008
by Birlinn Ltd
West Newington House
10 Newington Road
Edinburgh
EH9 1QJ

www.birlinn.co.uk

1 3 5 7 9 10 8 6 4 2   07 08 09 10 11

ISBN13: 978 1 84158 760 8
ISBN10: 1 84158 760 5

A CIP catalogue record for this book is available from
The British Library.

Typeset by AJT
Printed and bound by CPI Antony Rowe, Chippenham

CONTENTS

1
Opening Fire

Tony McGovern did not have time to turn off his headlights. The first shot shattered the driver's window of his black Audi. The dull percussive thuds of three more shots followed instantly. The gunfire brought his friends from inside the New Morven pub where they had been waiting for him. As they emerged, a white car reversed at speed away from the pub, a man was seen sprinting in the opposite direction and McGovern was slumped, dying, in his car.

He had already visited the pub earlier in the day, drinking sparingly – a beer, possibly two. He was known to just about everyone in the Morven although only a handful of drinkers would say hello, catching his eye fleetingly, giving small nods and mumbled acknowledgements. He had spent some time in the backshop, the office behind the bar, but soon returned out front to the gaggle of drinkers who were splitting their Saturday afternoon between the pub and the bookies.

McGovern stood at the side of the bar with his arms resting on the counter. Side-on to the main door, partially hidden by the jangling fruit machines, he spoke quietly to a few men, who approached him in turn. His words were only just loud enough to be heard above the growing clamour. When the others spoke, McGovern's gaze was directed down towards the floor but his eyes would flicker to and from the swing doors whenever they opened.

THE ICEMAN

The date was 16 September 2000 and it was cold enough outside for McGovern to be wearing a jacket. It helped to conceal the heavy bulk of a £400 Kevlar stab-proof vest that he wore beneath. He had not left his home without strapping on the body armour for weeks – not since June when someone had tried to shoot him dead one Friday afternoon while he showered at his bungalow in nearby Bishopbriggs.

McGovern, thirty-five, had learned to be a careful man but if he felt safe anywhere it was there, at that rough public house between Springburn and Balornock, north of the M8 motorway that bisects Glasgow. Sited like a fort on a hill at the top of Edgefauld Road, the white-painted pub stands in isolation off the main road. Four stone steps lead up on to the small concrete concourse and surrounding car park while closed-circuit TV cameras, encased in steel mesh, perch high on each of the building's corners. Tony had not voiced any particular fears that day and had no special plans for the night ahead. He left the bar after an hour or so, arranging to return to the Morven after 10 p.m. to meet some family, some friends, some associates.

His speeding £30,000 Audi A6 overtook another car on Syriam Street at 10.15 p.m. The driver remembered seeing the car as it headed towards the Morven half a mile away. McGovern phoned his wife Jackie on his mobile while driving. It was to be the last time she would speak to him. There were other men near the Morven making calls. Other arrangements were being made.

In Hornshill Street, cutting up from the busy Barmulloch Road towards the Morven, a white car was parked with a number of men inside it. As McGovern neared the pub, a white Vauxhall Astra was seen speeding down Boghead Road towards McGovern's Audi as he drew up in front of the pub at 10.20 p.m.

The Morven was busy enough but it should have been busier. For every drinker from the surrounding streets buying pints and shorts at the bar, another was spending time and money elsewhere. The New Morven was a McGovern pub. It might not have the names of Tony and his three brothers on the deeds or the licence but their business and reputation might as well have been posted on the glass-fronted noticeboard outside that plugged the acts brave enough to accept a booking. The McGoverns' business was selling class A drugs in the council estates and high-rises of north Glasgow. Their reputation was for savage, murderous violence.

McGovern was a regular visitor to the Morven, sometimes for pleasure, sometimes for business, more often a combination of the two. He had already collected his money from the men dealing drugs inside – heroin to the junkies, Ecstasy to the kids heading into town – and he'd checked his tick book, the scrawled record of outstanding debts, for drugs distributed or money lent. He parked his car in Littlehill Street, in front of the Morven, facing away from Edgefauld Road. If he'd faced the other way, he might have seen the car drawing in behind. He might have noticed the well-built man half-walking, half-jogging the twenty yards towards the black Audi. If he had seen his killer approaching, McGovern might have had a chance, an opportunity to flee or to fight. Instead, he was still seated in his car when the first bullet shattered the driver's window before three more were pumped into his groin.

His headlights were still glaring in the darkening gloom when his friends ran from the pub. A white car was seen reversing, engine screaming, out of Littlehill Street on to Edgefauld Road and away. A man was seen sprinting through the pub's small car park towards the council houses of Burnbrae Street before he disappeared into a garden, into the darkness.

The 999 call was made at 10.22 p.m. and, within minutes, an ambulance, blue lights flashing, drew up at the Morven. Emergency treatment was administered before McGovern was slid on to a stretcher and into the ambulance. The crew sped along Petershill Road, turning left on to the carriageway of Springburn Road to Glasgow's Royal Infirmary less than a mile and a half away. It was there that Tony McGovern was pronounced dead at 11.23 p.m.

At the scene of the shooting, uniformed officers were taping off the streets around the pub. Their colleagues took details from drinkers, from the residents of homes nearby and from taxi drivers ranked on the main road just yards away – details but no information. No one had seen or heard a thing.

In a few days' time, Detective Superintendent Jeanette Joyce, leading the murder inquiry, told reporters, 'At this time, we have no motive. There is no obvious reason why Mr McGovern was murdered.'

Few of her officers would agree as even those with only a passing knowledge of the bloody feud that was being played out in the northside of Scotland's biggest city already knew there was only one suspect for this most clinical of gangland hits. He was not always an enemy of McGovern. The two had once been best friends, best men at each other's weddings, partners in crime, allies in the venal drugs trade laying waste to lives and neighbourhoods in their home city.

His name was Jamie Stevenson and he was to become better known as The Iceman.

2
Busted at Dawn

It was still dark when officers started arriving at the squat police station in East Kilbride town centre and, by the time the briefing began, 150 officers had assembled. Only fifteen of them knew why.

The small group of officers from the Scottish Crime and Drug Enforcement Agency (SCDEA) understood that morning's work would signal the beginning of the end of an operation stretching back almost four years. The secret offensive against Scotland's biggest drugs trafficker had taken officers around the world and back again. It had involved months of uncomfortable, nerve-jangling surveillance – months of covert observation and secret recording of some of Scotland's most dangerous and ruthless men. It had already led to the seizure of twelve tonnes of drugs worth £61 million, nine convictions for drug trafficking and money laundering and disruption to the criminal operation streaming heroin, cocaine, speed and cannabis into the country's cities, towns and villages. As the sun came up on 20 September 2006, the police operation, code-named Folklore, was about to enter a final, decisive phase.

Twenty addresses were to be visited that Wednesday morning, in Lanarkshire, Glasgow, and Amsterdam. The Scottish task force were split, briefed and ready to move by 6.15 a.m. Some left by the back door into the station car park where the fleet of marked and unmarked cars and vans was waiting. Colleagues, drafted in from other stations, left by the front door where multicultural messages etched into the glass door panels spell out 'Welcome' in twenty-four different languages. There would be no similar greetings at their destinations.

The SCDEA's team, led by the elite agency's crime controller Detective Superintendent Stephen Ward, attended the briefing that detailed officers to each of the target addresses and revealed the identities of the six men and two women to be taken from the houses and flats scattered across the West of Scotland. There would be no surprises or omissions. The agency's surveillance teams – officers on the ground and the specialist teams of electronic eavesdroppers – had been watching and listening, plotting the location of every target.

But Ward did not follow any of the units rolling out of the car parks around the station, opposite the district court and council buildings. Instead, he returned to the agency's headquarters. There, in the control room of the nondescript red-brick Osprey House, hard against Glasgow Airport, he would follow the endgame of Folklore. His attention was focused most on two of the homes whose occupants were about to be abruptly woken.

Afterwards, Ward would tell reporters:

Today has seen us target several individuals. This type of operation, which involves painstaking intelligence gathering over many months, is the way forward as far as we are concerned. Organised crime is led by ruthless and dangerous individuals who seek to make profit from the pain and suffering of the most vulnerable people in our communities. The public rightly expect our response to this to be co-ordinated and robust.

Most of the police teams had headed out of East Kilbride but the vehicles of one of the tasked units drove south, in convoy, along the deserted carriageways of the new town, to one of the modern estates on its southern borders. Lindsayfield is popular with parents looking for a safe haven to raise their children. Good for schools, handy for a Morrisons superstore, it seems no different to the commuter town's other tidy, new-build estates. It was here, in the scheme where the streets bear the names of famous Scottish mountain ranges, that the police team headed, ghosting slowly over the road bumps deterring speeding drivers and passing the neatly trimmed lawns where kids' forgotten scooters lay in the dew. They pulled up just before entering the cul-de-sac of Campsie Road, out of sight of number 44.

Sleeping inside the double-garaged villa, backing on to fields and facing down the streets inspired by the Pentlands, the Cheviots, and the Cairngorms, were Gerry Carbin Jnr, twenty-six, his partner Karen Maxwell, thirty-one, and their two children, aged one and six. They had also been home one Saturday evening eight months earlier when, as detectives listened in, Carbin unwillingly took delivery of a holdall containing £204,000 of drugs money. The bag, unsuccessfully hidden first in a cupboard and then in a study, would provide the breakthrough the Folklore team had been working towards for four years.

Seven miles away, across East Kilbride and the green fields dividing it from Greater Glasgow, another team had arrived at their destination. It was an equally unlikely setting for the climactic raids of a landmark police investigation into international drugs trafficking and money laundering. Burnside, lying on the south-east rim of the city, is also popular with young families. Many are drawn to the tree-lined sandstone terraces on the edge of Rutherglen, just a few miles from the city centre.

Fishescoates Gardens is half-hidden in the heart of Burnside. A small development of modern flats, it lies in an L-shaped corner plot, just off the main road to East Kilbride.

A funeral home opposite the development's main entrance strikes the only jarring note. Signs warn that the well-kept communal gardens are private and that dogs are not welcome. The recycling bins are neatly lined up for collection. Strangers are noticed and not particularly welcome. A sign on the rear door of number 21 urges residents of the nine flats to make sure it is locked at night. The officers preparing to visit the couple living quietly in one of the flats on the second floor came through the front.

Armed response units were nearby. Thousands of hours of taped conversations, recorded by hidden bugs inside their homes, suggested the gang were not reckless or foolish enough to stash guns there but no chances could be taken that morning. The 150-strong force also included the so-called 'Angry Men', the Strathclyde officers trained and equipped for forced entries in the face of extreme hostility. Wearing protective clothing, visored and carrying mini-rams, the teams were ferried by van to each of the homes. The synchronised raids began at 6.40 a.m.

The doors were forced opened and stayed open as officers entered the homes, detained the suspects and mounted inch-by-inch searches. As cupboards were emptied, drawers rifled and carpets lifted, officers found almost £8,000 in Carbin's home, along with eight luxury watches. A further thirty-six high-value watches were found in the simultaneous raids, some valued at more than £30,000. Those searches already underway even before the suspects had been taken from their homes, would help secure their downfall. One officer involved in the arrest of Carbin and his partner in East Kilbride said:

> It was early. They were still half asleep but they knew who we were and why we were there. We had gone to Carbin's in January looking for a bag of cash and he had lost the plot, shouting and bawling. This time, he just kept it shut and got dressed.

In Burnside, Carbin's stepfather was equally subdued. Like the others, he was driven to the high-security police office in Govan on the southern banks of the Clyde and detained. He called himself a self-employed car valet and a sometimes jewellery trader. According to his tax forms, his business was slowly growing, earning him £38,083 in 2003 rising to £80,885 two years later. His returns to the Inland Revenue did not include the dirty millions raked in from his true occupation – being a career criminal commanding Scotland's biggest-ever drugs importation business.

By 8 a.m. on 20 September 2006 – six years and four days after the fatal shooting of his former best friend and gangland ally – Jamie Stevenson was behind bars. He had nothing to say.

3
Here's Jamie

'Get yourself tae fuck!' boomed the dark-haired youth at a nearby policeman.

The officer was perplexed since, up to that point, he had not even noticed the swaggering teen.

This was one police officer's introduction in 1982 to Jamie Stevenson, then a seventeen-year-old with a growing reputation as an aspiring man of violence in an area with no shortage of them.

The smarter criminals knew better than to fall out with the police, quickly grasping that there was truth in the half joke about Strathclyde Police being the biggest gang in the city – and one with a very long memory. But Stevenson, later a model of understated discretion at the sharp end of a global organised crime network, had yet to learn that it often paid to keep his mouth shut.

One Scots-Italian crook in his twenties was soon to make Stevenson's acquaintance in an even more memorable way. It happened while he was hanging around a Springburn petrol station which was a haunt for the street-level drug dealers just when Scotland's heroin epidemic was first taking hold. Stevenson's fast, brutal and efficient knife attack left scarlet splashes of his victim's blood on the diesel-stained forecourt. To most people, it was a cowardly and terrifying slashing but, according to gangland legend, this was the moment when Stevenson had 'arrived'.

At the time, the police were certain that this act of violence, deliberately performed in the view of a gaggle of small-time dealers and their desperate customers, was Stevenson's way of making it clear that he was not to be messed with. One veteran officer said:

> Parts of the west of Scotland are like the old Wild West. In the cowboy films, everyone wants to take on the fastest gunslinger and if you're the local hard man, in Govan, the Gorbals or Greenock, people want to have a pop.

In those early days, as the crime gangs bullied, stabbed and slashed their way around their streets, Stevenson's menacing confidence was just the kind of thing the gangsters ruling his area were looking for in new recruits. And the police say that, even at such a young age, he already had a reputation as being willing and able to use a knife to hold up shopkeepers on the orders of two older criminals. In fact, even back then, many recall how older, cooler criminals were needed to rein in the reckless bravado of Stevenson. One police officer said:

> Stevenson became an enforcer and a chib man but he wasn't very smart with the police as he had a big mouth. Clever criminals didn't stand there sneering at you and drawing attention to themselves for no reason. He got noticed by behaving like that and it wasn't clever because all it does is harm business.

James Stevenson, always known as Jamie, was born in 1965 to Emma and James Snr, a general labourer who was not around during his son's upbringing. By 1969, Emma and her toddler son were living with her new partner who she would later have a daughter with and marry in 1984. Stevenson's first home at 37 Monkland Street in the Townhead area of Glasgow has long gone. In fact, not only is the family's tenement flat away, the entire street has been wiped off the map, long buried underneath developer's concrete.

Most of Stevenson's childhood was spent in the Red Road high flats in the Barmulloch area in north Glasgow. His Petershill Drive tower-block home was built in 1969. Futuristic looking for its time, it was amongst the tallest buildings in the city. To a child in the late 60s, these new concrete monoliths would have been every bit as exciting as the Empire State Building in Manhattan.

He wasn't exactly a model pupil at All Saints Secondary School – a school which hit the headlines in 2004 when an eleven-year-old refugee boy from East Africa died after a scuffle in the canteen.

Another ex-detective remembers arresting fifteen-year-old Stevenson following one of his first brushes with the law. He said:

> In those days, Stevenson was just a skinny wee boy who lived for a spell near Maxwell Road in Pollokshields in the southside of Glasgow. He broke into a car and was spotted by a security guard who was ex-military. We arrested him and he appeared in court for that. I suspect that it does not appear on his record because a lot of the old paper records were routinely binned when the system became computerised. In future years I knew him as part of a serious criminal gang with a rising reputation. I was amazed that it was the same boy.

The petrol station slashing earned Stevenson a place in a Springburn gang led by the feared McGovern brothers. One of them, Anthony, had followed Stevenson's arrival into the world eleven days later, at the same maternity ward, at Robroyston Hospital. By the time Jamie and Tony were teenagers, they were already as close as brothers and would remain inseparable for years to come. Only death would divide them.

4

Chips Off the Block

On light summer evenings, the queue of customers would snake out the door of Santi's fish-and-chip shop in Springburn Way. Much of the business was local but the lure of Santi's suppers was enough to draw passing trade from the type of people who would not normally have cause to stop in Springburn. These hungry middle classes would head back to comfortable homes in the more affluent suburb of Bishopbriggs via the A803 dual carriageway – an ugly scar cutting through the centre of Springburn. They would warily sidestep the youths who clearly regarded the patch of pavement outside Santi's as belonging to them.

It was 1980, long before the shell suit and baseball cap became the uniform of the Glasgow schemes, these teens were wearing the latest skin-tight stonewashed jeans and jackets and colourful Kickers on their feet. The sharp-faced, streetwise kids would stand outside Santi's sharing cigarettes, joking with each other and making their presence felt as they eyeballed the well-to-do outsiders waiting in line for their chips.

Amongst this gang of around twenty boys and girls were the teenage McGovern brothers who had already gained notoriety, not least because previous generations of their family had also been steeped in crime. Their parents Joe Snr, a taxi driver, and Elizabeth Mitchell, a sewing machinist, tied the knot at St Aloysius Church in October 1962. Their

Catholic wedding was perhaps prompted by the arrival five months later of their first son Joe Jnr.

In 1980, their eldest boy was seventeen and already an unmarried dad to a son also called Joe. His brothers were Tony, fifteen, Tommy, thirteen, James, nine, and Paul, seven. At this time, the family, including sixteen-year-old sister Jackie, lived in a cramped council flat at 42 Blackthorn Street in Springburn, in the north-east of the city.

Springburn in the nineteenth century had been an industrial powerhouse where thousands of men and four great works – Cowlairs, St Rollox, Hyde Park and Atlas – produced most of the steam engines, carriages and wagons that connected Britain with her global empire. By the 1970s, that industrial past was a ghost and much of the area had sunk into a pit of crime, grime, despair and violence although many good people were proud to call Springburn home.

The area's most famous face is Michael Martin who in 2000 became the first Roman Catholic Speaker of the House of Commons having been the local MP since 1979. His nickname of 'Gorbals Mick' reveals only the geographical ignorance of the sneering London commentators who coined it since he has no connection to that part of Glasgow. The pomp, ceremony and grandeur of the Houses of Parliament must seem like a different planet compared to the streets where the people who vote for him live.

Today much of Glasgow is booming and the city has enjoyed a cultural renaissance and ongoing improvements. But, no matter how much cash is spent, pockets of inner city deprivation stubbornly remain – some of them amongst the worst in Britain. A National Health Service study in 2004 revealed the extent of Springburn's appalling health problems. On average, men could expect to live to sixty-six-and-a-half years against a UK average of seventy-seven. In the whole of the UK, Springburn was only beaten by Glasgow's Shettleston area which had an average male life expectancy of sixty-three – the same as India and Iraq. Taking third place in this unenviable league table was neighbouring Maryhill. This report prompted eminent public health expert Professor Ken Judge of the University of Glasgow to remark, 'There are parts of Glasgow that should be thought of as Third World communities.'

Two years earlier, another study, this time by the Child Poverty Action Group, also exposed the neighbourhood's despair. Measuring life expectancy, unemployment, income levels and illiteracy, it found the same three parts of Glasgow – Shettleston, Springburn and Maryhill – to be the three most deprived areas in Britain. Poor diet, smoking, excess alcohol, lack of exercise, poor housing and amenities, not to mention drugs and violence, still shape much of modern Glasgow.

It is little surprise that the ruthlessness, greed and casual violence required for the life of a drug dealer should be nurtured in places like these. The McGoverns' extended family was scattered around the same area but, when people quietly spoke in tones of respect, fear or hatred about the 'McGovern family', they now usually meant Joe, Tommy, Tony, James and Paul.

One former neighbour remembers Tony as being a bright boy who, even in his schooldays, had an eye for making money. He said:

> He obviously became heavily involved in drugs but, like a lot of these guys, he was great on a personal level – he could be kind to his pals. When he was a kid, he had a go-cart and would charge other boys ten pence to have a shot on it.

Such fond childhood moments may not have been typical for this family but even those who knew of the McGoverns' reputation back then would have been unlikely to predict the sheer scale of violence that would cling to the family, their friends and their enemies in later years. As the late 1980s and 1990s exploded into a perpetual chain of shootings, slashings, beatings and fire attacks, those teenage days of bragging and joking outside Santi's must have seemed like a more innocent age.

It was outside the popular chip shop that the McGovern boys first discovered that crime did pay. They also realised that, in a city where it is estimated that one in three adults receive state benefits, they would never join the respectable ranks of the commuting chip shop customers. These middle-aged customers were not the most street-smart and the McGovern boys were adept at clocking a wallet carelessly poking out of a back pocket. The kids would take it in turn to try to remove the wallet by stealth and, even if their victims caught them in the act, they would rarely be quick enough to do much about it. Once safely in the back lanes of nearby tenements, the thief would count the spoils which would be used to pay for that night's carry-out of cheap cider, vodka and 64p packs of cigarettes.

For one police officer, who was to have many encounters with the McGoverns throughout his career, the radio call to attend a pickpocketing outside Santi's soon became routine. As usual, when he and his colleague pulled up to deal with the irate victim, all potential witnesses claimed to have seen nothing. Anyone in Springburn who was seen to be helping the police would land themselves with the potentially dangerous tag of 'grass'.

The police knew that their light-fingered suspects would almost always include the young McGovern boys but there was rarely anything they could do about it and, from an early age, the McGovern boys enjoyed getting away with it.

5
Blackthorn Street to Amsterdam

Police officers sometimes claim that those who are born into the McGovern family learn to steal before they can speak. But that dig does not do justice to the sheer scale of the family's long-running love affair with shoplifting, pickpocketing, till dipping, distraction thefts and however many other ways there are to say the word 'stealing'.

One retail crime expert said, 'It's almost like a mental illness or genetic fault where they just cannot help themselves. Even with thousands of pounds in their pockets, they would still instinctively want to take a Mars Bar without paying.'

To the present day, the brothers' cousin Jean McGovern – born between Tommy and Tony – along with her partner-in-crime Annette Daniel, from an equally notorious Glasgow crime family, ran the most professional team of shoplifters in Scotland. Despairing defence lawyers would look sheriffs in the eye and offer mumbled pleas in mitigation that it is just the way they are made as they try to talk their clients out of a stint inside Cornton Vale Prison.

The McGovern and Daniel teams routinely get away with helping themselves to entire rails of expensive garments from some of the finest designer stores in Glasgow's Buchanan Street, Edinburgh's Princes Street and London's Oxford Street. In seconds, thousands of pounds' worth of stock from Birmingham to Braehead and Dundee to Darlington can disappear only to be later eagerly snapped up for half-price around the pubs and bingo halls of Glasgow or more anonymously disposed of on eBay.

Long before these brazen shopping molls became the scourge of security guards and retailers the length and breadth of the land, it was the boys who were making piles of cash – simply by taking it out of shop tills. Nabbing wallets from outside a local chippy was one thing but their daring till-dipping trips were soon to attract the attention of the now defunct Scottish Crime Squad and even Interpol. The McGoverns were about to enter the big league.

One police officer said:

> They started out by going round big stores in Scotland like Marks & Spencer and staging what appeared to be a real fight between a couple of kids who had been brought along for the purpose. When the woman leapt out from behind the till to try and stop the boys from killing each other, one of the gang would calmly lean over and clean out the till. The McGoverns made this scam their own. They then started to get their hands on till keys. It was usually the case that the same keys fitted every till in every store in a UK-wide chain. It was a free for all.
>
> The boys were dabbling in drug dealing at this point as well and the money from the stealing helped to finance their first bulk purchases. Such was the scale of their till dipping that they soon became known to police forces across Scotland. That led to the former Scottish Crime Squad taking an interest and, as the heat increased on them here, they would travel into England but that was even more serious as it was cross-border crime. Before long they were travelling to Europe and hitting places like Amsterdam, Paris and Brussels.

These brash young men with their pockets stuffed with cash were well suited to the late 1980s environment of yuppies and excess in which they operated. It was coming to the end of Margaret Thatcher's era and, at the time, the biggest comedy character was Harry Enfield's yobbish Loadsamoney who taunted people with his own wad of banknotes.

An ex-police officer said:

The problem was that we were always a step behind them. I remember being part of a Scottish Crime Squad team that followed them by car to the ferry at Hull. As they got on the ferry, they had a right laugh by waving at us as we stood watching, unable to do anything.

They often used Hull but were smart enough to use various English ports. They would drive south and hit stores in all the big English cities along the way – you could follow their progress from the trail of crime reports.

Sometimes they would use a stolen car to travel. There was no shortage of people in Springburn willing to sell them their driving licence for as little as £30. That way, they could just dump the car which had been hired in the other person's name at Amsterdam's Schiphol Airport and fly back to Glasgow. The sergeant at Glasgow Airport was told to look out for them and he must have pulled them a hundred times. This was before the Euro was introduced in 2002 so they would have piles of different European currencies like Dutch guilders or French francs. It was also before the Proceeds of Crime Act came along so there was nothing they could do about all this cash even though it was obviously stolen.

One former McGovern family ally said:

They always worked in teams of four in a car and Tony was the boss. He made sure the best boys came with him and, if they weren't up to scratch, they would be put on the sidelines for a spell.

They had a rule that they would not return home until they each had £5,000 in their pockets. They could turn over up to £30,000 from a trip to Europe which, even today, is a staggering amount of money. They had passports planked over there in case they had to flee in a hurry.

They would put on different accents, such as Irish, French or English, to confuse any witnesses who would have no idea they were actually Scottish. If they got cornered by a store guard, there was always one of them able to knock him out as they were capable and fit. On some occasions, they even wore disguises like fake moustaches or beards and would put on hats and coats that old men would wear. They might have looked odd but it served their purpose well.

It was clever and well executed and they continued doing it long after they started dealing in drugs at a serious level. They would come back from these trips like some kind of Elizabethan explorers decked out in top-quality designer clothes that we had never seen before. They also had booze and piles of cash. In fact, the money from these robberies helped them buy their way into the higher level of dealing.

Another former police officer, who had previously arrested Stevenson in south Glasgow over the car break-in, despaired at the lack of police reaction to this well-planned criminality at a time when the force did not even acknowledge the existence of 'organised crime'. He said:

Stevenson was involved with the McGovern teams at that time and I was surprised because I had last dealt with him over the car incident a couple of years earlier and this was a different ball game.

The problem was that we had masses of intelligence on the overseas operations – who they were, their methods and a very accurate level of how much money they were making which was at least £500,000 a year. But the senior officers didn't act. They didn't know what to do about it because they had never come across it before. Whether someone is making half a million quid from drugs or any other type of crime, we should have still pursued them. It was ignored and the chance was missed.

In the mid 80s, on one trip, Tony and two of his team escaped alive from a car crash in central Europe when the driver died after falling asleep at the wheel and hitting a tree. A former Strathclyde Police intelligence officer said:

The driver was a McGovern associate and he had £6,000 in his pocket despite being unemployed.

The problem got so bad that we put together a book of mugshots and details on all the travelling thieves which was circulated across Scotland. The sheer numbers that originated from north-east Glasgow, in particular Springburn and Possilpark, were unbelievable. Before long, the UK police forces all had a copy of the booklet and then Interpol distributed it around Europe.

Every other week, we took calls from police officers in Europe asking us to look at CCTV of suspected Scottish store thieves. We knew it was going to be the McGovern gang before we even looked at it.

One thing such trips did was to expand the criminal horizons of the McGovern boys and take them to places such as Amsterdam which, as one of Europe's illegal drug industry hubs, would later become crucial in their operation.

But the hard-bitten Glasgow CID men who tried to keep a lid on the gangs of youths in places like Springburn and Possilpark, known as Possil, were not impressed by this upstart gang of cocky, cash-rich criminals. A handful of these officers were also the type who did not always follow the rules when it came to dealing with crooks who revelled in getting away with it.

In 1985, one officer arrested Tony over a minor outstanding warrant and he was taken to the city's Baird Street police station. The former detective said:

> He was brought in all cocky so I decided to make up some fake tenner bags of heroin with magazine paper and cling film. They looked just like the real thing. I walked into the interview room and threw the wraps down in front of him and told him he was getting done for them. He was still in his late teens at this point and he just burst into tears. There was a real battle going on at that point because they thought they could do what they wanted. They also thought that a few of us would do anything to jail them so, when I did that, his arse collapsed.

This unofficial but systematic CID campaign of hounding family members as they swaggered between their Springburn pubs, controlled drug dealing and enjoyed their European spoils did not have the desired effect. The officer said:

> We were stopping them at every opportunity which began to really disrupt the smooth running of their drugs business. Then one day this delegation of around half a dozen members of the McGovern family, men and women, trooped in to complain about what they described as harassment by two particular cops.
>
> We couldn't believe it when one of the officers was put back to uniform and the other was stuck away in the warrants office. The troops felt that the bosses should have commended them for making life hard for the McGoverns.

If your kids were growing up in a Springburn awash with McGovern smack, you'd want the police to be harassing them. But the bosses didn't have the backbone to tell them where to go and the easiest answer was just to cave in.

These recriminations within the ranks were a major coup for the crime clan. Yet again, the McGoverns were getting away with it.

6
Taste for Drugs

The young Scot in the red-and-white football scarf was not the only Liverpool fan heading to Merseyside for the big game. There had even been a few exiled Scousers on the 10 a.m. train from Glasgow Central and, two hours later, hundreds of fans were on the platform at Preston, waiting for a lunchtime connection to Liverpool Lime Street. Jamie Stevenson, who could not have named many of the Anfield team, blended in perfectly.

One associate remembers:

It would have been 1985 or so and the McGoverns had started into the drugs business. They had suppliers in Glasgow but were also dealing with the Liverpool gangs. They were not taking huge amounts from Merseyside so it could easily fit into a wee rucksack or even a jacket pocket. They'd send a courier down to collect the stuff and bring it up the road. It was often Stevenson. He was a pal of Tony's at that stage but still way down the pecking order in terms of hierarchy. He was more or less a gofer for the brothers – a tea boy.

Whenever a delivery coincided with a Liverpool game, he would time his trip to mix in with all the fans coming and going on the trains. He'd wear the scarf and everything. I think he enjoyed the pantomime.

Of course what the McGoverns didn't realise was that he

was down there meeting the boys in Liverpool and making contacts of his own. The McGoverns thought they were sending the boy down for the messages but all the time he was seeing how the business worked. He learned a lot and, when the time came to go on his own, it showed.

Liverpool was one supply route for the McGovern gang as they realised the profit from drugs could easily outstrip the fortunes they were raking in from their European robbery sprees. But another supplier was far closer to home.

There are many stories about Arthur Thompson – and just as many drink-soaked bores and gangland apologists to tell them. He was the Godfather, the courteous old-school criminal who dominated Glasgow's underworld for decades. He never spoke to the police. He never hurt civilians. And he would never touch drugs.

If his legend seems to grow each year since his death in 1993, the reality remains unspoken. He was one major criminal among many in the city. He was a hugely violent man who was capable of inflicting terrible pain, injuries and death both on his own and by order. Many innocents were harmed by his awful business. And he *did* deal drugs. The malignant Godfather was one of the first suppliers of heroin to the Springburn brothers who were wanting to secure a toehold in the trade.

The start of the 1980s witnessed a rapidly changing criminal landscape. Old bank robbers and burglars were the equivalent of office workers with forty years' service. They had become yesterday's men. They either adapted to the new drugs scene or became redundant.

At this time, heroin was seeping into the schemes of Scotland. The authorities were far from prepared as the first ripples of what would become a tidal wave of the drug crashed on to Scotland's cities. In Edinburgh, for example, an official clampdown on the distribution of hypodermic needles was meant to reduce addiction but only helped fuel the spread of HIV and AIDS. The gangsters did not exhibit the paralysis and confusion shown by the authorities. Switched-on mobs like the McGoverns were perfectly placed to stake an early claim on this highly profitable yet poisonous action.

One Thompson family associate recalls how, in the mid 80s, 'the McGovern boys were taking six ounces of smack each week. That soon went up to nine ounces. Gangsters like Tam Bagan and Paul Ferris were working for Thompson at the time and they were aware of the McGoverns' rising reputation.'

Today, an ounce of heroin costing £1,000 will produce 160 'tenner bags' – a pea-sized cellophane wrap of brown powder sold as a £10 deal, which is enough for one hit. Once that ounce has been cut with whatever substance comes to hand, a door or street dealer will easily be able to make up 300 tenner bags. That means £3,000 will be recouped for their initial £1,000 outlay. In the 1980s, the profits were even greater because there were fewer competing dealers.

With the McGoverns' ongoing overseas robbing trips bringing back up to £30,000 each time, bags of heroin were a logical investment choice for criminals. Putting the cash into property, shares or tax-free savings accounts would not land you in prison but it would also never yield instant profits of 200 per cent. Heroin has since plummeted in price due to a glut on the market meaning there were even fatter profits then than today.

At this time, the McGoverns' HQ was Thomson's bar which was strategically placed in the middle of their Springburn heartland. It was a comfortable pub and not typical of the more unwelcoming gangland howffs scattered around the city. One former regular said:

Ordinary people drank there because it was well run and they had a football and dominoes team. It was more like the Queen Vic in *EastEnders* than somewhere like old Arthur Thompson's Provanmill Inn where strangers dared not enter. Of course, there was rarely any trouble because everyone knew that it was a McGovern pub.

However, one teenage peddler of stolen goods around pubs in those days has mixed feelings about the place. He said:

You would always make money in Thomson's because, no matter what time you went in, the place was busy. It was a guaranteed pub for a few quid but one time I had this £5 watch and a guy from Thomson's put it on and said he was keeping it. When I said he could keep it only if he paid me, he reached inside his jacket as if he had a blade. I had to back off.

Those early heroin deals were mainly conducted by twenty-one-year-old Tony and Tommy, then nineteen. In this drugs business, Tony was the MD while Tommy was his number two. Tony was the brains while Tommy was the brawn. Tony could charm while Tommy would growl. Others regarded the less visible eldest brother Joe as a more mature controlling influence, almost like the chairman of the board. Fourth son James was aged fifteen and just months away from being shot while the youngest, thirteen-year-old Paul would murder a man three years later. At this time, Tony and Stevenson, then one of the mob's key enforcers, were stuck together like glue and people often mistook them for cousins. It was clear that, when it came to business, Tony was the boss.

In the early 1990s, the McGovern mob of brothers Tony and Tommy along with Stevenson were a force to be reckoned with. Before the trendier glass-fronted private health clubs spread across the city, they used what was then called the Springburn Sports Centre to keep fit. The most successful gangsters usually possess a mental toughness but the Springburn gang understood that physical strength and fitness would give them an extra edge over potential rivals, who could be flabby in mind and body. Stevenson would maintain his enthusiasm for gruelling physical workouts throughout his career.

Often the police would pull up Tony in his red top-of-the-range four-wheel drive outside the municipal gym but they would rarely be able to pin anything on him. There was no chance that the police would ever be able to make him cry again. Even in years to come, when he led a tight team of armed robbers who struck at a series of banks, the charges often failed to stick.

Others in the McGovern gym squad at that time included the powerful figure of Willie Cross, who was around four years older than Tony. In 2007, Cross would be standing in the dock alongside Stevenson. This health-conscious enforcer had previously worked for an older generation of Glasgow gang boss, a security firm owner called Bobby Dempster, nicknamed The Devil, before choosing to join the McGoverns.

Also on the scene at the sports centre was Colin McKay who is just a few months younger than Tommy. Even his friends describe him as a 'psychopath' and, almost as an afterthought, a very talented football player. He was later accused of using his particularly large hands to strangle his friend Chris McGrory to death in September 1997 but walked free from that thanks to Scotland's controversial 'not proven' verdict. McGrory died just after he had returned from his honeymoon. When he got married, McKay had been his best man. In 2005, McKay was to be cleared of a second gangland slaying. This time the victim was twenty-five-year-old Richard Holmes who died after being shot on Halloween 2004 and children out guising witnessed the clinical murder. The gunman, McKay's co-accused, got eighteen years.

Later, McKay fell out with the McGoverns and did not seem too bothered by their growing reputation. He would deliberately swagger past the windows of Thomson's bar as an act of provocation. Those inside would race to the door but McKay would gesture with a hand reaching towards the inside of his jacket that he had a knife, causing the mob to slink back into the pub, shouting threats and insults behind them. Some fights were worth the hassle but this one was not.

Along with McKay, the other alleged McGrory killer was robber, dealer and dog fighter Frank McPhie, who, at the age of fifty-one, was himself killed in 2000 by a sniper's bullet, following a feud with the Daniel family. The audacious hit on McPhie at the entrance of his Maryhill flat remains unsolved.

Tony and Tommy's brother-in-law is Russell Stirton. People joked that it would take a brave man to go on a date with the McGovern sister, Jackie – can you imagine having those five brothers coming after you if you broke her heart? Enemies say that Stirton climbed up the greasy gangland pole thanks, in no small part, to his in-laws and the reputation of their name but he was also a capable operator.

He later began dealing in the hidden world of mail order boxes, flogging porn and sex aids, allegedly as an early way of trying to launder the profits of drug deals. It is equally possible that this tacky Love Boat business's presence in Amsterdam could have had as much to do with the availability of drugs as porn.

Many of the McGovern crew could be found at the leisure centre at a time when Stevenson really began to stick out. It seems that he still had not learned to keep his mouth shut. One person, who also attended the gym for several years, said:

Tony was the boss – he was the director of everything. Tommy was always nearby as was Stirton but Tony was the chief. Tony was a fit young man in those days and he was into general keep-fit while Jamie was more into pumping his muscles up. He was more interested in looking the part. He was quite sleekit and never made eye contact. He was a big, cocky, arrogant young guy with a real swagger and had the bad habit of being crude towards some of the women customers. He would say things like 'I would shag that!' in a loud voice, certainly loud enough for the girl to hear. He wasn't exactly Prince Charming.

Some days, Jamie would turn up and batter on the gym door if it wasn't open and try and intimidate the staff. Tony would then calm it down and most people would be fine with that but there were plenty of boys capable of taking on Stevenson at that time. In the gym, they didn't talk business but everyone knew they were full-time criminals. They were into drugs, armed robbery and the like and were usually to be found in Thomson's which is just seconds away.

If it came to a square go between Tony and Stevenson, my money would be on Tony because, despite being smaller, he was a real street fighter.

This was a few years before the 1996 release of the cult movie *Trainspotting*, a darkly comic look at a group of Edinburgh heroin addicts. The opening credits feature scenes of the film's anti-heroes Renton, Sick Boy, Spud, Tommy and Begbie waging a particularly dirty game of five-a-side football but even that was a friendly kick-about compared to the weekly battle that took place in Springburn.

Every week, while thousands of boys, youths and men across Scotland enjoy casual games of football with their pals and colleagues for a bit of exercise, the McGoverns played for money and hard men, like Tony and Tommy McGovern, Stevenson, McKay and Cross, would play dirty to win.

One bystander said:

This was like five-a-side fighting rather than football even though they were mostly decent players. They would kick lumps out of each other. To make it even more interesting they would play for money with the winning team pocketing £100. They would sometimes pay £50 to ex-professional players to appear as ringers which only made the game more fierce.

A member of another crime gang said:

They were making a hell of a lot of money but Stevenson was actually not their most dangerous member. They had one other guy doing their dirty work who had a slight lisp and had a much worse reputation for violence than Stevenson. All these types of guys do the damage on behalf of who they think are their pals and end up getting the jail for it. Very rarely do any of them realise they are getting a using to make other people money.

Sometimes old Arthur would need to send a couple of boys to remind Tommy to get his money paid by the end of the week so they were by no way the kingpins at that point. They knew their place in the pecking order.

But, by the early 90s, this cocky, fit and streetwise mob were effectively running their Springburn heartlands inspiring a taste for power as well as money. Their swaggering sense of command was such that they sometimes walked into the council-run gym without paying despite having pockets stuffed with cash. They did it because they could.

7
Takeover

By 1990, pumping dance music and glassy-eyed smiling faces were no longer limited to the rave generation as Ecstasy swept the mainstream nightclubs of Britain's cities. In Glasgow, clubbers aware of their identity would be disconcerted to see men known for violence – men like Stevenson and Tony McGovern – grinning like Cheshire cats and embracing while high on the little white Doves that, in those days, cost around £25 each. Nowadays a pill can cost £2, less than a packet of cigarettes, which only underlines how the large-scale importation of class A drugs has driven down prices on the streets.

The venue for much of the McGoverns' partying was a club that was to later burn down. Called Peggy Sue's, it was in West George Street in the centre of Glasgow, just along from Queen Street Station. The boys wore the best designer gear, they swigged bottles of trendy foreign lager or, if they wanted to show off, bottles of champagne would be casually summoned with the click of a finger, with one round often costing more than some people earned in a week.

They would rub shoulders with the footballers and pretty girls in the VIP section of venues like Peggy Sue's, Hollywood Studios and the *Tuxedo Princess*, a rusting former ferry docked in the shadow of the Kingston Bridge on the River Clyde that was the height of cool when it opened in 1988.

Tony and his crew would consider themselves a cut above and those wanting Ecstasy or a little bit of cocaine – then still a preserve of the rich – knew they would always be able to provide.

It went without saying that the McGovern crew would stroll past the nightclub queue and be ushered inside by bouncers who rarely showed the same respect towards the paying customers standing patiently in line. Not that such hedonistic evenings were completely without incident and nor did the wave of Ecstasy-induced happiness mean an end to the occasional slashing, beating or even murder.

One night in October 1989, a Peggy Sue's bouncer called Mick Kane, from Possil, died in an ambulance after being found in a pool of blood having been stabbed at the club. It was a twenty-seven-year-old McGovern associate who was to be arrested shortly afterwards and charged over the murder of the thirty-five-year-old doorman.

One associate said:

> The charges were eventually reduced to culpable homicide and the McGoverns liked to make out that they pulled strokes with people in authority to get it dropped from murder. The truth is that his lawyer got the deal based on the facts of what happened and not because of string-pulling by the McGoverns.
>
> At the time, he was actually unhappy because he felt the McGoverns had abandoned him. He ended up getting seven years jail.

One Strathclyde Police detective said:

> This type of claim is often made by organised crime gangs. To brag that they can pull strings with the police or the procurator fiscal may be rubbish but, by doing so, it simply adds an extra dimension to their perceived power.

In another Peggy Sue's flashpoint, the McGoverns scrapped in the street with a rival gang led by Ian 'Blink' McDonald. Associates put this feud down to an old argument over a firearm provided to the McGoverns by Arthur Thompson. The gun was handed over through Blink – reputedly nicknamed because he'd slash you in the blink of an eye – but a major fall-out ensued when the McGoverns, perhaps unwilling to relinquish the weapon, claimed to have lost it. One clubber recalls the battle well. He said:

> It was a mob of English boys led by Blink who was capable and had a reputation for slashing people, sometimes they would be near enough scalped. Him and his pals just steamed in which was a pretty bold thing to do given the McGoverns' reputation at that point. There was a construction site on the street and everyone was grabbing scaffolding poles or anything else that would make a weapon before the blue lights and the sirens put an end to it.
>
> Blink also owned The Talisman pub in Springburn around that time so I think there were ongoing issues about territory as well as personality.

Murders and pitched battles aside, these weekend sessions were a way for the McGovern crew to unwind, much like any other professionals. They regarded themselves as businessmen and anyone looking at their turnover and profit might understand why. While they were clubbing with the beautiful people, just a few miles north and east in the grey housing schemes, they were still earning as tenner bag after tenner bag of poor-quality, heavily cut heroin was injected into yet another arm, leg or groin. Every day or so, the papers would report another drugs death at a time when fatal overdoses were still rare enough to be newsworthy.

In the first half of the 1990s, the McGoverns spread out of Springburn, much like any successful small company expanding into new territories after taking over its home patch. A former detective said:

> At this point, they were putting all of their money into drugs. They were spreading from Springburn into areas like Roystonhill, Sighthill and Balornock and the Garngad. Their recruits in these areas were also well capable of violence. They would be the local faces and would become almost like agents or franchisees of McGovern Drugs Plc. Tommy had moved to Maryhill around then and made contacts with some of the older teams. They had piles of cash and what did cash buy them? Heroin. The profits in heroin at that time were huge.
>
> The McGoverns were gradually taking over the schemes and they realised that, once you did that, the money would start pouring in. They also realised that they were good places to operate in because the police found it so difficult to get information from them.

The platform that allowed the McGoverns to make the leap from bossing their own backyard to taking over the heroin trade in the surrounding housing schemes was built on the logistics of the drugs supply chain. Just as the countries that control oil and gas often wield disproportionate global power, so the McGoverns' new-found heroin supplies from the well-organised Liverpool-based smuggling gangs propelled them into the big league. From pinching wallets to dipping tills and dabbling in drugs, the boys had become serious and organised criminals. Life was to get altogether more serious.

8
Long Live the Kings

His lawyer Sir Nicholas Fairbairn once called him 'the coolest Godfather Glasgow has ever seen'. He was, according to the flamboyant QC who defended him on a number of occasions, 'smooth, silken, slow and deadly'. Fairbairn continued:

> He had eyes like a cod. He never blinked and he never stopped licking his lips. He had a very spine-chilling presence. Of all the gangsters I have met, he was the most frightening, the most threatening. He was also one of the most mannerly clients I have ever had.

The minister leading the hundreds of mourners at Arthur Thompson's funeral in March 1993 was slightly less fulsome than the flamboyant Queen's Counsel. Thompson, he told the congregation gathered in the chill wind and rain at the gangster's graveside, was a man to whom dignity and pride were important. His widow Rita – once herself jailed for stabbing another wife, from another gang – had to be held back as she tried to hurl herself towards the open lair. But, apart from her hysterical sorrow and the huge floral wreaths spelling out Arthur, Darling, Papa and Pal, there was little overt grief among those assembled. One who was there remembers:

> It was meant to be this old-school send-off for an old-school criminal – like the Krays and their black-plumed

horses and all that rubbish. His funeral might have been a bit bigger but it was really no different to any other gangster's – a lot of guys in cheap suits and scars. Most of them only turned up to make sure the old bastard was really dead.

The need for witnesses to Thompson's certain demise was understandable given the Godfather's charmed life up until that point. He had survived three known attempts to kill him only to die of cardiac failure, aged sixty-two, in bed around the corner from the cemetery where he was buried. He died at home, the infamous Ponderosa in Provanmill Road, where a row of terraced houses had been knocked through, extended and stone clad and seemed, like him, to belong to an earlier era. But that era was certainly not a more innocent time. The loan-sharking, robbing, gun-wielding Thompson was as vicious as any of the gangsters who followed him. And he knew about drugs, the business and its consequences. His daughter Margaret had died of an overdose in 1989, a death reputedly blamed on her drug-dealing boyfriend of the time, Gerry Carbin Snr. His own son, Arthur Jnr, was jailed for eight years for dealing and would be gunned down on weekend leave from prison in 1991.

The gangster's death may not, as his eulogists suggested, have marked the end of an era. But it coincided with a new age of criminality as a tidal wave of hard drugs broke over the schemes of Scotland and left thousands of shattered lives in its wake. The scale of the fortunes to be made as the heroin trade pushed into new markets would have been unimaginable even to Thompson. The gangsters who followed him did not even pay lip service to the old-school hokum of dignity, pride and honour among thieves. They were too busy making money.

By 1993, a decade or so since the drug had first appeared in the schemes of Glasgow, Aberdeen and Dundee, heroin use had spread alarmingly. Abuse and addiction were reaching new markets far from the inner city housing estates. Young clubbers, who would have never touched smack ten years before, were smoking the drug – 'chasing the dragon' to come down from Ecstasy and speed. No neighbourhood was a safe haven from it and no family was immune as heroin use soared. The problem persisted in Glasgow but Grampian was suddenly showing the highest official rate of addiction. Government statistics, published in 1997, suggested 57 per cent of drug users admitted taking heroin, compared to 45 per cent in 1995. It was in 1995 that Strathclyde Police confirmed a record 103 drug deaths, most related to heroin, with the annual death toll regularly reaching three figures throughout the decade. The banning of the notorious 'jellies' – the gel-filled capsule form of sedative Temazepam – in 1996 did not seem to slow the death rate.

A confidential Scottish Office memo admitted in 1997 that heroin was now the main drug of 49 per cent of users compared to 29 per cent just twelve months earlier. The hugely successful black-marketing campaign waged by the dealers was detailed in a Home Office report the following year. It said that while the perception of heroin users in the 1970s was of hippies pursuing an alternative lifestyle and in the 1980s of society's losers, by the 1990s dealers were deliberately targeting young people already taking softer, recreational drugs like cannabis and Ecstasy. It was no coincidence that these years saw the emergence of the 'tenner bag' of heroin, putting the drug on a par with the price of an Ecstasy tablet.

The Home Office researchers concluded:

> The message of course is that heroin is no more expensive and little different from other recreational illicit drugs. The heroin outbreaks spreading across Britain are primarily a product of purposeful supplying and marketing. The precursor to this has been the strong, sustained availability

of pure, inexpensive heroin primarily from south-west Asia.

There is little doubt that a second wave of new young heroin users is emerging. With 80 per cent of areas confidently identifying outbreaks within their communities and providing such a consistent picture and profile of new users, it is, unfortunately, reasonable to suggest that we are facing a second heroin epidemic.

In their Springburn stronghold, business had never been better for the McGovern family firm and its junior partner Jamie Stevenson.

9
High Life

All the pretty teenage barmaids were told to make an extra effort that night by dressing as sexily as possible for the grand opening of Cafe Cini in the town of Greenock, a half-hour drive from Glasgow. It was the summer of 1999 and the one-time shipbuilding hub was buzzing with activity. The sun was shining and the visiting Tall Ships Race gave the rundown town a sophisticated feel-good glow.

That summer saw the arrival in the town of Cini which was the last word in cutting-edge cool with a waterfall cascading down behind the bar and as good a sound system as any London nightclub. The fridges were full of perfectly chilled champagne and cocktails were on the menu. The original Cini was already established in Glasgow city centre and it was a favoured haunt of the Rangers and Celtic footballers with signed jerseys hanging from the walls. One such item was a white Chelsea shirt bearing the autograph of Italian footballer Gianfranco Zola with his hand-written message 'to all at Cafe Cini'. Years later, when the buzz of that opening night in Greenock had long faded, this shirt was one of many lots disposed of through a liquidation auction caused by the collapse of the pub chain. Many years later, in 2007, pub boss Jim Milligan was still trying to sell Glasgow's Renfield Street building that houses Cini.

In the 1990s, fast-talking Milligan was on the way up. He owned these two sleek style bars and other less glamorous pubs in Glasgow's Springburn area – Thomson's and the New Morven. At least that is the impression that was given by the paperwork for parent company Jimmy Nick's Properties Ltd which was lodged at Companies House. The people of Springburn knew that, no matter what such documents may have said, these were McGovern pubs.

In 1998, Thomson's, the family's pub-cum-HQ, was raided by police as part of a high-profile crackdown on the blatant peddling of drugs that the McGovern crew allowed to go on inside with impunity. The police action did not seem to hurt their business – neither the selling of drink nor their illegal trade in drugs.

Milligan's business partner was Charlie Nicholas, a former Celtic, Arsenal and Scotland striker whose love of the bright lights of London clubland had earned him the nickname Champagne Charlie. There is nothing, however, to suggest that Nicholas knew of his business partner's close relationship with the McGovern crime clan. He was known to take a back seat, allowing and trusting the more astute Milligan, who used to date one of Charlie's female relatives, to get on with running their business. Nicholas, now a Sky Sports football pundit famous for his often-mangled commentary, did not attend the VIP opening night in Greenock.

Cocaine had, by now, entered the mainstream and was no longer a rich man's drug. One Scottish celebrity's headline-making enthusiasm for the drug did more than most to reveal coke's ubiquity on the club scene. He was another ex-footballer of the Nicholas era, the former Celtic and West Ham striker Frank McAvennie. Later re-invented as a caricature of a ladies' man thanks to a comedy impersonation by Jonathan Watson, McAvennie famously described the cocaine found during a police search as 'a little bit of personal'. More seriously, Customs and Excise investigators seized £100,000 of McAvennie's cash in 1995 and a judge agreed that the money was going to be used to finance drug smuggling despite the ex-footballer's bizarre claim that the money was to fund a hunt for sunken treasure.

Milligan's plan was to introduce the glamour of the London nightclubs frequented by the likes of McAvennie to Greenock. One ex-worker said:

> All the best-looking young girls were hired and told to show off their legs and cleavages. This was to be the sexiest venue for miles around. The money that was spent at the new Cini was completely over the top. The waterfall alone cost an absolute fortune. Milligan was the boss and he would make frequent visits. Sometimes Charlie would be with him but not all the time.
>
> It was a strange decision to pick Greenock but Jim and Charlie had spoken publicly about their ambitious five-year plan to open twenty pubs around the country. They had even registered the name Planet Football for a chain of themed restaurants but that never took off.

Milligan's appreciation of a pretty pint-puller was revealed a decade later when it emerged that he was being chased for maintenance by a Cini barmaid who claimed he was the father of her child. The despairing mum even accused Milligan of trying to cheat responsibility by getting a pal to take the DNA paternity test.

On that late summer opening night in Greenock, Milligan welcomed the invited guests, most of whom had travelled west along the M8 from Glasgow. They included a young self-made business tycoon called David Moulsdale who had made his fortune through his nationwide chain of optician shops. Moulsdale, an entirely legitimate businessman, was a personal friend of the slightly older Tony McGovern who affectionately nicknamed him Noodles. In 2000, the *Sunday Times* Rich List estimated Moulsdale's personal fortune at £100 million. It was no surprise that so many women fell at the feet of this multimillionaire and his gangland boss friend – money and power are eternal aphrodisiacs. At one point, Moulsdale got engaged to the daughter of an assistant chief constable but the relationship ended soon afterwards and the wedding was never to take place. One of his many ex-girlfriends was to later marry drug dealer Justin McAlroy who was shot dead in front of his wife at the age of twenty-eight in 2002.

Staff at Cini in Greenock were gradually beginning to realise that their exciting new workplace was not all that it seemed to be. One manager, later sacked for wrongly thinking the management's stock of champagne was free, told workers in hushed tones that they should never speak about who owned Cini as secret microphones had been installed to monitor for disloyalty. This warning was either a wind-up or paranoia resulting from his enthusiasm for 'a little bit of personal'.

As the sweep of stretch limos drew up outside the bustling venue, it soon became apparent what type of guests Cini would be welcoming for the opening night when admittance was strictly by invitation only – bulky men looking awkward in £1,000 Hugo Boss suits, scar-faced guys in their twenties wearing the softest of leather jackets and bleached-blonde women with hardened faces, who were squeezed into slinky size tens and wearing Prada shoes.

One worker said:

It was like an Oscars' night entrance outside with all these guys and their girlfriends arriving as if they were Hollywood A-listers. But anyone could see them for what they really were – Glasgow gangsters with scars, tattoos and that constant look of being a split second away from turning violent. The men weren't much better.

Another outwardly respectable figure at the centre of the McGovern circles in the 1990s was a maverick criminal lawyer called James McIntyre who is now a television scriptwriter. Wearing a gold stud earring, he revelled in his abrasive courtroom style and enjoyed antagonising the stuffy legal establishment. Even while studying to become a lawyer, McIntyre found himself on the wrong side of the criminal fence. He would sneak into people's homes to steal their goods in order to help fund his student lifestyle and he has three convictions for housebreaking to his name from those days.

At an early stage in his legal career, McIntyre forged links with the McGoverns – some say this was through family connections. In 1993, he was stabbed in the leg and thigh at his office near to Glasgow Cross but he told the police that he could not tell them who had attacked him. In 1989, he was convicted of reckless driving while charges of attempting to murder a drugs squad officer at the same time were dropped. Every trainee lawyer knows the importance of maintaining a firm boundary between themselves and their clients but, for men like McIntyre, it seems that the glamorous lure of gangland was irresistible. There was money and excitement in abundance to be had acting as the on-call lawyer for one of the city's rising organised crime gangs.

He was not the first lawyer to get in too deep and nor would he be the last. In 2006, female solicitor Angela Baillie ended up in jail after ferrying drugs to an organised crime gang in Barlinnie prison.

McIntyre's own spectacular downfall was for guns not drugs and, when it came, those who knew how close he had got to the McGoverns were not surprised. However, he was not the gang's solicitor. He appeared at the High Court in Glasgow in late 1997 in front of Lord Marnoch after police, armed with Heckler & Koch sub-machine guns, had stormed

his home in the respectable small town of Linlithgow, West
Lothian, in August 1996.

They recovered a pair of .22 pistols – one loaded – along
with ammunition wrapped up in his pyjamas and stashed in
his underwear drawer. It is not what a lawyer usually means
when he says he is taking some work home with him.

Knowing that his career would be finished if convicted
of possessing the weapons, McIntyre pleaded not guilty. He
said a client had wanted him to hand them to police during
a firearms amnesty but the jury did not believe him and he
was sentenced to three years in prison and later struck off
from practising as a lawyer. The judge told him, 'You were,
at some stage, in possession of these items in various public
streets and, when the firearms were discovered, one of them
was found to be loaded.'

What the judge and jury did not hear in evidence or
from McIntyre were the details of who exactly he was looking
after the guns for. The McGovern family made it known that
McIntyre's loyalty in not mentioning them would be well
rewarded. The very least they could do was send a limo to
the gates of Edinburgh's Saughton Prison at the end of his
sentence.

One former friend said:

> McIntyre took the fall, did the time and not once did
> he turn on the family. He was eventually struck off from
> acting as a solicitor by the Law Society of Scotland and,
> if anyone's qualified to write TV crime scripts, he is. There
> can't be many people with such personal experience on all
> sides of the law.

These were the type of people who joined the McGovern
gang at play that night in Greenock. The family had millions
pouring in from heroin, cocaine, Ecstasy and cannabis. They
had pubs and clubs fronted by what they thought was the

trusted figure of Milligan. Recent figures released by the fledgling Serious Organised Crime Agency, described as Britain's FBI, estimate that proceeds of crime totalling £370 million go through Britain's licensed trade annually. At least £29-million worth of drugs money and other dirty cash is filtered through pubs and clubs across Scotland, mainly Glasgow. It is an industry that is greased with dirty money.

As the McGovern brothers mixed with footballers, businessmen and other people of high standing in society, they were confident that the police could never catch them. What could go wrong?

While Tony McGovern and Stevenson shared a bottle of Bollinger champagne that night in Greenock, they would have quietly toasted the dirty business on the streets of Springburn that had bought them this status and success. They had been through a lot together and, in the drugs business where loyalty was as fleeting as fashion, they trusted each other like brothers. Little did either of them know then that, the next time Stevenson would have cause to return to Cini in Greenock, he would not be stopping for a drink.

10
In the Blood

An ordinary fifteen-year-old, three years off the legal drinking age and with school the next day, would not have been sitting in a smoky Glasgow pub at 11 p.m. on a Sunday night. On 5 April 1987, in an age of just four TV channels and no internet, most kids that age would have been at home watching *The Russ Abbot Show* at 7.15 p.m. followed by Esther Rantzen's *That's Life!*. But young James McGovern was not an average schoolboy. As a member of the notorious crime family, no one paid much attention to the baby-faced youth drinking alongside his nineteen-year-old brother Tommy and twenty-year-old cousin Stephen McGovern in the corner of the now-demolished Vulcan Bar in Springburn Way.

Young James's presence may have been of no concern to the groups of men as they drained what was left of their pints and cheap house whisky chasers with one eye on the clock as drinking up time neared an end but, as the barmaid's piercing order to 'finish your drinks off' shook the old drunks into action, a youthful gunman strode soberly through the door. He knew exactly who he was looking for. As he hovered over the three McGovern boys, everyone froze. The spell was broken as his shotgun unleashed its deafening roar and ferocious spray of lead pellets.

The youngest person there took the worst of it. Screaming out, James collapsed on to the pub's grimy carpet with

47

blood pouring from horrific face wounds. His cousin Stephen was also caught by the blast while Tommy, the boss of the trio, escaped unscathed as glasses shattered, tables toppled and McGovern blood marked the walls. A third man aged thirty-four, with no connections to the family or what was behind this particular feud, also felt the shotgun's blast. His injuries were not serious.

The gunman, who had fired from point-blank range, fled before anyone could react. Within a few moments, the spring evening was filled with the wail of sirens. Most of the drinkers tried to escape into the night before the CID arrived to lock them in the pub and ask questions they had no intention of answering. Tommy didn't hang about either. Police would say that the rising hard man had lost his bottle and abandoned his stricken brother but it is perhaps more likely that he went to rally the people and the weapons that would be required for instant retaliation.

James and his cousin were taken to the nearby Royal Infirmary but medics there took one look at their injuries and sent them to the specialist Canniesburn Hospital for emergency plastic surgery. Stephen, from the 'poor relations' side of the family, was to die of a drugs overdose in later years. The surgeons did what they could to rebuild James's badly damaged face but, when he was eventually allowed home to the familiar surroundings of Blackthorn Street, he was scarred for life. From that moment on, James was nicknamed 'Elephant Man' although the cruel jibe was never made to his face. One associate said, 'He has a nasty scar which distorts one side of his face. For that to happen to a teenage boy must have been very hard to deal with.'

In the higher levels of Strathclyde Police, a decision was made to put a lot of time and effort into investigating who was behind the pub shooting. The motivation was partly as a way of finding out as much as they could about the increasingly powerful McGoverns. One officer said:

We decided to throw everything into the shooting enquiry because we wanted to get into the family and gather as much knowledge as we could. It turned out that the person who did it was in his late teens and unknown to the police yet he had got hold of a weapon and had done the business. He acted after Stephen had threatened or assaulted his brother over something to do with drugs. He intended to shoot Stephen but James got the worst of it.

This crime would have been remarkable had it been inflicted on almost any other family but, for the McGoverns, the shooting of James and Stephen was just one incident in a maelstrom of serious violence. Sometimes they are the victims but more usually the perpetrators.

In the lawless Balkan state of Albania, blood feuds are an ancient custom whereby families avenge previous murders with murder. This lawless approach causes a perpetual chain of violence. In parts of Glasgow, families like the McGoverns seem to have adopted the same tribal blood-feud mentality. One officer said:

If you want to get to the top and stay at the top of the Glasgow drugs trade you cannot afford to lose face. You must always come out on top. For many years, the McGoverns would attack anyone who crossed them or got in their way but often they were far too extreme in their reaction which bred a lot of hatred towards them.

The boy who did the Vulcan Bar shooting was charged but it never got to court as the McGoverns refused to co-operate. The intelligence at the time was that the gunman left the country shortly afterwards because it was certain the family would seek revenge.

Less than two years later, on 5 November 1989, James's younger brother Paul McGovern inflicted a frenzied fatal knife attack on popular and hard-working forty-seven-year-old school janitor Thomas Cushley. Thomas was heading to Santi's chip shop that afternoon when he was jostled outside Springburn Sports Centre by McGovern and two of his pals but it was more serious than that and Thomas shouted to passers-by that he had been stabbed. He then shouted at McGovern and punched him.

This punch caused sixteen-year-old McGovern to run back towards his victim and attack him with a knife. As unarmed Thomas lay stricken on the ground, McGovern knelt on him and slashed his face over and over again. Pathologists found eighteen stab wounds on his body, with the two fatal blows landing in his lower back. On Springburn Way, McGovern was quickly arrested for the murder.

What drove the feral sixteen-year-old McGovern boy to steal the life of this father of two has never been explained but what is certain is that the Cushley family's suffering was only just beginning.

The McGoverns simply did not get convicted and to this end, like many of the bullying Glasgow crime clans that terrorise their own neighbourhoods, they used witness intimidation as a first resort. One Cushley family member, recalling the lead-up the to the 1990 trial which, against all the odds, resulted in Paul being jailed for life for murder, said:

> During the trial, the McGovern family intimidated the witnesses and members of our family. Paul McGovern would even snigger and laugh at us when we walked past. He showed no remorse.
>
> There was one male witness who could hardly speak because they had got at him. One young mum with two kids identified Paul McGovern as did a couple of others. They were the crucial reason that justice was done for Thomas.
>
> After the trial, Thomas's widow Mary and their kids

Thomas and Carol had to move away from the area. It is repellent that ordinary people should have their husband and father murdered for no reason and then be forced to abandon their homes. People should remember that when they even think about making excuses for the McGoverns.

Woman jurors had wept after the guilty verdict against this baby-faced killer was delivered, their maternal sympathies unclouded by the facts.

A decade later in 2000, the Cushley family's pain returned when it was revealed that Paul McGovern had been freed from prison and was the owner of the security company that was guarding the construction site of the new Springburn Academy – the same school where Thomas used to collect his wages.

Glasgow City Council blamed the contractors for the indefensible decision to employ his company. The *Sunday Mail* had spent years unmasking the organised crime gangs behind the flourishing so-called security industry in Scotland. The firms were actually drug gangs with business cards and they were running glorified protection rackets. Construction firms were offered security and refusal meant that their sites would be mysteriously targeted by vandals and fire-raisers. Such attacks would eat into their profit so they had little choice but to grudgingly pay up. Some of the security firms were also fronts for money laundering.

Shortly after being released, Paul had formed M&M Security along with the other 'M' in the company name – George 'Geo' Madden who himself had been shot while drinking in the Spring Inn in 1996. Madden's shooting was in revenge for a pub fight but, after being told that major surgery would be required to remove the .22 rounds from his leg, he walked out of the hospital. His brother Charlie had been stabbed to death in 1985 not long after he had fathered

a son with shoplifting boss Jean McGovern, a cousin of Paul
and the brothers.

M&M courted further controversy when it was revealed
that North Glasgow Housing Association had hired the
security firm at least twice – once to patrol the streets like
some kind of pseudo police force.

In 1991, a police officer on routine patrol spotted a dark
blue Ford Transit van parked outside the Highland Fling pub.
Another known haunt of the McGoverns, it is located in an
isolated spot in Springburn. The officer parked up, stepped out
of his car and walked up to the driver's side window where a
man was doing his best to pretend he was invisible.

'What are you doing, Abie?' asked the officer.

Once the window was wound down, all Abie Monaghan
could do was shrug.

The officer told the one-time promising footballer, then
involved with his brother Terry in a Possil pub, to get out of
the van.

The officer recalls:

The van had a bench-style seat in the front and, when we
looked behind it, we recovered this very long, very sharp
and very lethal samurai sword.

Monaghan, desperately trying to talk his way out of a
tight spot, confided that he was there to kill 'that McGovern
bastard' but refused to say which one.

After some back-up had arrived, the officer strolled into
the pub where two McGoverns were in attendance – Tony
and Tommy. They gave the lone policeman a bit of cheek,
asking him if he wanted a pint and jeering him out of
the door. He left, still unsure as to which of the two had
escaped a potential beheading.

It was a close thing because Abie had links with
prominent Glasgow gangsters like Arthur Thompson and
Bobby Dempster. He was more than capable. He later said

he could have used a crossbow but that he took the sword because he wanted to see the whites of his victim's eyes as he chopped his head off.

Whether it was Tony or Tommy, they had a narrow escape but, at the time, they didn't even realise it. We later found out that he was working for a major criminal figure who had sent him to do it.

During the early 1990s, Tony McGovern and his by-now best pal Stevenson were running ice-cream vans out of Possil. This cash business was one of gangland Glasgow's first forms of money laundering but it had been tainted by the so-called 'Ice-Cream Wars' of a decade earlier. The battle between rival ice-cream van operators resulted in the 1984 murder of six people including an eighteen-month-old baby in a cowardly arson attack on a flat in Ruchazie.

Two men who had been convicted of the killings were later cleared after one of modern Scotland's most infamous miscarriages of justice. Not that the atrocity meant that ice-cream wars were over. In 1992, Tony McGovern was accused of stabbing a rival operator. However, the man failed to pick Tony out of a police identity parade. But it is unclear whether this was because the victim was genuinely unsure or because the McGovern intimidation tactics had been successfully deployed.

By the following year, Tony and Jackie, then his wife of just a year, had moved into a smart new-build home near to Hogganfield Loch around three miles east of Springburn. In the early hours of the morning, the fire brigade were called to their home after a petrol bomb was hurled through the living-room window as the couple slept upstairs. One policeman turned up at 5 a.m. to see Tony and brother-in-law Russell Stirton on the pavement at the front of the house. In his opinion, they seemed to be having a serious conversation and possibly plotting something.

One detective said, 'There was so much going on with the McGoverns at that point that I don't think we ever got to the bottom of the petrol bomb attack.'

In 1995, another McGovern brother was to be accused of murder. On 9 April, a forty-five-year-old taxi driver called Jimmy McHugh was shot three times at the entrance to the packed Ashfield Club in Possil. Karen Kennedy, the sobbing girlfriend of Celtic-supporting Jimmy, branded the killer a coward who had executed the wrong man. Jimmy's stepdaughter Michelle, then just sixteen, urged people with information to speak out while her mum refuted claims that the victim was a drugs war casualty. She said, 'Jimmy was a kind, caring man. There is no way he was involved in drugs.'

A teenage boy standing in a takeaway shop that Sunday night witnessed the gunman run from the scene and jump into a waiting getaway car. Before long, the street drums started beating a familiar rhythm – the hit was down to the McGoverns. It was suggested that Jimmy was shot dead simply because he had come off better the previous night in a pub fight with one of the family and this had wounded their pride. If so, it was an extreme way of saving face. Police appealed for information about a taxi driver who may have taken the gunman to the club after picking him up at the Spring Inn, another family haunt.

Tommy McGovern was eventually arrested for the murder and stood trial at the High Court in Glasgow where he was represented by Donald Findlay QC, one of the finest criminal defence lawyers of his generation.

One police officer recalls having to phone Findlay, then vice chairman of Rangers Football Club, as he was about to board a club flight to Romania for a European Champions League match against Steaua Bucharest. The detective told the lawyer that the police had information to suggest that the McGoverns were 'up to their necks' in serious and concerted attempts to locate and intimidate witnesses.

The prosecution eventually threw in the towel and the case against then twenty-eight-year-old Tommy was dropped due to lack of evidence. Jubilant Tommy had been identified as the gunman by one witness but another told the court that he had lied about seeing him at the scene. This witness, Raymond Bainbridge, then twenty-four, also revealed that his life and the lives of his family were in danger because of what he had seen. He had been got at.

It was also claimed that one potentially damaging witness was given cash to go on an exotic holiday but had actually spent the lot on heroin. Whatever the reason, he was a no-show at court.

By helping to secure Tommy's freedom through the intimidation of witnesses, the family's rule of fear had grown even stronger over a decade when their name had become a byword for extreme violence. From a tactical point of view, such behaviour also helped keep any predatory rivals from circling their territory.

One detective said:

> The one thing about the McGovern team is they didn't make idle threats. If someone crossed them, they just came down on them hard without any warning – unlike some crooks who sat around all day saying what they were going to do. Over those years, you would come into work in the morning and, every other day, there would be something that had happened that was to do with them, whether it was a beating, slashing, fire or shooting.

As the 1990s drew to a close, the dawn of a new millennium was greeted with worldwide optimism for a brighter more peaceful tomorrow. Few in Springburn could share that hope.

11

The McGovernment

If their entrance was intended to make a statement, then it worked. The venue was the home of Celtic Football Club in Glasgow's East End. The occasion was the unveiling of the club's new £17-million north stand. The guests were Newcastle United and their Toon Army. With rock star Rod Stewart opening the new section of the stadium and Celtic manager Tommy Burns fielding debut German midfielder Andreas Thom, there ought to have been no distractions for the tens of thousands of pairs of eyes. Yet one Celtic-supporting police officer remembers the pre-season occasion that was to end in a 1–1 draw for a very different reason.

Several minutes after this late summer afternoon game kicked off amid a burst of colour and deafening noise, a group of well-dressed young men slowly picked their way to their seats in the new stand. It was 5 August 1995 and Jamie Stevenson and the McGovern brothers had arrived.

The officer said:

> I was sitting in the crowd and, just after the game kicked off, this McGovern team led by Tony swaggered out of the executive lounge. Everyone looked as they made their way past the directors' box towards their expensive seats. They were like the Mafia. There is no doubt in my mind that this was intended as a statement. They were clearly saying, 'Look at us. We're here and we're number one.'

Had they sat down before kick-off like everyone else, no one would have noticed them but it was not just the timing, it was the way in which they carried themselves.

Tony and Tommy were there as was Stevenson and a handful of other key members. They were letting people know that they were the top men and there were several other well-known Glasgow villains watching this. They would have got the message.

In the second part of the 1990s, the McGoverns were to emerge as the number-one wholesalers of drugs in Scotland. Every small town would have a dealer who was aware through the underworld drums that hash, pills and almost anything else was available from the boys in Springburn. They had taken over vast tracts of the heroin trade in north Glasgow and had standing with the gangs of Liverpool and London. They were seen as good people to do business with. They could be trusted. Most important of all, they had the cash.

Some drug dealers make a moral decision not to deal in heroin because of the fatalities and misery that it creates. Others are repelled by the clientele and opt out because of the headaches involved in dealing in the meanest of streets. But, to the McGoverns, it seemed to come naturally.

Another veteran drugs squad detective said:

They had made millions of pounds by the mid 1990s and they ended up running Scotland in the years that followed. It's always the same story – whoever controls the supply into the country becomes the kingpin and, as soon as they lose that, someone else steps in.

The family had put money into pubs, property and other businesses like taxis, car washes, petrol stations and even a laundry business. At this stage, they were on the receiving end of very serious attention from not just the police but also Customs and the Inland Revenue. Generating millions of pounds was futile unless you could put it through the books of a legitimate business in order to make it clean and they had in place the advisers and infrastructure to do that.

They also learned some golden rules such as never lay your hands on the 'product' and never have anything incriminating in your home.

With henchmen like Stevenson ready and willing to dish out violence to late-payers and rivals, few mobs would look to upset the McGoverns who had begun to call themselves The McGovernment. This arrogant self-regard would later contribute to their dramatic decline but, at that time, they seemed to view themselves as true lords of crime.

Each icy Guy Fawkes' night, on 5 November, they would stage a massive bonfire and fireworks display for the locals on a patch of waste ground near to their former Blackthorn Street home which, in recent years, has been demolished. It was said that, on one occasion, the colourful rockets and deafening bangers going up in smoke had been stolen from a delivery truck destined for a DIY warehouse. The McGoverns even laid on a couple of ice-cream vans for the spectators. Some of the drugs money was going into such vans and, a decade after the gangland atrocities of the Ice-Cream Wars had gripped Glasgow, many of the vans touring the city's streets were still run by those involved in organised crime.

Many people could be forgiven for not expressing unconditional gratitude for this apparent generosity. Just how many people died through their dealing is impossible to say. Others would have experienced the bullying and beatings dished out by the McGoverns. The shooting out of house windows was their trademark warning and they would do this with no apparent thought as to who might be behind them at the time. Some would also have been repulsed at the mob's flashing of dirty cash while they struggled to feed their families and heat their homes.

One said:

> There were a lot of atrocities done in their name. One guy who had a bit of debt with them was stabbed in the throat. It was over the top. You can't show any sign of weakness but the smarter mobs know that you don't do things that will alienate you amongst your own people.

By now, the McGoverns had taken over a local private-hire taxi firm. It had the second biggest fleet of cars in Glasgow and, on paper, this profitable business was owned by a former Glasgow private-hire car inspector. Along with some colleagues, he had been driven out of his job because of gangland threats – the gamekeeper had become the poacher. Many private-hire car firms in the city and in places like Lanarkshire, Renfrewshire and increasingly further afield have succumbed to an offer that could not be refused from Glasgow-based organised crime gangs. Usually the drug-dealing owners find a respectable front man to put on the Companies House paperwork.

The brothers' involvement meant that their elderly parents enjoyed a round-the-clock free chauffeur service. One driver suffered a serious beating in the street when, having failed to recognise that his passenger was one of the senior McGoverns, he made the mistake of not showing him the customary deference.

The McGoverns also dealt in cocaine. No longer the preserve of the very rich, it had become a hugely profitable drug for a mass market. Like Ecstasy and heroin, cocaine is yet another substance to have dramatically dropped in price thanks to the volumes of it pouring through the country's ports and airports. Comedian Robin Williams' old gag that cocaine is 'God's way of saying you're making too much money' is redundant in an age where teenagers can afford a few lines and crack cocaine's grip tightens on Scotland's cities much like heroin's two decades before.

And, in the mid 90s, it was the cocaine market that was next to be targeted by the McGovern outfit and, in Brian Doran, they saw an opportunity to break in. This bespectacled Glaswegian hairdresser and linguist was a key figure in a major cocaine smuggling gang that dealt directly with the Colombian cartels. He was a most unlikely but hugely effective drugs baron. In the months leading up to a massive two-year Customs operation that tore Doran's gang apart in 1995, he was the man in the UK to speak to about the supply of large quantities of coke.

One such meeting was arranged between the McGoverns' brother-in-law Russell Stirton, acting for the McGovern family, and a middleman who had direct access to Doran's crew. Strathclyde Police drugs squad knew about the meeting which was due to take place in a cafe on Glasgow's Great Western Road.

If Doran could be persuaded and terms agreed, the McGoverns could become major distributors of a drug that was beginning to appear not just in nightclubs but also at the dinner parties of smart, middle-class professionals. Glasgow city centre's drugs market for Ecstasy and cocaine was a cash cow and the first step towards success was to secure the supply lines. The next was to take over the doors on the clubs and that way you controlled who sold what, where they sold it and how much for.

Stirton immediately realised that the meeting was compromised. His instincts told him that almost every table was occupied by undercover officers. To anyone else, it would have looked like a normal café. There was a mixture of single customers with their noses in newspapers and chatting couples but Stirton could smell the police a mile off – he even spotted the pair in the corner who were apparently staring love-struck into each other's eyes. Had he done business that day, he may also have taken a heavy fall when Customs swooped on Doran shortly afterwards.

One officer said:

> Stirton was treble wide. He seemed to have a sixth sense when he was being watched or followed and he made it very, very obvious that he had clocked all the cops. The meeting was off. It was a shambles.

Three years after their bold entrance at Celtic Park, the McGoverns were to have their first experience of media attention. It was prompted by their own knack of fighting with each other. This was a trait that had surfaced during their rise, continued during their successful years and was kept going through to their eventual fall – a demise that was precipitated by a man joining them that bright August day to enjoy the football.

The *Sunday Times* newspaper cast a light on the family's rapidly expanding drugs empire in August 1998, referring to them only as the mysterious 'M Family'. The article told how two unnamed brothers (Tony and Tommy) had clashed following a bitter fall-out. The newspaper predicted bloodshed but it omitted to mention one non-family member who would be central to the murderous drama that was to unfold in the months ahead.

While the McGovern name was now being talked about by police, reporters, nightclub crowds and amongst the Glasgow underworld, Stevenson was staying firmly in the shadows. The teenage wide boy with the big mouth had grown up and had learned the value of keeping quiet.

12
Best Men

The senior policeman in charge of the Friday afternoon operation did not find the joke funny. He led a small surveillance unit whose job on 31 July 1992 was to discreetly monitor the wedding and reception of drug dealer Tony McGovern. The officer's blood pressure began to rise when some in the team half-jokingly suggested getting closer to the action by joining the wedding party for a pint in the hotel's public bar. That idea was firmly rejected.

McGovern, then aged twenty-seven, was to marry Jackie Craig, a publican's daughter, who was one year younger than her husband-to-be. To an outsider, it was a romantic but otherwise unremarkable exchanging of vows between a groom, who described himself as a 'recovery vehicle driver' on his wedding certificate, and his shop-assistant bride.

The ceremony at St Aloysius Church in Springburn was conducted by Father Noel Murray – the priest would also perform the groom's funeral service eight years later. Best man on that summer's day was Tony's closest pal and business partner, Jamie Stevenson. They were as close as brothers. Also witnessing the exchanging of vows was Tony's sister Jackie who was, by then, the wife of Russell Stirton.

After the happy couple tied the knot, the wedding party crossed the River Clyde to a hotel in Shawlands on the southside of Glasgow for the reception. The choice of this rather modest venue was all about Tony being smart enough to keep it discreet. By now, his prominence in the city's drugs trade was enough to merit the police surveillance operation. The team from Strathclyde Police's Pitt Street headquarters created their own album of wedding snaps although they were never to be seen by the happy couple.

This was the police's chance to see who Tony was friendly with and, just as tellingly, which criminals had not received an invitation through the post. Car registrations were clocked, names noted and faces photographed – all scraps to be stored away for future reference in the intelligence files.

Six years later, on a Saturday in August 1998, it was Stevenson's turn to leave single life behind. Tony McGovern was the obvious and only choice to reciprocate the best-man duties for the ceremony at King's Park Church in the southside of Glasgow.

Stevenson's mother was not there to see her only son getting married, having died just a few months earlier at the age of fifty-four. Stevenson, then aged thirty-three, was to marry Caroline Adam, who was just four days away from turning forty. Their wedding certificate has both of their occupations down as 'ice-cream van salesperson'.

The couple had recently moved into a comfortable detached home in the Glasgow commuter town of East Kilbride. Up until that point, Stevenson had lived in a flat in Aberfoyle Street, in the Dennistoun area of Glasgow's east end.

One guest at the 1998 wedding was New York construction firm owner Anthony Sarcona, whose wife, a relative of Caroline, moved to the US at the age of twelve. He has only just learned about the groom's more recent drug-smuggling activities. Anthony said:

This is a big surprise to me. As far as I knew it was just a regular wedding. I talked to Jamie when I was there. He wasn't a big guy or anything like that. In fact, he was smaller than me and had a regular build. You really wouldn't think he was involved in anything like this. I had no clue what he did other than have some candy trucks or something like that. My wife says to me that, in Scotland, you're either a criminal or you're poor. Everyone has a hard time making a living.

Two years later when best man Tony was gunned down and Stevenson, the groom, emerged as the prime suspect, Strathclyde Police were to take an even keener interest in this 1998 wedding day. Detectives probing the murder of Tony in September 2000 obtained a copy of the video taken at the wedding. They watched happy faces full of life and the two best pals clowning with each other for the camera. Police trawled through the tape, identified all the guests, tracked them down and interviewed them.

One police source said, 'This illustrates better than words just what kind of people we are dealing with. Tony is dead and Jamie is the only real suspect yet, not so long ago, they were best men at each other's weddings.'

However, by the time of Jamie's marriage, the seeds of destruction had been sown as simmering resentments and petty niggles over drugs had caused an irreparable split in the McGovern camp. Tony's brother Tommy was not at Stevenson's wedding – he had been frozen out. Increasingly, Tony and Stevenson were becoming more of 'a gang within a gang' as rows over territories and money took their toll. On that wedding day, Tony and Stevenson were happy to look into a future without what they saw as family baggage but that was before Tony had a very dramatic, and ultimately fatal, change of heart.

Witnessing the ceremony, as Stevenson and his new bride tied the knot, were divorcée Caroline's two children from her first marriage, son Gerry, then nineteen, and daughter Carrie, twenty. Her first husband, who she had divorced seven years earlier, was not there to see Caroline remarry although he had only very recently returned to Scotland after years spent on the Costa del Sol. Days before his former wife remarried, Gerry Carbin Snr had strolled through the arrivals hall of Edinburgh Airport wearing a T-shirt bearing the legend 'Bad Boy'. As police in Scotland and Spain would testify, the logo across his chest was no understatement.

13
Name of the Father

He may have become Jamie Stevenson's stepson but Gerry Carbin Jnr's pursuit of a life of crime was in his genes. His father Gerry Snr was a career criminal. A small-time thief and thug, he had become an audacious international drug smuggler and suspected killer.

Some said his Cyclops nickname stemmed from a bungled cataract operation that left him blind in one eye. Others blamed a gangland fight. Whatever the truth, wide boy Carbin's good eye was always on the main chance. Emerging from the Castlemilk housing scheme which sprawls over the southern edge of Glasgow, he quickly realised the profits from drugs would far outstrip what could be made by robbery.

He married Caroline Adam, a bottle blonde with a pretty face, in 1977. Two years later, the couple had a son, Gerry, named after his dad. In the years that followed, his father's reputation for having a violent raging temper had enabled him to move to a higher level of drug dealing but this had strained his relationship with Caroline to breaking point. The couple split, divorcing in February 1991.

One friend of the couple said:

Carbin had not treated her well. Caroline is a real mixture. She's as hard as nails and a bit of a waif at the same time. She's a tiny wee thing, four foot ten or so, and I think guys wanted to protect her. I don't know if she needs it. She's a keep-fit fanatic now – runs for miles. Loves her sunbeds. Hates the police.

She's like a gangster's moll out of central casting. It's all she's ever known – her family in the east end, Carbin and then Jamie Stevenson. They had known each other for a while before getting together. I think Jamie maybe felt a wee bit sorry for her after she split from Gerry and took her in. But he really loves her. That's the thing you have to remember about the two of them – they really love each other, absolutely mad for each other, besotted. And Jamie took on Gerry Jnr like his own boy. That was a big thing for Caroline. She loved him anyway but she really loved him for that.

Meanwhile, after splitting from Caroline, Carbin Snr briefly hooked up with Margaret Thompson, daughter of Glasgow Godfather Arthur, but the door into the gangster's inner circle slammed shut after Margaret's death from a heroin overdose was blamed on her dealer boyfriend. He left Scotland soon after for the Costas to join a McMafia who were already enjoying the sun while jemmying open entry points into the cannabis-smuggling operations that were streaming drugs from Morocco to the southern Spanish coasts and onwards to Britain.

Carbin, no stranger to Her Majesty's prisons, was not there long before he discovered what the inside of a Spanish jail looked like. He spent fifteen months in custody over the murder of a Norwegian disco owner in 1990. He was arrested after Torbjorn Heia disappeared and bloodstains were found at his villa. His body was discovered months later at the bottom of the property's 120ft well and police blamed his death on a row over a drugs consignment.

Carbin was eventually cleared but then he was immediately extradited to face cocaine charges in Scotland. He was again acquitted. He had also walked from drugs charges in 1988 when he was caught in a car with 40 kilos of cannabis. He was arrested again after leading an audacious hash-in-a-can operation based in the Costa del Sol. This involved smuggling cannabis hidden in food and drink cans into Scotland. Carbin, then thirty-eight, was held along with a fellow Scot, Mick McKay from Govan in Glasgow, after a raid on a luxury villa at Benalmadena, near Malaga, in October 1994.

A makeshift canning factory was concealing kilos of cannabis in tins of olives and tomatoes that were being driven to Glasgow in a fleet of vans. Hours before the raid, Carbin had been spotted buying sixty-five wholesale-size tins of food from a cash-and-carry six miles from the villa. The raid uncovered hashish worth £1.6 million and equipment used to cut open the cans, insert the drugs in waterproof wrapping and reseal them. Each run to Glasgow netted the smugglers £100,000. The bust at the villa came after the four-month Operation Lata – Spanish for 'tin can' – led by the Spanish Civil Guard and involving Scottish Customs officers. Investigators believed the hash was being brought into Spain by speedboat from Morocco before Carbin's gang stashed it in the cans to be driven to Glasgow.

Just days before the bust, the brass-necked Carbin said, 'The police think I'm Public Enemy Number One. They'll do anything to put me behind bars but I've been in jail enough. Now I just want to live quietly in Spain.'

The operation was first uncovered when French police stopped a van load of Stella Artois cans in transit. An officer opened one of the cans and became suspicious when the lager did not fizz. He ordered the cargo to be opened and the drugs stash was exposed. Carbin's gangster pals would enjoy Spanish holidays before driving the vans back to Glasgow for £1,000. Speaking from behind the bars of Alhaurín de la Torre prison, near Malaga, in January 1995, Carbin said, 'I have admitted the lot. It was my operation.'

He left Alhaurín de la Torre jail in a black Mercedes after being released in 1998, having served two thirds of his six-year sentence. He was then charged with dealing heroin during his time behind bars and fled to Scotland while on bail. After strolling through Customs at Edinburgh Airport, wearing the 'Bad Boy' T-shirt, the fugitive went into hiding. He came home to Scotland for the last time with nothing but a heroin habit – an addiction that was to lead to his death from the flesh-eating bug, necrotising fasciitis, in December 2003.

By then his son, who shared his father's facial features and build, had followed him into the family business of international drug smuggling. Carbin Snr may have been unable to show his boy the ropes but, in his stepfather Jamie Stevenson, he had an equally capable mentor.

14
It's War

The phone call from Liverpool was short and to the point. 'We don't give a fuck whose fault it is. We want our money. He used your name so it is your problem.'

For Jamie Stevenson it was a very big problem. One of his trusted Merseyside wholesalers was owed £80,000 for a consignment of cocaine. The person who had taken delivery was Tommy McGovern but he was refusing to pay. Tommy had got the drugs on credit by using Stevenson's name as a reference. Therefore, it was Stevenson who had to come up with the cash – or deal with the defaulter.

A former family associate said:

> It was a contact of Stevenson's but Tommy just decided to blank it. He had it on tick but wasn't going to pay. The Liverpool boys were not happy and it was up to Stevenson and Tony to get it sorted. There was a big fall-out and they both went up against Tommy. The only way to sort it would be to kill Tommy but Tony could not cross that line. The family would never have agreed to that.
>
> If you bump your supplier, you must be seen to be doing something about it. If you don't, then the English boys will take it up with you.

Long-running brotherly squabbles between Tony and Tommy, separated in age by only two years, had long been a feature of the McGovern household but this sibling rivalry was about to reach a new low. Tony and Stevenson had begun to do more side deals of their own. Tommy resented being cut out. He was often called upon to do the dirty work but increasingly suspected that he was not getting his fair share of the money.

The McGovern mob bought large quantities of heroin, coke, cannabis, Ecstasy and speed, mainly from Liverpool, sometimes London and occasionally directly from Europe. This was cut and distributed – tenner bags to junkies, pills to clubbers, dope to students and coke to the professionals. The profits were fantastic so to squabble over one batch of coke was just stupid. Tommy's non-payment was seen by Stevenson and Tony as a deliberate act of provocation and neither was the type of person to back down. It was war but, in this particular conflict, one of the generals was to change sides in mid battle.

In the early summer of 1998, the opening salvo, however, was directed at Tommy after Tony and Stevenson were blamed for Tommy being run over by an ice-cream van and suffering leg injuries. Later that month when Tony was best man at Stevenson's wedding, Tommy did not even get a bit of wedding cake, let alone an invitation.

Throughout that summer, police received intelligence of other minor skirmishes between the sides and, when they arrested Tommy for attempted murder, possession of firearms and perverting the course of justice, it neatly put a lid on the brotherly battle. His conviction also pleased the police for other reasons – they had been infuriated at the witness intimidation that had seen Tommy's 1995 trial for murder collapse.

Tommy was sentenced to four years in prison at the High Court in Greenock for the various charges in March 1999, although the attempted murder charge had by then been reduced to assault. With Tommy out of the way, Tony and Stevenson could get on with business without distraction and were able to appease the Liverpool contact. Meanwhile, Tommy had time to plot his next move following his eventual release from his cell in the newly built private prison in Kilmarnock, Ayrshire.

It was during his time behind bars that the McGovern family intervened in the dispute. With so many genuine enemies, they could not afford to fight amongst themselves. Eldest brother Joe is credited with forcing Tony and Tommy to form a peace pact but Tommy could only accept this deal on one condition – Stevenson must be killed.

It will never be known when Tony made the conscious decision to sacrifice his best friend for the sake of peace with his brother, in effect signing his friend's death warrant, but, by early 2000, the bonds of friendship had lost out to family loyalty. Blood was, after all, thicker than water.

For those in the police and the underworld tracking the feud, a High Court case in March 2000 revealed exactly how the McGoverns would use any means necessary to score points.

Joseph Carbin, a relative of Gerry Snr and Jnr, who stands at six foot four, was sentenced to nine years for a knife attack on five-foot-tall John Callaghan, a cousin of the second-division Lyons crime family. As Carbin, fuelled by alcohol and drugs, stood over his victim holding two razor-sharp boning knives above his head, he told Callaghan, 'Your lungs are getting it.' It was no idle threat. Carbin plunged the blades into Callaghan thirteen times, leaving him disabled. It was a miracle that Carbin was not facing a murder charge.

What seemed most relevant to those monitoring the feud between the McGoverns and Stevenson was that Callaghan co-operated with police and, had Carbin not pleaded guilty, he would have been willing to give evidence against him. It was widely held that the McGoverns sanctioned their associate Callaghan to do so. The reason? Stevenson was married to

Gerry Carbin's ex-wife and he had a good relationship with his stepson Gerry Jnr. This meant that Stevenson and Joseph Carbin were natural allies which, in turn, meant Carbin became an enemy of the McGoverns. Callaghan's co-operation helped to land Carbin in jail for nine years.

A court observer said:

> It was strange that Callaghan would co-operate and the reason for that was because the McGoverns had sanctioned it because the feud with Stevenson had begun and this was a member of the Carbin family. Had this happened a year earlier, it would never have resulted in a conviction. It's a trick that's been used by various groups – they will encourage and protect other people to give evidence in order to put a rival away while they are not being personally seen as grasses.

The play in court was only one weapon in the gangland foes' armoury, however, and there were far less subtle mechanisms for securing success. On the afternoon of Friday, 30 June, Tony McGovern was showering in his comfortable house in Bishopbriggs – the type of house that the pickpocket victims of his youth might have lived in – when someone walked in and shot him. The gunman, who had entered through the unlocked back door, fired at least twice, possibly three times, in the steamy tile-lined bathroom, shattering the glass shower cubicle door. At least one shot hit Tony before he ran, injured, naked and shouting, into the street.

The gangland figure was rushed to hospital but his injuries were not life threatening. Police were quick to suspect Stevenson. Tony refused to co-operate with detectives but forensic experts recovered some of the rounds used in the shooting. The ammunition was of poor quality. Investigators believed the bullets were home-made and had probably been fired from a converted replica firearm. The amateurish ammunition suggested that whoever shot Tony either lacked the contacts capable of supplying a better gun or was in a hurry and had grabbed whatever weapon was immediately at hand.

One newspaper the following day devoted fifty-six words to the incident but mistakenly reported that Tommy McGovern, rather than Tony, was the shooting victim who was recovering in hospital.

One detective who worked on the case said:

> I got a call on the day after the shooting from a contact who supplied the full details about the fall-out between Stevenson and Tony. I reported this information to a detective inspector but he was not that interested. It was not until the following Monday morning when an assistant chief constable found out that it was taken seriously. The ACC realised that this was an ongoing vendetta which had the potential to become a lot more serious.

In the months that followed, there was more tit-for-tat violence. In the early hours of one Sunday in July, Cafe Cini in Greenock was torched. Just one year after its glitzy gangland opening, hundreds of people were having to flee from the McGovern-controlled style bar. All that remained as morning broke was a smouldering shell. Police warned staff to be prepared for similar attacks at other pubs in the Jimmy Nick's chain. CCTV images showed the culprit to be a man who appeared to be of the same height and build as Stevenson but there was never enough evidence to make an arrest. The McGovern family did not require the same standard of proof – they knew who was behind the attack.

The escalating feud widened. Stevenson is devoted to his stepson Carbin who, at the time Tony was shot, was aged twenty-one. In the same year, a member of the McGovern crew brandished a gun in Stevenson's stepson's face at the

Ashfield Club – the same venue in Possil where taxi driver Jimmy McHugh had been shot dead in 1995.

Following Tony's eventual murder, one frustrated detective said:

> There was an incident at the Ashfield Club. There was allegedly a firearm present. It's a matter that still has to be resolved. Police were called to an incident at the time but we don't have an official complaint. I'm aware that the person involved is the stepson of Jamie Stevenson. As to whatever exactly happened, I don't know. There were few witnesses. It's amazing how many people can get into a pub toilet at one time.

By the time Tommy stepped through the prison gates to freedom on 9 August, he finally understood the consequences of his refusal to pay his Liverpudlian drug debt. His stunt had propelled his family into all-out war. The most crucial act in this long hot summer of spiralling violence happened just days before Tony was shot at while in the shower. Indeed, it had been the catalyst for the attack.

Just four weeks before Tommy headed back to Springburn, Stevenson was persuaded to go for a drive in the country. He was not meant to return.

15
In the Jungle

It's called Tak-Ma-Doon Road but the only thing about to be taken down that night was Jamie Stevenson. He had been told it was to be a meet, a drive north out of Glasgow to a secluded spot to discuss business with a trusted contact. It was July 2000 and the rendezvous was agreed in a bid to end his war with the McGoverns. He knew his companions and felt no need to go armed. It was almost a fatal mistake. Who, he thought, would try to kill you at a peace summit?

Leaving the north of the city through darkened back roads, the car headed into the countryside behind Kilsyth and parked up near a reservoir. Then a handgun was suddenly pulled, aimed and fired straight at Stevenson's head. He tells people that the pistol jammed in the steady hand of the would-be assassin. Friends of those in the car that night say that a shot was fired but it merely burned their intended victim's neck. They insist the injury was bad enough to later need hospital treatment but admit it was never life threatening.

Stevenson was shocked. Fight or flight? In a split-second, his human instinct for self-preservation to flee prevailed over a bare-handed attack on two men, one of whom was armed. He tumbled out of the car door, rolled over and then was back on his feet. Over a fence and into a field, he was running, the adrenaline thundering through his body. His would-be assassins followed him but lost him in the darkness.

After stumbling across the boggy fields of this unfamiliar rural Stirlingshire terrain, Stevenson eventually came to the house of a businessman acquaintance, a Glasgow publican. Entering the garden from the rear, he knew he had found a temporary haven but realised there would be no permanent safety until he had dealt with those who had tried to kill him – the McGoverns.

One of the men in the car that night was allegedly Terry Monaghan, an 'elder statesman' of Glasgow gangland and a man who had the authority and the trust to broker a potential deal between the McGoverns and their nemesis – in particular, he could do a deal that might save face on both sides and stop the war escalating to the stage where it would begin to hurt business.

Monaghan, however, is reluctant to go into exact details about the night when, allegedly, he, Stevenson and a third man, who is now in prison, went for a drive in the country. Perhaps he hoped that, having so much to deal with, Stevenson's memory has begun to fade. When tracked down, Monaghan asked:

Is this anything to with a gun? Is it something to do with him getting shot in the back of the head? I wonder what happened there. I know that it was when Wimbledon was on. The police know about it – they'll tell you. He had to go to hospital – it was a private hospital. Everyone can speculate and the dogs in the street seem to know that it is me.

A Monaghan ex-associate said:

After this happened, Terry was very worried about repercussions. Stevenson obviously trusted him enough to get into a car unarmed and head out the back roads while in the middle of a war with the McGoverns – not the kind of mistake you'd make twice.

Ironically, nine years earlier, Terry's brother Abie, a promising footballer who, as a boy, had played alongside the legendary Kenny Dalglish, had been caught outside the Highland Fling with a samurai sword, as he was preparing to chop the head off one of the McGoverns.

A Stevenson associate said:

Jamie was not injured and he was not armed. If he had been, things would have been different. For years they ran together and worked together and Tony had been a proper friend, a china. Tony knew that Tommy was a loose canon but Stevenson knew that, if it ever came to the crunch, Tony would always side with his brothers. Even before the fall-out over Tommy bumping his Liverpool contacts for money, Stevenson had been growing apart from them.

Pushing his hands forward like train lines, he added:

Up until the late 1990s, they had worked together like that but there had been a gradual moving away even before this. Stevenson understood that the McGoverns would hold him back. They were liberty-takers – slashing people, stabbing people. Tommy was snorting most of their profits. The youngest brother Paul was about to come out of jail after doing his time for murdering the janitor and he would be looking for a piece of the action.

It might just have worked itself out if they hadn't tried to kill Stevenson first but, after that, there was no going back. Stevenson felt bad about it but he knew it was him or them and he was not about to let it be him. It was both business and personal.

Stevenson felt bad about Tony and, after he died, he just said, 'If you walk in the jungle, you had better be ready to bump into a tiger.'

Stevenson had been shocked by the attempt on his life. In the nights that followed, he admitted as much to one criminal associate at The Tunnel club in Glasgow, a venue where he and Tony had spent many happy times together.

Another close friend said:

> He could not believe it when they tried to kill him out on the back roads. For several nights, he talked about it and he had tears in his eyes. At first, he didn't know what to do but quickly realised there was only one course of action he could take. A few days later, Tony was shot in the shower.

Many in the police were already certain that one side or the other would suffer a fatality. Stevenson was undoubtedly dangerous but most observers thought that the McGovern brothers would ultimately triumph in this most brutal test of strength – after all, Stevenson was just one man. They thought wrong.

Tony was shot dead on the evening of 16 September 2000 while he was sitting at the wheel of his black Audi A6 which was parked outside the New Morven. It would be one of the most significant gangland murders for years and one that signalled an audacious gangland putsch.

In the days after McGovern was murdered, Stevenson trailed other members of the McGovern family, including the brothers and their parents, covertly taking their pictures. They were soon sent the photos in the post.

The associate recalls:

> The McGoverns wanted revenge. They would have been baying for Stevenson's blood but sometimes self-preservation comes before anything else. And, when they got those pictures, they got the message very quickly. They were feared but not respected and suddenly somebody wasn't scared of them or what they might do. Stevenson

took the war right into their backyard, into their heartlands, and away goals count double.

Another north Glasgow underworld figure said:

After Stevenson did what he did, the whole perception of the McGoverns changed. They were running about like headless chickens offering people money to do things for them but people asked why could they not do it themselves. Their reputation was in tatters, this entire facade of invincibility just melted away like ice.

Their plan had spectacularly backfired. In the countryside north of Glasgow, the damp shallow grave that lay open in readiness for Stevenson's warm corpse would remain unfilled.

16

Vengeance

Big Duncan McIntyre asked the barmaid for another large vodka before scrutinising his palm for a coin to feed into the Thomson's bar jukebox. McIntyre, a long-standing McGovern henchman, was mourning his good friend Tony.

For several weeks after the killing, his routine was the same. Each afternoon, he would steadily dispatch vodka after vodka, soothing his pain with the clear spirit. His personal soundtrack for the grieving process was repeatedly selected from the jukebox, as if on a loop. The melancholic tune that reminded McIntyre of Tony was 'Sometimes We Cry' by Tom Jones featuring Van Morrison. The lyrics that McIntyre immersed himself in during those long weeks of autumn 2000 were certainly appropriate. The haunting song ends with the lines:

> Sometimes we live,
> Sometimes we die,
> Sometimes we cry,
> Sometimes we cry.

One regular recalls how McIntyre, a known McGovern enforcer who had survived being shot three years earlier, symbolised the feeling in Thomson's after the murder. He said:

He would play that song at least once a day, usually more depending on how much he'd had to drink. He was emotional about what had happened to Tony. This went on for months. A lot of us would joke that it would be us that would be crying if we heard it again – it got on your nerves after a while. We were careful not to let big Duncy hear us say that.

Tony's murder sent shock waves through the Springburn community and the Glasgow criminal underworld. In Springburn, many would feel a secret happiness about the end of a man whose heroin had claimed the lives of many sons and daughters. They knew about the many teenage girls, once the babes of proud parents, who were now forced to sell sex on The Strip in Glasgow in order to scrape together cash for another tenner bag, which allowed Tony to live the high life. Others openly welcomed his departure. They had tasted the family's violence and drug dealing first hand. Some, however, were happy to remember Tony as a married family man rather than a violent thief and drug dealer.

In the other major criminal heartlands – places like Possil, Paisley and Pollok – rivals kept a close eye on events as they watched and waited for the inevitable violent repercussions and the equally inevitable grab for power. Most now believed that the power and influence of the McGoverns was waning, with the family unable to control Springburn never mind further afield.

Stevenson was the prime suspect, indeed the only suspect, after the murder of his former friend. Amassing evidence of his involvement was the unenviable – some would say impossible – task of a murder squad that was working long hours but making little progress. There was some hope in the form of witnesses who included those attending a nearby function and a teenage thief who had been on the flat roof of a shop near to the New Morven. When asked, none could – or perhaps would – be certain of what they saw.

Some police officers joked about how the overtime generated from the large-scale murder enquiry was helping to pay for a new TV or that summer's family holiday. It did not help their task that the McGoverns banned the police from releasing a photo of Tony. The public only got to see his face after an old police mugshot found its way to the *Sunday Mail*.

Thomson's bar was a hub of activity in the weeks following the murder. People like thuggish Billy Ferris, who was later convicted of a cowardly killing, started to appear on the scene like vultures circling a corpse.

One regular said:

Tommy would slip in now and again but he was quiet and drawn, he wasn't saying much. The brother that most people seemed to defer to was Paul. He was soft-spoken and, as a young guy with trendy clothes and a fancy big four-wheel drive, you wouldn't think he had just got out after doing a life sentence for murder. He never made a big deal about who he was or his reputation – unlike the other brother, James. The only one that kept out of the way was Joe. Guys like George Madden were always about.

Above the gantry at Thomson's were snapshots of Tony, his wife Jackie, family, friends, famous footballers and pub regulars in happier times. In those days when talk of banning smoking in pubs would have been laughed at, lighters were for sale bearing the words 'Jackie welcomes you to Thomson's bar'.

The mother to Tony's three young children, Jackie was now a widow. Strong, quiet and dignified, she would occasionally visit the bar to tie up loose ends. During these visits, any talk of Tony's reputed girlfriend was respectfully muted.

For those monitoring events, it was not until the following year that the violent ripples from Tony's murder began. Mourner-in-chief McIntyre was one of the first to feel the waves. He had sunk his usual vodkas at Thomson's over that Monday lunchtime in June 2001 before going into the barber's shop next door for a haircut. As he made his way along the street with his wife Linda, the hit man struck.

McIntyre, then aged thirty-eight, was shot in the head. The handgun was thrown to an accomplice who made off while the gunman escaped in the most bizarre of getaway vehicles – a Number 45 bus. A passer-by took McIntyre to the local Stobhill Hospital from where he was sent to the Royal Infirmary for life-saving surgery. Typically, he would not talk to the police, instead vowing to deal with it himself.

This daylight attack on McIntyre took place just one week after Tommy McGovern had been the target of a gunman. Four shots were fired at Tommy in a Springburn car park, each one missing the intended target. Tommy, armed and ready, fired shots back but they also failed to connect. The two Glaswegian gunslingers took poorly aimed potshots at each other. It was only good fortune that no innocents in the vicinity were maimed or even killed in the frenetic and inept crossfire.

Many people thought that Stevenson was behind the attack on McIntyre because he was so well in with the McGoverns. But the truth was even more incredible – McIntyre was shot because he was deemed responsible for setting the trap from which Tommy had escaped the previous week. He was blamed for trying to lure Tommy to his death. He had been accused of switching sides because he feared Stevenson and recognised that the McGoverns' influence was waning.

The failed attack on Tommy was another clear signal that Stevenson was intent on taking the war to the McGoverns – as the saying goes, the best form of defence is attack. Turning McIntyre to his cause was yet another signal of his rising influence but he knew that, to guarantee his safety, he needed to deal with the two brothers most capable of seeking revenge – Tommy and Paul.

Several months later, just over a year after Tony's murder, a botched attempt was made on Paul's life. By now, Paul was a 'businessman', running a security firm with his partner Madden. Whether the amateurish move against Paul was the work of Stevenson or perhaps rivals in the gang-corrupted security industry is not known.

If there was ever a time for the McGovern clan to stand united, this was it. A sibling feud had not only led to the death of one brother, it had brought about the public exposure of their criminal empire and the near-collapse of their business. However, there was to be no united stance. Their knack for inflicting mutual harm triumphed over the requirement to maintain solidarity in the face of common enemies. In the same month as he fled a gunman, the youngest of the five brothers, Paul, had a blazing fall-out with eldest brother, Joe. Paul blamed Joe's twenty-one-year-old son Joe Jnr for stealing a drugs haul worth around £30,000. Not long after Tony's murder, the boy had featured in a BBC prime-time documentary about car theft. The fly-on-the-wall programme had shown a traffic policeman cornering the sweaty youth in a Possil bingo hall after he was seen fleeing from a stolen car. The glove under his table matched the one in the car but the charges were dropped. It did not help that the bingo hall's CCTV cameras failed that night. Even now, Joe Jnr tags along with the family-run shoplifting gang and often trawls the pubs selling their weekly haul from the high street. For years, his mum Anne has been one of the members of the Jean McGovern and Annette Daniel organised shoplifting gang.

When accused of the drugs theft by his furious uncle, Joe Jnr claimed that they had been stolen from him and his dad backed him up. Paul McGovern did not believe a word of it and, even if the story was true, it did not do the family's reputation any good if a mystery man could simply swipe drugs from the brothers without reprisal. Joe Snr did not take kindly to the youngest of his four brothers, ten years his junior, impugning the honesty of his son. At least this particular family fall-out stopped short of violence.

17
Paying Respect

Some in the McGovern family were not happy. It was the day after Tony's funeral and that day's newspaper reports were suitably scathing about this gangland send-off. Several McGovern members also had issues with the priest who had conducted the service. They suggested that someone ought to have a word with Father Noel Murray, the same priest who had married Tony and Jackie in 1992 and married elder brother Joe in 1989.

Eight long weeks after Tony's murder, his body was finally released by the authorities. This had given the local florists plenty of time to prepare for that cold Monday morning in November. The biting weather was well suited to the pinched faces in attendance. The previous day, Tony's multimillionaire pal David Moulsdale had stated his intention to attend. In the end, he did not and ex-footballer Charlie Nicholas was also absent.

Tony's oak coffin was carried from St Aloysius to the strains of the Celine Dion ballad 'Immortality' before being taken, in a slow-moving cortege, to Lambhill Cemetery.

Father Murray was to later take a phone call from one female McGovern relative who was critical of what he had said – and what he had not said – about Tony. The priest, now in his eighties, who retired in 2005, said:

> A family member phoned up and said that I didn't praise him for being a good family man. In the circumstances, I

didn't think I could start saying anything positive. I kept it quite theological or spiritual and said we were all children of God and that it was not for us to judge. I wasn't going to start praising him – he was up to his eyes in criminal activity as far as I could gather.

The problem nowadays is they expect a eulogy but what could I say about him? I just said to myself, 'Keep it on the ground.' I remember other clergy saying I had got out of it well. Some older priests in previous times might not even have let the body cross the chapel door.

Many saw the funeral as a way of the family flexing its muscles – showing people they were still not to be crossed – but, in terms of gangland power, they had taken a major hit with the loss of Tony.

Stevenson was on the run, out of reach and mocking them. Many in the former McGovern camp were switching sides. They could see a more attractive future as part of Stevenson's new mob. Men like Willie Cross jumped ship. He would later join his new boss in the dock.

Soon, pub boss Jim Milligan was to flee when the family began taking a keen interest in what exactly he had been doing with much of their illicit income for all those years. Partly motivated by self-preservation, he also moved towards Stevenson.

No matter how badly Tony's murder had harmed their reputation and ability, the family were still actively involved in drug dealing. In January 2001, four months after Tony's murder, they planned what they hoped would be a spectacular show of strength.

The New Morven, where Tony had been shot as he sat in his car outside, was to be the venue for a massive tribute to him. Buses from Liverpool, with the McGoverns' long-standing criminal allies on board, made the trip up the M6 and many gangland cronies from Glasgow and Ireland made the effort to attend. The Saturday night blowout was billed as a 'rebel-oke' – like a karaoke but mainly with songs of an Irish Republican theme. One source said:

> Stevenson had already been doing a bit of business with a few Ulster Loyalist types by then. The McGoverns had long enjoyed links with those close to the IRA and other Republicans heavily involved in crime. In the late 80s and early 90s, a Glasgow-based IRA criminal called John Friel, along with his then girlfriend Maureen McLaughlin, had helped to show them the ropes in the pub and property trade. Glasgow's modern criminals have rarely split down sectarian lines but, around that time, it seemed to have the potential to go that way. Some of the brothers like Joe thought it was a bad idea. This event showed people that, even without Tony, they could do the business.

Also around this time, the gang would hold 'board meetings' on the pavement near to their Blackthorn Street childhood home. One witness said:

> Every week, this big fleet of flash cars – BMWs, Range Rovers, Mercs – would suddenly appear from all directions. The cars were virtually abandoned in the street while the guys gathered round the pavement and stood talking. Maybe they were worried about their phones being bugged.

The big funeral, the New Morven tribute and the pavement meetings were all designed by the McGoverns to say one thing: 'We're not finished.' Stevenson, their friend-turned-nemesis, was, by then, too busy to listen.

18
Last Orders

Jim Milligan's ears should have been burning. 'Guys like him are all the same. They start off OK but then start believing that they're gangsters too. The bubble usually bursts soon after that.' The gangland figure delivering his opinion of the McGoverns' erstwhile business associate could have been speaking of many of the businessmen – and businesswomen – running firms in Scotland that had been launched with criminals' dirty money and were busy laundering more of it.

In the underworld village, where gangsters of a certain level know each other and often do business when convenient, most will know a man who knows a man who can help an associate. In Glasgow, like any city in Britain, there are bankers, lawyers, accountants and estate agents happy to take on new business. They do not ask awkward questions because they already know the awkward answers. The motive of these corrupted professionals is most often greed but, in a few cases, their co-operation is assured through blackmail. Their new clients may not only keep a keen enthusiasm for cocaine or prostitutes a secret but may be helpful on the supply side too.

The other staff that must be recruited urgently are the frontmen, people with no obvious criminal connections whose names can be used on official company documents – preferably plausible business types capable of talking a good game. Jim Milligan fitted the bill perfectly. The one-time electrician always fancied himself as a 'player' – a term only used by those who believe gangsterism should be worn like a badge of honour. It was not long before this wide boy from Springburn would get involved with the McGoverns. He was soon running Jimmy Nick's Properties Ltd. Controlling a maze of five other firms, the chain owned Thomson's bar and the New Morven, both in Springburn, and trendy Cafe Cini style bars, one in Glasgow's city centre and another in Greenock.

Milligan's business partner was ex-Celtic footballer Charlie Nicholas who often visited Milligan for lunchtime social visits in the company's Springburn office. His silent partners were the McGovern family. Milligan had long been a friend of Nicholas. He had even lived with the footballer's parents for three years and they treated him like a member of the family.

Milligan and Nicholas had met in 1981 at the former Warehouse disco. Milligan was a bouncer while Nicholas was a fresh-faced Celtic star. Many years later, Nicholas admitted in court that he'd been 'young and naive' to go into business with Milligan. Both men were interviewed by the police officers investigating Tony's murder outside the New Morven. The pub's licensee was John Fox, a man who later fronted M&M Security for murderer Paul McGovern.

For Milligan, the first sign of trouble came in June 2000 when hundreds of fleeing customers ran for their lives as flames destroyed Cafe Cini and the nearby G1 nightclub in Greenock. The intense fire, started in the empty flats above Cini, took two hours to control. It was part of the tit-for-tat attacks between Stevenson and the McGoverns but Milligan was quick to lie in public about the motives behind the blaze. With as straight a face as he could muster, he said, 'This isn't about gangsters – it's about people in Greenock who have never accepted us here from the outset.'

The fire prompted a public vow from a sickened Nicholas to get out of the pub game after fifteen years. Following Tony's slaying several weeks later, Nicholas said he had sold his 50 per cent stake in Jimmy Nick's. Having one pub torched as part of a gang war was bad but a mobster getting shot outside another bar was altogether worse.

For Milligan, the morning after the night of Tony's murder must have been more painful than the worst hangover in his pub chain's history. The game was up. His complex creative accounting was set to unravel. Behind the smoke and mirrors, the McGoverns were to discover a seven-figure black hole in their fortune. Milligan would have a lot of explaining to do or he would have done if the McGoverns were the type of people who were in any way interested in explanations.

He attended Tony's funeral a worried man but, by the time the Clydesdale Bank pulled the plug on Jimmy Nick's Properties Ltd, he had fled Scotland. In February 2001, the chain of companies went spectacularly bust, owing up to £1 million.

Milligan's large and luxurious family home overlooking a golf course near Gartcosh in Lanarkshire had been hurriedly emptied of personal effects before being abandoned. When the McGovern team arrived at the house, there was no sign of Milligan so they trashed his home, making it uninhabitable – not that its occupant planned to return.

Rumours of the McGovern family threatening Nicholas were never substantiated but they did put word out through contacts. 'If you know where Milligan is, let us know immediately. If you don't, then you'll get it as well.'

It was no surprise that Milligan drifted towards the protective sanctuary of Stevenson. For several years, he dared not risk returning home. There was an endless list of countries in which this Glasgow gangland fugitive was supposedly holed up.

LAST ORDERS

Years after Milligan's hasty departure, the McGovern anger has still not abated. One former associate said:

> A couple of years ago, they knew he was coming and going and would have done him on sight. They reckon they are owed £1 million of Tony's money and there will be no room for negotiation. He was well trusted.

Following the company collapse, it was not just the McGoverns who were out of pocket. Brewery company Interbrew UK Ltd, later renamed Inbev, was owed £318,000 from two loans that it had made to Jimmy Nick's in 1999 and 2000. The scrawled name of the person underwriting these loans was apparently that of Nicholas but he denied ever having signed them. Undeterred, the brewers attempted to freeze the Sky Sports TV pundit's wages, forcing Champagne Charlie to go to court where he scored a pleasing victory.

Nicholas told the court that he had invested 'about £60,000 or £70,000' in Milligan's business in the late 1980s when it bought its first pub but had no paperwork of any kind to prove this – no contract or agreement. Nicholas said he had previously been forced to raise legal action against his pal Milligan in the 1990s after discovering that the older man had forged his signature, personally guaranteeing a loan from another brewery. However, this 'very unpleasant experience' was not enough for Nicholas to end their personal and business relationship.

This time around, Nicholas again had to prove that he had not signed the two loan guarantees. His lawyer conjured up a written confession from fugitive Milligan in which he admitted faking his old business partner's signature. Milligan said that he first signed his pal's name during a meeting at a Glasgow law firm while Nicholas was distracted on the phone and a lawyer had briefly popped out of the room.

The second time, Milligan apparently told a lawyer that he would take the document through to another room for Nicholas to sign. He then claims to have signed it himself. Nicholas denied ever being at that meeting. Despite Milligan's courtroom confessions of fraud, no prosecution was ever undertaken.

Milligan could not be cross-examined, explained Nicholas's QC Heriot Currie, because he feared being arrested if he turned up and 'there are also people who wish to find him whom he does not wish to be found by'.

The company's accountant Richard Cleary told the court that, in the aftermath of the collapse, he feared for his own safety. 'It was scary stuff,' he said.

Not that Milligan was the only person surrounding the pub chain's collapse who was to disappear. Lawyers for Inbev pointed out that the other people who they had been unable to find were Jimmy Nick's company secretary Frank Boyle, a solicitor who had acted for Nicholas called Frank Collins and Nicholas's personal accountant Jim Murphy.

Several months after hearing the evidence, Lord Menzies had come to a decision and he ruled in favour of Nicholas.

His written judgement said:

> I am satisfied that, on the balance of probabilities, the pursuer was not the author of the two questioned signatures on the personal guarantees dated 20 January 1999 and 17 May 2000 and that these signatures are forgeries. Although strictly it is not necessary for me to express a view as to who was the author of these signatures, taking all the evidence together, I am of the view that it is probable that Mr Jim Milligan forged these signatures.

Interbev's lawyers were 'surprised and disappointed'. Nicholas no longer faced having his wages seized and Interbev would need to think again about how to get their money back.

The fact that Nicholas had any kind of contact with Milligan was enough to raise hackles in Springburn. One family associate said:

> The McGoverns didn't like the fact that Milligan could be traced and they had known nothing about it. The only good thing about it was that it kept Milligan's face in the papers and reminded people that he was still a wanted man.

19
On the Run

Even as police investigating Tony McGovern's murder sited a caravan outside the New Morven, hoping witnesses might wander in with case-breaking information, they knew the prime suspect was in the wind.

In the incident room at Baird Street police station, Stevenson had been recognised as their number one target for the gunning down of Tony McGovern within hours of his former friend's clinical execution. For a very few days, some of the forty detectives working on the investigation looked at the possibility that his own brother Tommy might have ordered the hit, even if he had not pulled the trigger himself. But, although there had been a history of violent conflict between the brothers in the past, detectives knew this shooting was no family affair.

By the Tuesday, just three days after the murder, Stevenson was identified as the prime suspect in press reports. However, journalists were unable to reveal his name and, instead, used his nickname 'The Iceman' which, some say, dated from his time running ice-cream vans. He was also known as 'The Bull', but both nicknames had more currency in the media than in the tight circle of family, friends and associates that surrounded him. Certainly, The Iceman seemed most appropriate in the wake of the cold-blooded execution. The stories detailed his long criminal alliance with Tony McGovern, how his former friend had sided with his brothers against him and the bloody consequences.

As the Strathclyde force waited in vain for someone, anyone, to enter their caravan, Stevenson went on the run and murder squad detectives designated him a TIE – a suspect to be Traced, Interviewed and Eliminated.

A month after the murder, the caravan had yet to receive a single visitor. By this time, Detective Superintendent Jeanette Joyce, the officer initially in charge of the case, had been moved to lead her force's complaints unit and Detective Superintendent Alex McAllister took charge.

Stevenson, meanwhile, stayed out of Scotland, first in a safe house in the Republic of Ireland that had been arranged by his friends in Belfast and then in Spain. He disappeared in the holiday resort of Fuengirola on the Costa del Sol, twenty minutes from Malaga airport where his old pal John 'Piddy' Gorman, an Ayrshire dealer, had a home. Like exiled royalty, Stevenson would receive visitors from Scotland while he continued to keep busy, smuggling boatloads of cannabis from Morocco to the Costas' secluded beaches.

One former associate said:

> There was a tremendous amount of loyalty towards Stevenson. People clearly knew what he was capable of but, even above that, he had a knack for getting people on side and keeping them there. Of course, that loyalty was not tested because the McGoverns had been broken and everyone likes a winner.
>
> People knew he had come through the ranks and they knew he wasn't a liberty-taker.

He showed up in Glasgow sporadically in the months following the New Morven shooting but no one except a few trusted lieutenants knew of his imminent arrival and even they only knew he was leaving after he was gone. After receiving a rare tip-off, the police pursuing him came close to catching him but, in a late-night raid on a house in Glasgow's

Croftfoot neighbourhood, they missed him by minutes. His wife Caroline would remain in their home in East Kilbride while Stevenson hid. Her son Gerry Carbin also stayed in Scotland to the surprise of many aware of the McGovern brothers' vocal insistence that there would be a bloody settling of scores.

One associate said:

> Carbin kept very low to the ground. He would have been a fool not to. Stevenson was fairly confident that the McGoverns had got the message but, if they still had any appetite for revenge, Carbin would have done in his stepdad's absence. In fact, Stevenson would have rather been attacked himself than have anything happen to Carbin.

The McGoverns put on a public show of defiance after their brother's humiliating assassination in their own heartlands. Approaches were made to the city's most influential mobsters demanding they declare themselves friends or foes in their feud with their former ally. They received some words of comfort but not the truth. As ever, the gang bosses had loyalty to nothing but the next pound. They were content to wait until the gun smoke cleared and then deal with whoever survived. And few were now betting against Stevenson being the last man standing.

If the warning that was implicit in the sinister snapshots delivered to the McGoverns in the days after Tony was murdered had not been clear, a series of late-night calls in the months that followed spelled it out. The caller, instantly recognised by Tommy McGovern, would taunt him during his brief but brutal telephone conversations, saying, 'I know where you are but you don't know where I am. I'll shoot you just like Tony.'

The McGoverns had plenty to think about – their brother's killer, their missing pub boss Milligan and the black hole in their drugs fortune.

Meanwhile, police hunted Stevenson. For eleven months, he remained elusive. That was about to change with Blackpool, the Lancashire resort popular with generations of holidaying Scots, providing an unlikely backdrop. As August edged towards September, the Scots had returned home for the season but the English schools were still on holiday and Blackpool remained busy although a little less raucous. The summer season was nearly over at the resort but the Tower and the famous Pleasure Beach were still bustling with tourists. The seaside town, traditionally a holiday magnet for Scots on a budget for generations, had attracted a less likely visitor. Mingling among the crowds as he went shopping in the clutter of streets at the foot of the Tower was Stevenson.

He was unaware of the plain-clothes officers, watching and waiting, as he strolled around the shops among the tourists and office workers looking to grab a sandwich just after noon. Glasgow detectives had arrived in the town two days earlier after following a trail from London where Stevenson's stepson Carbin had used a credit card to hire a car. Bolstered by detectives from the Lancashire force and with an armed response unit on standby, they had finally caught up with Scotland's most wanted man.

At a co-ordinated signal, the net closed. Stevenson tried to run but officers on foot chased him down as colleagues jumped from pursuit cars before the wheels had even stopped turning.

One witness told reporters, 'We were walking along the road with the kids when we heard shouting and running feet. They finally grabbed a guy and wrestled him to the ground before throwing him into the back of one of the motors.'

After eleven months of movement, of fleeting homes, of living on the run, Stevenson had finally been captured and was immediately driven north to Glasgow in an unmarked car. The next day, Thursday, 23 August 2001, he stood in the dock charged with murdering McGovern. Giving his address as Macdonald Avenue, East Kilbride, Stevenson made no plea or declaration and was remanded in custody until another appearance scheduled for Glasgow Sheriff Court in eight days time. But, by then, he was out, having been released from the remand wing of the city's Barlinnie jail in a move that did not surprise anyone aware of the paucity of evidence against him. Publicly, police and prosecutors insisted the case was live. Privately, they confessed that, in the absence of forensic evidence or a single witness placing Stevenson at the murder scene, they needed a miracle. They did not get it.

Despite being charged with the country's most notorious gangland assassination, he stayed free and, eleven months later, in July 2002, prosecutors confirmed what was already clear – Stevenson would not stand trial.

In a terse statement, the Crown Office said, 'Counsel have concluded the evidence presently available is not sufficient to indict anyone for the murder of Anthony McGovern at this stage.'

With the threat of charges lifted, Stevenson stopped running – and went to work.

20
Loose Ends

The bodies were found on a Wednesday afternoon. Two elderly men out walking, despite the autumn chill and threatening rain, found them down a Lanarkshire dirt track.

John Hall, forty-five, and his pal David McIntosh, thirty-three, had been gagged and their hands were bound behind their backs. They had been pushed at gunpoint to a nearby scrapyard where they were forced to kneel before being tortured. Petrol was poured over them. Then their killers fired a shotgun into the back of their heads. They were shot again in the back. Their bodies, along with the black Volkswagen Golf that McIntosh had driven to the scene of his death, were set alight.

With some sense of understatement, Detective Superintendent John Carnochan, leading a team of fifty officers hunting the killers, told reporters, 'It's reasonable to conclude the way they died was not as the result of some petty argument.'

It was October 2001, just over a year since Tony McGovern had been murdered and just three months since Stevenson had been charged with the fatal shooting of his former friend and ally in one of Scotland's most clinical gangland coups. In the immediate aftermath of these murders, the theories explaining why Hall, a professional car thief, and McIntosh, a former army marksman, were killed with such calculated barbarity split and multiplied day by day. Some said they had quickly got out of their depth after making a tentative and ill-fated entry into the drugs trade. Some said they were innocent pawns in a gangland power struggle and sacrificed in a merciless show of strength. Others, particularly some detectives still trying to build a case against the assassin of Tony McGovern, wondered if Hall and McIntosh had simply known too much? If they were potential witnesses to be silenced? Loose ends to be tied up?

One detective, who had investigated Stevenson's involvement, said:

> There was certainly speculation that Hall and McIntosh not only knew about the McGovern murder but had actually been at the scene. Men were seen in a car nearby who were never identified. It was only speculation and their murders were never formally linked with McGovern's but that was a suggestion and one that was taken seriously.

Another who knew Hall well said:

> He was a professional car thief who stole a handful of expensive models each week. He stole them and sold them as they were. He wasn't involved in ringing. He used to say that he could earn £10,000 a week from this and was happy for that to fund his bets and a drink. I was amazed when I heard what had happened to him – he had clearly got out of his depth.
>
> Frankly, I don't think he would have had the bottle to be at the scene of the McGovern murder but it's possible he could have supplied a stolen vehicle for the killer's getaway car.

On the first anniversary of his death, Hall's widow Moira, forty-nine, begged for information and appealed for someone, anyone, to reveal why her husband died. 'I pray that someone will open up. Our lives are ruined and someone out there knows something. I just hope that someone can find it in their heart to come forward.'

On the same day, his eldest daughter Clare, twenty, said, 'The one question we have is why?'

A year after the killings, police seemed little nearer to finding the answer. By then, officers had interviewed hundreds of people and looked at thousands more. They had scoured hours of CCTV film. They had even spoken to the residents of tower blocks on a Motherwell estate a mile and a half away from the crime scene, just in case anyone with exceptional eyesight had a bird's-eye view of murder. They were getting nowhere.

On the anniversary of the murders, Detective Superintendent Carnochan insisted that just one person could unlock the investigation. He said:

> I have spoken to people who, if not there on the night, know who was and the reason it was done. I don't have any doubt about that. I have evidence that will help to prosecute, if we get the help. If someone walks out of the darkness, I'm confident I have enough evidence. All we need is the final piece of the jigsaw.

In the years since that double shooting, Stevenson has been relentlessly linked to the killings in his Lanarkshire heartland and newspaper reports also suggested that Paisley drugs baron Grant McIntosh may have had some involvement. Like the dead men, he had an enthusiasm for greyhound racing and, like them, he had graduated from car crime to drugs. Unlike them, he was, and is, a gangland survivor capable of doing whatever is necessary to protect his business. He went to their funerals.

The last sighting of the men was at the Halcrow Stadium, a greyhound track in Gretna, the night before their bodies were found. Police believe they met their regular drugs supplier there. Sources suggest the deaths of Hall and McIntosh in the disused scrapyard near Larkhall may have been linked to the £120,000 they owed their supplier for five kilos of cocaine. The drugs had been seized by police before they could sell them on, leaving them dangerously in debt and with no means of settlement.

Whatever the motive, the double murder had clear and, for detectives, disturbing similarities to another gangland shooting almost exactly two years before. The charred bodies of robber-turned-dealer John Nisbet and his pal William Lindsay were found in 1999. Like Hall and McIntosh, they had been tortured and shot several times before being set alight. They were found up a farm track at Elphinstone, East Lothian, but police believe the men had been murdered over forty miles away in a field near Chapelhall – in the same scattering of North Lanarkshire villages where Hall and McIntosh would be found two years later.

Nisbet was just twenty-five when he died but he was already a hardened criminal. In 1994, he had been cleared of an attempted murder in his home estate of Craigneuk, Wishaw. The victim was paralysed after being shot in the street. Nisbet got lucky again three years later when he escaped jail after being charged with a bank robbery in Torquay when his co-accused pleaded guilty.

The year before, in 1996, he had been prime suspect in an audacious £1-million heist on a security van. Nicknamed the 'Blondie and Clyde' robbers, the gang held up the cash couriers after a blonde woman, possibly a man in drag, crashed a stolen car into the Securicor van in Kilwinning, Ayrshire. She pretended to be hurt but, when a guard went to her aid, four hooded robbers grabbed him and his colleague, threw petrol over them and warned them they would be set alight if the van was not opened. No one was ever convicted of the robbery but Nisbet reputedly used his share to secure a lucrative foothold in the drugs trade.

The hair-trigger thug had survived two attempted hits in the months before his death and was armed at all times. Detectives believe he must have known his killers to have been lured to the scene of his death. They shot him and his driver Lindsay, twenty-six, once in the head and three times in the body with a powerful handgun. The prime suspect was one of Nisbet's underworld cronies, another young gangster with a fearsome reputation for violence.

Nisbet had been a guest when Lee Smith had married his wife Claire at a lavish wedding at Chatelherault, the spectacular hunting lodge set in a 500-acre country park, near Hamilton. Police scouring mobile phone records discovered the last call made by Nisbet before his death was to Smith on one of the eight mobile phones the young gangster had in use.

Smith, a car-thief-turned-drug-dealer, was twenty-five at the time and had already been jailed for two years for a machete attack that left a stranger scarred for life. He got another two years for a knuckleduster assault. He and an associate, Andrew Cairns, were questioned by police hunting the perpetrators of the double killing and theirs were the only names to appear in a report to the procurator fiscal but neither were ever charged.

Five years after her son William Lindsay was murdered for being in the wrong place at the wrong time, his mum Elizabeth said, 'I've great faith in the man above. I hope something will snap into place.'

In August 2006, Smith, thirty-two, was found dead in a caravan at the Craig Tara holiday park, near Ayr. He died of a suspected drugs overdose linked to a severe cocaine addiction. He had been forced to hand over assets worth £750,000 – including his home, three flats and a Jaguar car – to underworld asset strippers before his death. The Civil

Recovery Unit said their investigation into his criminal wealth would continue.

Stevenson was never charged, questioned or formally named as a suspect by officers investigating either of the double killings. His business could continue without interruption.

21
Game On

The City Inn on the northern banks of the Clyde at the end of Glasgow's Broomielaw is in the vanguard of the riverside development that is intended to transform the derelict docks and shipbuilding basins of the waterfront. Popular with businessmen, conference delegates and overnighters in town to see a show at the nearby Scottish Exhibition and Conference Centre, the hotel is a sleek and airy testament to the developers' dreams of creating an upwardly mobile affluent neighbourhood where the city's shipyards once stood. It was an unusual venue for the very public pronouncement of the end of a gangland dynasty.

The one-time McGovern associate and erstwhile business partner of Charlie Nicholas, Jim Milligan, had disappeared in the wake of Tony McGovern's murder. He remained disappeared while the hunt for the mobster's fortune raged in vain. He had holed up in Ireland for a while but, by June 2005, he had returned to Scotland and was enjoying lunch in the City Inn's popular restaurant.

He was just having coffee on the wooden decking overlooking the river when he was confronted by a reporter from the *Sunday Mail*, Scotland's biggest-selling newspaper. The hotel is just a few hundred yards from the newspaper's offices. Milligan did not welcome the attention but, as he made his hurried departure clutching the property schedules he had been discussing over lunch, he insisted he had nothing to fear from the McGoverns. Indeed, he went further, saying no one should be scared of the Springburn brothers, once the most feared crime gang in the city. Fumbling for his car keys, he blurted out, 'The McGoverns are finished.'

It seemed a bold statement by a man seemingly uncon-cerned by possible reprisals for his outspoken assessment of the power shifts in Glasgow's underworld but it was only a public acknowledgement of what detectives had realised months before. The McGoverns' dominance across tracts of the city was over. The brothers were continuing the battle to hold on to their drug-dealing heartlands just north of the M8 but they had lost the war.

Two years earlier, Stevenson had stepped up the scale and pace of his operations, leaving the McGoverns and every organised crime gang in Scotland in his wake. With the threat of prosecution over Tony's murder lifted and the dead man's family hemmed in by the need to protect what was left of their business, Stevenson had made his move. He stayed in Glasgow, buying a flat in the southside before moving to East Kilbride. In a characteristically arrogant gesture of absolute confidence in his own abilities, he is said to have sent the McGoverns change of address cards. He did not expect them to visit.

He was working out again. Tall and well built, physical strength had always signalled his authority but he now stepped up his exercise regime. Daily workouts on the weights and running belts at the gym in East Kilbride's Hilton Hotel, where he was a member, were augmented by regular runs around the nearby man-made loch at Stewartfield. He was never short of running partners with three or four heavy-set associates often joining him in their shorts. The burly joggers often did not seem to be enjoying the exercise as much as their boss but, even given his apparent gangland dominance, Stevenson was not foolhardy enough to go out running alone.

He started trading in gems to hide his earnings from drugs and his big plans, shared only with his wife and a clutch of trusted associates, would see those profits escalating dramatically in the months ahead. His intention was not only to take charge of the drugs trade in Glasgow but also to cement his position as the biggest trafficker Scotland had ever seen. His confidence, contacts and operational knowledge acquired during his months in exile had encouraged his belief that one man could effectively become Scotland's drugs wholesaler – a one-stop shop selling to the dealer gangs from Dumfries to Peterhead.

His strategy was, in theory, simple and one often adopted by businessmen pursuing a bigger share of the profit. He intended to cut out the middlemen. Drugs have traditionally travelled into Scotland from England. After being sold by English gang bosses to their Scottish counterparts, they are taken over the Border by train or, far more usually, driven up the M6. But, under Stevenson's ambitious business plan, heroin, cocaine, speed, hash and the rest would arrive in Scotland by the same route except the English gangsters would have no involvement, no responsibility and no cut. Stevenson would deal directly with the international organised crime gangs. From now on, he alone would take the risk of transporting the drugs into Britain, arranging the transport, finding the drivers, co-ordinating the deliveries, distributing the consignment and making the millions.

Of course, other Scots had smuggled drugs without the involvement of the gang bosses of London, Manchester and Liverpool. Gerry Carbin Snr, the father of Stevenson's stepson, had led one of the first and most innovative methods with his Costas-based 'hash-in-a-can' supply route shipping cannabis directly from Spain to the streets of Glasgow. People such as Tam McGraw, Brian Doran and Les Brown had all been linked to direct smuggling routes into Scotland. It was the sheer scale of Stevensons' ambition that set him apart. He was about to bring in more drugs more often than any Scotland-based criminal had done before. The scale of his operations would eventually reverse the traditional north-south transport of drugs in Britain as addicts in England's northern towns and cities were soon buying drugs sourced and transported by a Scots gangster.

One senior detective, who has tracked Stevenson's criminal career from the gangster's teenage years, says:

> After the McGovern murder, he took it up a level and the money he was raking in was absolutely phenomenal. You cut out the middlemen and your risk goes up but so do the profits. In the year he was away after McGovern, he was making contacts. When he came back, he thought he was absolutely bombproof. It was game on.

Stevenson's business strategy of making key contacts and forming makeshift alliances on a deal-by-deal basis put him in the vanguard of a trend that had been noted by crime analysts – the rise of powerful individuals in an international underworld traditionally dominated by organised, ethnically-based gangs. *The Organised Crime Threat Assessment*, produced by the crime-fighting agency Europol in 2006, described the rise of 'one-man armies' like Stevenson and the commercial tactics of this new breed of entrepreneurial drugs baron. It concluded:

> Modern research is increasingly shifting its focus from criminal collectives … to the individual 'organised criminal'. Studies have revealed very flexible and fluid patterns of association between individual criminals. The existence of criminal organisations or networks should not be taken for granted.

One observer, with his expert knowledge of Stevenson's deals in the crucial months following his full-time return to Scotland, was stunned by his audacity and ambition. He said:

> Stevenson spoke no languages but that did not deter him from seeking out the contacts that could deliver a foothold with the foreign gangs. He made it clear that he had the funds to purchase very large shipments and had the organisation to move the product efficiently. He paid when he was meant to and caused suppliers no problems.
>
> Stevenson is personable and has a good manner with people. They liked him and they liked doing business with him. You cannot do what Stevenson has been doing for so many years without making enemies but he has made fewer than most men in his position. Generally speaking, he did what he said he was going to do when he said he was going to do it and that is appreciated whatever business you're in.
>
> But he can turn the charm off and on like a tap. People can think they're his pal and only find out they're not when it's too late.

22
Breaking In

They are Stevenson's kind of people, the expat Turkish fixers of Glasgow. They live quietly, modestly, stay close to home, keep their own counsel and are loyal, secretive and ruthless. The criminal gangs of Turkey have forged a fierce allegiance of their members scattered across Europe through a sinister amplification of the wider codes of their society – codes of loyalty, respect and family.

It is no surprise that Stevenson, keen to bring in huge quantities of heroin, sought out the men who quietly frequented the cafes and gambling clubs of Britain's Turkish communities. He knew that, amongst them, were those who were capable of opening a channel of communication with their countrymen who ferried opiates across the continent. His reputation and personality ensured he found them. One informed police source said:

> In 2001, he started to search out the people who could help him. He was good at building relationships. He was very good at that – just by talking to the right people and winning confidence. He's physically a big man and, within Glasgow's underworld, absolutely feared. He made contacts with Turks and Asians that would be fundamental to his business.

Turkey is at the crossroads of Europe, Asia and the

Middle East and the country's crime syndicates ruthlessly exploit their geographical good fortune to traffic lucrative contraband, from drugs to guns to humans. Most of the heroin – 75 per cent, according to official estimates – streaming into the towns and cities of Europe passes through Turkey and most of it is destined for Britain.

Opium poppies grown in two areas are used to produce most of the world's heroin – the Golden Triangle of Myanmar (formerly Burma), Thailand and Laos and the Golden Crescent of Afghanistan, Iran and Pakistan. Myanmar and Afghanistan are the biggest producers of poppies with an estimated 70 per cent of the 135 tonnes of heroin sold in Europe each year originating in Afghanistan.

The harvested poppy heads harden and dry before the malleable raw opium is rolled into balls. A gram will be sold by the farmers of Afghanistan for three pence. The criminal wholesalers might pay £27 for it and an addict in Scotland will need £50 to buy the same gram. Raw opium is usually transported to Turkish labs through Pakistan or Iran where the opium base is processed to produce heroin. The drug shipments are bought and sold by different gangs along the route.

In 2001, as Stevenson was building bridgeheads to mainland Europe and beyond, the international trafficking network was stabilising after years of flux provoked by the civil war raging in the former Yugoslavia through the late 1990s and the rolling reverberations from the collapse of the Berlin Wall. A clampdown by the Iranian authorities had seen more heroin leave Afghanistan to the north through central Asia to Russia along the Silk Road, an ancient network of trading routes stretching from the Far East to Europe. Tajikistan was emerging as a new and popular transit point but, further down the line, the various branches of the traditional Balkan Route had been disrupted but not closed by the ethnic conflict.

Starting in Turkey, the principal overland connection between Asia and Europe, the 3500-mile-long Balkan Route, was once used by more than one and a half million lorries and four million cars each year. The highway through the former Yugoslavia was the principal conduit for the heroin smugglers until the bloody civil wars of the late 1990s forced the forging of a new road map. The collapse of the Berlin Wall made that easier.

Typically, battered trucks had carried heroin consignments from Turkey to Greece and on to Macedonia before a fleet of small boats ferried the drugs north to the Dalmatian Coast or across to Italy. After the Iron Curtain was raised, some drug shipments continued through Croatia and Macedonia but far more were detoured north through the Czech Republic, Romania, Hungary, and Bulgaria. A smaller number of shipments went through Hungary and Slovakia to Austria. In recent years, the McGoverns have often claimed Vienna's burgeoning wholesale drugs market had made it 'the new Amsterdam'.

Some opiates are smuggled by train, by plane (one estimate suggests 25 per cent of Britain's heroin is flown in from Pakistan) or by post but most is driven to Holland, Belgium and Germany for distribution hidden in buses, cars and, most often, container trucks.

As Stevenson prepared to launch himself into the marketplace, a secret report by the US Drug Enforcement Administration in 2000 revealed America's fears that the new European era of trade cooperation and open borders had kicked open the door for drugs traffickers. They said, 'Although this agreement is advantageous for trade, it is also attractive to drug traffickers.' The DEA warned that stocks of class A drugs were already being amassed in holding depots at key distribution points to ensure a constant flow of narcotics at stable prices. The agency said:

In the last few years, heroin has been increasingly stockpiled in some western and eastern European locations, enabling west European travellers to take delivery of the drug closer to home. Turkish heroin-trafficking organisations work in collusion with nationals from Eastern Europe who have established heroin depots to store large quantities of heroin and release it on demand. These storage facilities ensure a steady, uninterrupted drug supply to west European consumers.

The drugs are ferried north to staging posts and holding depots on the northern coast of mainland Europe, particularly in Holland and Belgium, awaiting collection by anyone with the cash and contacts to make the deal – someone like Jamie Stevenson.

The Turks do not have the monopoly as the Albanian gangs, in particular, show themselves capable of quickly drilling into the narrowest of openings to carve out new opportunities in drugs and human trafficking. But the Turks do continue to command the routes. Their countrymen living in Holland, Belgium and Britain control the importation and wholesale distribution of heroin and Stevenson knew they would hold the key to unlocking his own supply routes into Scotland.

In May 2006, Abdullah Baybasin was convicted in London for conspiracy to supply 2.23kg of heroin. His conviction showed what influence the British-based Turkish gangsters had with their countrymen abroad. While being sentenced at Woolwich Crown Court to twenty-two years behind bars, the Turkish Godfather smiled as Judge Gregory Stone told him, 'You used the application of violence and threats of violence and fostered a well-founded reputation for serious violence.'

Detectives had launched a five-year electronic surveillance operation against the crime boss, who arrived in Britain ten years before his conviction. They believe he was involved in arranging massive heroin consignments to come into the country. Asylum-seeking Baybasin was confined to a wheelchair after being shot in an Amsterdam bar thirty years ago. He ran his drugs and protection-racket empire from the Green Lanes neighbourhood in Haringey, North London – a business police link to twenty-five murders.

The Turks offered Stevenson the contacts to begin the wholesale importation of heroin in Scotland but he had other avenues to explore, other international contacts to be forged. The Balkan Route, or modern variations of it, is still used to transport most of the heroin eventually polluting the veins of Europe's addicts but some estimates suggest that around a quarter of the opiates arriving in Britain now passes through Pakistan. The international drugs brokers of Islamabad, next to the poppy fields of Afghanistan, are a force in the global marketplace. And for a Scottish smuggler with more money than he knew what to do with, Pakistan seemed like a nice place to spend a fortune.

A small, unassuming travel agency in the southside of Glasgow was about to become Stevenson's favourite shop.

23
Foreign Exchange

The tiny travel agency in Glasgow's southside seemed no different to any of the others specialising in low-cost air deals to Pakistan in the Pollokshields neighbourhood which is home to most of Scotland's Asians. The peeling green paint on the shabby shopfront of Makkah Travel concealed the tiny bucket shop's status as a multi-million pound business laundering Scotland's gangland millions.

Suitcases and holdalls with zips bulging would be delivered to the shop on the junction of Kenmure Street and Albert Drive next to the Spice Garden supermarket. The bags would be left there and returned on the next visit after being emptied of the dirty money of Jamie Stevenson and other millionaire criminals – grubby tenners and twenties bound into £5,000 rolls amassed from Scotland's addicts and users.

Once handed over by couriers, the money would be transferred to Pakistan under *hawala*, an informal worldwide banking network used by families and firms throughout Asia for centuries. Of Arabic origin, *hawala*, also known as *hundi* – commonly accepted as meaning 'transfer' – is a cash pipeline used by millions of expat Pakistanis to send money home to their families or to give monetary gifts to friends. Built on trust and an international network of unofficial money-movers, its attraction to Stevenson and other Scots gangsters is obvious. There is little or no paper trail left by the millions being sent abroad and no official records at its destination. The recipients, named in the sparse paperwork, remain untraceable and uncheckable. It is fast, reliable and based entirely on trust. Money promised by a *hawaladar* in Scotland will be delivered by another, thousands of miles away without any physical movement of cash. The debt will be settled in time. Often the money owed will be sent out of Britain later in apparent settlement of an invoice for goods imported from Pakistan. The invoice will have been falsely inflated to incorporate the debt.

Money transfers by anyone other than official banks remain illegal in Pakistan, but foreign bankers estimate up to £4 billion a year floods through the *hawala* system every year. International law enforcers fear that this includes millions being laundered by organised crime gangs and terrorist groups. Most transfers are conducted by phone, fax or e-mail.

Neil Livingstone, of the Washington-based international financial investigators GlobalOptions, said, 'It's a great way to move a lot of money around while preserving anonymity.' And anonymity is just what Stevenson and his associates in Pakistan wanted.

Professor Nikos Passas, in a 2004 article in the *Journal of Financial Crime*, explained the potential problems facing investigators following the trail abroad from a British-based *hawaladar*. He wrote:

> *Hawala* ledgers are often insubstantial and in idiosyncratic shorthand. Initials or numbers that are meaningful to the *hawaladar* are useless if they reveal nothing about transactions, amounts, times and names of people or organisations.
>
> The co-operation of *hawaladars* in such cases is of vital importance. Personal ledgers are sometimes destroyed within a short period of time, especially where *hawala* is criminalised. In some cases, particularly when *hawaladars*

know that their clients are breaking the law, no notes or records are kept at all. In other cases, *hawaladars* may serve customers without asking many questions about their true identity, the origin of their money or the reason for the transfer. In such cases, even if *hawala* operators decided to co-operate with authorities, they would have no knowledge or useful knowledge to share.

At the other end of the money chain, *benami* or false name accounts will also camouflage where the money has been sent. Professor Passas continued:

In some cases, accounts may be held by a lawyer, accountant, friend or even persons unaware that someone else is using their name. Sometimes the owner of the *benami* account may be simply fictional, making the tracing of the beneficial owner impossible.

One of Stevenson's associates said:

It worked like a dream for him but everybody was into it. You basically gave the shop the money and they sent it out to the Pakistani equivalent of Mr Mickey Mouse. It's picked up the next day in Islamabad or wherever and there is absolutely no way of anyone discovering who really sent the money or who really received it. You're easily talking about millions and millions of pounds every year.

Some of Stevenson's money streamed out of Scotland to Islamabad to be cleaned and hidden in legitimate accounts or property deals. Some went to the United Arab Emirates and some to China. Huge sums would also be steered to the money-changing shops lining the streets of Peshawar and Quetta, along Pakistan's border with Afghanistan – the cities where opium brokers do business. Brokers were happy to trade with Stevenson – delighted to make the deals that pumped heroin on to the streets of Scotland.

The Home Office estimates that £2 billion of dirty money remains in Britain each year while £3.3 billion is sent abroad. Many of the millions flooding out of Scotland in a stream of electronic transfers were being delivered to Makkah Travel by underworld bagmen. Customs investigators who eventually shut down the money-laundering pipeline suspect that Zohaib Assad, twenty-six, and his accomplice Mohammad Ahmad, fifty-three, transferred £10 million of drugs money in just fourteen months.

Investigators staked out the shop in April 2003 after the National Westminster Bank raised the alarm over the massive sums being sent abroad by the tiny travel agency. Bankers had even advised the shop to hire a security firm to transport the fortunes in cash being handed over their counter. Launching an inquiry, codenamed Seraph, Customs monitored Makkah for months as expert financial investigators discovered £2.2 million had been moved by the tiny travel agency in one seven-month period.

After a five-week trial that ended in March 2006, Assad and Ahmad, who, like his co-accused, had no criminal record, were convicted of seven charges under the Proceeds of Crime Act. It was the first trial in Scotland based on the 2002 legislation. More were to follow, although legal teams for Assad and Ahman immediately appealed their convictions. After being freed pending a hearing, the men were due to return to court to attempt to overturn the guilty verdicts in summer 2008.

As the men allegedly behind Makkah's money laundering were being convicted, another travel agent was also being jailed in a case only underlining the astonishing scale of the cleansing operation run through the *hawala* system.

Shahid Nazir Bhatti, owner of the Bradford Travel Agency, was sentenced to three years. Customs investigators believe that his shop helped launder £42 million in just two years but suspect that, in just over four years, a total of £500 million of drugs money had been laundered through the cash pipeline from West Yorkshire to Pakistan. Bhatti, forty-five, was the last of eleven accused to be sentenced since the huge cash-cleansing racket was uncovered in 2001. Scots gangsters were among those around Britain sending their millions to Yorkshire to be laundered.

After uncovering the identical kind of money-laundering operation in Glasgow, Customs investigators recovered a total of £2,442,318 which had been received by Makkah and placed in Glasgow holding accounts ready to be sent abroad.

Sentencing the pair at the High Court in Edinburgh, the judge, Lord Dawson, told them:

> Over the weeks this trial lasted, it became clear to me that, without the services of people like you, serious organised crime could not exist. It is also clear to me ... that both of you knew full well what you were involved in. It may well be that someone else was pulling the strings and taking the lion's share of the money, but that in no way absolves you of responsibility for your own actions. It is my public duty to punish you and to attempt to discourage others who may be tempted to get themselves involved in this very nasty line of work.

Gordon Miller, the head of Customs' investigations in Scotland welcomed the verdict, hailing it as the country's first successful money-laundering prosecution under the Proceeds of Crime Act. He said: 'This investigation and trial demonstrates the success of the legislation. The act was specifically designed to take action against money launderers and take the proceeds out of crime, thereby depriving criminals of their illicit wealth.'

Money-laundering investigations, along with asset tracing and confiscation, are at the heart of HM Revenue and Customs' national criminal investigation strategy.

A third man had been accused over the money-laundering operation. Suspected underworld bagman William Gurie, thirty-nine, was accused of delivering massive amounts of cash to Makkah. One witness, James McDonald, a convicted counterfeiter, told the court that he had paid Gurie, described as an installation engineer, to deliver between £750,000 and £800,000 to the shop. McDonald, who is fifty-eight and from Stirling, is a self-styled legal adviser to some of Scotland's wealthiest organised crime figures. His portfolio of specialisms includes the identification of possible loopholes in both the proceeds of crime legislation and motoring law. McDonald often courts publicity for his legal coups and has few friends in Scotland's police and prosecution services. He is also one of Stevenson's legal advisers.

Customs had been watching Gurie as he arrived at Makkah on 23 September 2003 and switched a bulging holdall from his car to Assad's. Three days later, in a series of synchronised raids, officers found £384,720 in Assad's home in Darnley, Glasgow. The bundled-up cash was to be evidence at the trial and it took court staff two and a half days to count it. After being seized, the £5, £10 and £20 notes were analysed and 80 per cent were found to be 'saturated' with heroin as forensic scientists found the highest reading of drugs contamination on notes ever recorded in Britain.

Gurie, whose prints were on the cash and the holdall, walked free, smiling broadly after the jury found charges of money laundering not proven. McDonald is now trying to reclaim the money. He says he handed over the bags stuffed with cash to Gurie at Little Chef car parks and at the Showcase Cinema, near Coatbridge, Lanarkshire, but claims the money was to finance a call centre in Pakistan and to fund an invention allowing cars to run on water. He said the cash belonged to Abdul Gahfoor, a director of the defunct Alphascot Ltd, based in Sauchie, Clackmannanshire. In 2004, Gahfoor had been exposed for using Alphascot to launder money for multimillionaire VAT fraudster Michael Voudouri.

Asked why he had not delivered the money to Makkah himself or used a more conventional method to transfer such huge sums, McDonald replied, 'As I have convictions for counterfeit money offences, I used someone else. I could have been compromised with large sums of money. I had sent $14.57 million to the USA and someone managed to steal $14.1 million.'

He insisted the notes must have been contaminated with heroin after being seized by Customs saying, 'The jury must have accepted my evidence that £384,000 was legitimate. Why else was I not in the dock?'

Before Assad was sentenced, his lawyer, Donald Findlay QC, told the court that it 'is not for the first time that it is the soldiers, not the officers, who end up in the dock'.

24

Open for Business

It is only a guess, no more than a hunch, but law enforcers in Britain, like their colleagues on mainland Europe, estimate that they stop only one in ten of the drugs consignments being trafficked across the continent.

In 2005, police in Scotland seized drugs that would have sold for £48 million in the country's villages, towns and cities. If that is multiplied by ten, it amounts to a drugs trade worth £480 million and that is assuming that as much as one-tenth of drugs are stopped in transit. Many, in the police and outside, fear that figure is hopelessly optimistic. No one knows but a criminal economy worth £2 billion a year in Scotland, possibly even double that, is easily possible. It's a tide of billions of pounds washing through the blackest of economies, most of it founded on drugs. During 2005, the majority of those tonnes and tonnes of drugs was brought into Scotland by one man – a man living quietly in a small flat on the outskirts of Glasgow with an import business stretching across the globe.

One Strathclyde officer believes Jamie Stevenson's pre-eminent position in Scotland's drugs trade cannot be doubted. He said:

> He was a force before the McGovern murder but, when the case collapsed and he came back to Scotland, he took his thing into a wholly different league. He was doing more,

more frequently than anyone we've ever seen. Basically, for those five years or so, there would have been few major consignments of drugs coming into Scotland that he was not responsible for – very few.

Armed with contacts in Turkey and Pakistan who were capable of delivering drugs to the gateway towns of northern Holland and Belgium, Stevenson was ready to make his transport arrangements. He turned to the truckers. He was not the first Scots crime boss to use the HGV drivers criss-crossing the continent, picking up and delivering legitimate cargo, as cover for his drug runs. Some had a few drivers, doing a few runs, for a few thousand pounds but the scale of Stevenson's ambition required far more. He became a haulage boss.

Sometimes he bought lorries for drivers and set them up on their own. Sometimes he liked a haulage firm so much he bought the company. Apparently legitimate transport firms and depots scattered to the north of Glasgow, complete with warehouses and mechanics tuning their fleet of container trucks, were, in fact, fronts for Iceman Inc. In addition, his associates in Ulster, the one-time terrorists now turned organised criminals, had their own haulage arrangements already in place and this offered another option to the Scots crime boss.

The route north from mainland Europe to the southwest of Scotland and the ferry ports serving Belfast offered convenient and inconspicuous drop-off points. A quick cup of tea in a Dumfries service station, ten minutes swapping a few innocent looking boxes from cab to car and the trucker was back on the road heading home to Northern Ireland while one of Stevenson's cohorts was heading up the M74 to Glasgow with another load of drugs, another few million pounds.

The drugs could be hidden in loads of fruit, fish or whatever else was on the driver's manifest. It did not matter to Stevenson although the flower markets of northern Holland offered some of the most convenient camouflage for drugs runs. Demanding frequent pick-ups and based in the heart of Europe's clearing house for class A narcotics, Holland's flower markets were a regular destination for the drivers being paid up to £20,000 a trip for making a small detour to meet one of Stevenson's friends on the Continent.

One source with expert knowledge of Stevenson's drugs runs said:

The drugs would be hidden in the walls of the truck, in the panels, in the silencers, in among the loads, among the flowers. Sometimes, in a bit of bluffology, the boxes were sitting all wrapped up in the driver's cab. It didn't matter – they were coming in.

The drivers had to be of a type – men capable of taking some strain. There had to be some confidence that they would hold it together if stopped at the ports. Some bam skidding through Customs in a cold sweat is not required. Stuff did get stopped but there was so much coming in that a load here and there could easily be written off. And these are loads that Stevenson had paid £300,000 or £400,000 for.

Stevenson would want to make sure there was no comeback from it. He'd want to be sure the drivers were squared off, with money, with threats or with both. But they were cannon fodder. The business never stopped. He never stopped making money.

A kilo of coke in Holland cost him £22,000. Selling that to some gang in Scotland would clear £35,000. That's £13,000 profit per kilo without the risks of street dealing. If, like Stevenson, you're bringing in fifty, sixty, a hundred kilos a run, you're talking a lot of money – an awful lot of money.

Stevenson smuggled heroin but was one of a new type of criminal highlighted by a Europol drugs bulletin in 2006 – the so-called 'polydrug' smuggler. They did not limit themselves to specialist traffic in heroin, cocaine or Ecstasy – they did the lot, usually with the help of contacts and operational outposts in or around Amsterdam. The agency said:

> The Netherlands plays a vital role in Europe as a centre for the transportation, facilitation and preparation of polydrug consignments. Non-Dutch criminals are basing themselves in the Netherlands to conduct polydrug trafficking business. They work closely with Dutch brokers to facilitate the supply of cocaine and other drugs to the United Kingdom and Ireland. Drugs are often professionally secreted in purpose-built concealments within the framework of vehicles or within the legitimate consignment of goods being carried. Special concealments either in the packaging or within the goods themselves have also been found.

Another report, this time written by the US Drug Enforcement Administration, underlined the importance of Amsterdam as the must-go destination for major international drugs traffickers. They said the city is 'rather unique in that every type of drug-smuggling and distribution organisation is represented for strategic and logistical purposes'. They also described the city as 'an organisational centre, a central brokerage point and a safe haven' where 'Dutch hashish traffickers are increasingly distributing heroin, cocaine and amphetamine to other countries. This polydrug activity is being encountered more and more frequently.'

Cocaine from South America, heroin from Afghanistan, amphetamine and Ecstasy made in the industrial drugs labs of Holland and Belgium were all available in the criminal wholesale market of Amsterdam and Stevenson, with a growing reputation built on regular hassle-free deals, was a welcome buyer.

'That's maybe the one thing that would still surprise people – the sheer scale of what he was bringing in and the millions and millions he was making,' says one police officer. He added:

It wasn't just heroin. He'd have a truck carrying one box of smack, another of cocaine, some amphetamine in there, Ecstasy . . . he was bringing in everything all the time – whatever was available. He'd be told such and such was available. He'd send the money, a bagman carrying cash to Amsterdam or a money transfer to Pakistan or wherever. The money goes out and the drugs come back.

Basically, for those five years, Stevenson was the drugs market in Scotland. He was the wholesaler to smaller dealers across the Central Belt and up and down the country. He was the one-stop shop for these guys.

He was Drugs 'R' Us.

25
Friends Across the Water

After his arrest, Jamie Stevenson was told police were still struggling to identify and target all of his international business contacts. He just smiled before saying, 'I hope they're collecting their Air Miles.'

The network that Stevenson used to bring thousands of tonnes of class A drugs into Scotland stretched around the globe. His dealings with traffickers trailed from the poppy fields of Afghanistan through Pakistan and Turkey, to cocaine from Colombia and hash from Morocco and through Spain. Domestically produced Ecstasy and speed from Holland joined wholesale consignments of heroin and cocaine from the holding depots near Amsterdam, Rotterdam and along the coast of Belgium. Sweden, France and Portugal were all weigh stations for Stevenson's loads.

Despite disliking foreign travel, he visited many of these countries. Much of his business could only be conducted face to face. Sometimes he travelled on his own passport. Sometimes he was Jeremiah Dooley, the identity on a counterfeit British passport the police found in one of his homes as they moved to dismantle his operation. The passport had been supplied by a contact in Northern Ireland – a former Loyalist terrorist who was a skilled counterfeiter and one of the most important links in the international supply chain streaming Stevenson's drugs on to Scotland's streets.

Given his deal-making abilities, it was no surprise that

his associates came from both sides of the sectarian divide. 'He would do business with whoever was sat on the other side of the table,' one source remembers, 'green, orange, or purple.' He continued:

> I don't know how common that is – not very, probably – but he did it. It was just business to him. He could be one thing for somebody, another for somebody else. His reputation in Scotland was always going to help. There's so much coming and going over the sea that the people he was dealing with knew what he was all about. He didn't need a lot of introduction.

Stevenson was born a Protestant but, after his mother remarried, a lot of the time when he was growing up was spent with Catholic relatives – particularly a favourite uncle, who died while he was on remand after the Folklore busts. One acquaintance from Glasgow said:

> Religion was not a big part of his life, in any sense. He used to go to the Celtic games but it was more about being seen and seeing people. He was a businessman not a football fan. He had some decent pals in Ulster – men he trusted and there weren't many of them in Scotland, Ireland or anywhere else.
>
> He was close to one guy in particular. He never mentioned his name but just called him 'The Musician'. He seemed to be right at the top of the tree – a serious criminal. He seemed to be one of the very few that Jamie would listen to, take a bit of advice from.

His friends across the Irish Sea had been Stevenson's first port of call after the McGovern murder. He travelled first to Belfast and then on to a safe house in the Republic before heading to warmer climes with his crony John Gorman on the Costa del Sol. Irish gangsters, from both the north and south of the island, also enjoyed the bars and clubs around the Fuengirola resort and many were to become the two Scots' partners in drinking and crime.

After his return to Britain and the eventual collapse of the McGovern murder charge, the terror-gangs-turned-drugs-runners of Ulster remained a key part of Stevenson's business. For years, all through the Troubles, there has been an exchange of money and goods between the criminal gangs of the West of Scotland and their counterparts in Northern Ireland. The ferry routes offered easy access and escape for visitors to do special favours for their friends before quietly returning home, unsuspected and untraceable. The favours often left men unable to walk . . . or breathe.

The terror groups of Northern Ireland had enjoyed a peace dividend when their guns fell temporarily and then permanently silent in the wake of the Good Friday Agreement of 1998. The paramilitaries of all shades no longer had to divide their attention between crime and terror. In any case, crime was more profitable. When the Northern Ireland Select Affairs Committee investigated Northern Ireland's criminal underworld in 2006, the thirteen members concluded that the terror gangs from both sides of the religious divide were running rampant. Their report revealed IRA Republican, Loyalist UDA and UVF and all related splinter groups were attempting to outstrip each other in their enthusiasm for drugs, armed robbery, protection rackets and smuggling. And Stevenson had already bought in.

One associate said:

> He had his own lorries coming and going to Scotland but all the Irish trucks heading through Dumfries to the ferries at Stranraer and Larne fitted perfectly. He knew guys who could get one of his drivers a job. He knew guys who knew guys in Holland. He knew guys all over the place in exactly

the same line of work as his. For a time, Northern Ireland was a big part of Stevenson's operation.

By the time Stevenson was arrested, the government's Organised Crime Task Force estimated that Northern Ireland's gangsters were raking in £600 million a year as police chiefs warned of increasing evidence of international links and the involvement of criminals from the British mainland. The elite agency revealed a master plan to target thirty outfits and these were only the most dangerous and profitable in the Province. An estimated 230 criminal groups have been identified by police.

The huge wealth generated by the sectarian gunmen-turned-drug-runners was only emphasised in November 2004 when the rural retreat of one of Ulster's most feared terrorists was put on the market by criminal asset strippers. The mansion, complete with its own stable block, belonged to Jim 'Jonty' Johnston, a leading member of the Red Hand Commando, after he was shot dead while going to feed his two pet donkeys. He had controlled the drugs trade in County Down, raking in an estimated £1.5 million, and been questioned over five drugs-related murders. The authorities were to seize £1.2 million after his death, including a property portfolio, investments and a tidy pension plan.

Former members of the Red Hand Commando had been among Stevenson's best contacts in the Province.

A source said:

> The Loyalists seemed far more deeply involved in drugs running than the other side – the actual process of getting stuff from there to here. So that's who Stevenson dealt with. But I know for a fact he did stuff with Republicans as well. If it suited him, if he trusted the others and if it paid, he would go in with anyone. That was how he worked – always.

26
Chairman of the Board

To the detectives tracking Jamie Stevenson through his labyrinth of international money transfers, supply network and freight deliveries, he was the chairman of the board. One officer, involved in the massive offensive against Stevenson, said:

> Drugs trafficking is a huge, international business and men like Stevenson are the chief executives. They might never see their product but they are the men with the overall sense of the business. They are forging relationships with contacts, making the deals, organising supply routes, arranging recruitment.
>
> Stevenson was as capable as any we have seen in Scotland in terms of the skills and talents that he brought to his work. He was very organised, personable, a risk-taker and proactive in dealing with threats to his business. He was, in effect, a very successful businessman. His business was the large-scale importation and sale of class A drugs and he was good at it. He knew about supply and demand. He knew about product, price, his place in the market and strategy.
>
> Like most of these men, Stevenson surrounded himself with a very, very small group of people he trusted completely. They were his operational directors and he would deal with them on a need to know basis. One would handle

one bit of business for him, another would handle another. In turn, they're busy organising the level below them. The management structure was a classic pyramid, fanning out from Stevenson at the very top down through a tight group of key associates, down to the gangsters buying wholesale from them, down to the street dealers selling tenner bags up some close.

He was doing the import stuff, the supply chain stuff, and working out the franchise arrangements. Some of the gangs he would be supplying were selling his drugs in his areas, largely the southside of Glasgow spreading east out to Lanarkshire, for his profits, others were buying the stuff wholesale and going away and doing their own thing. Either way, he was making money.

If, as the business textbooks insist, good management is about planning, organising, and controlling, Stevenson was a good manager. He was also, according to at least one source who has known him for years, a natural leader. As academic and leadership guru Fred Fiedler says, 'There is no one ideal leader personality. However, effective leaders tend to have a high need to influence others, to achieve, and they tend to be bright, competent and socially adept, rather than stupid, incompetent and social disasters.'

One source, a long-term acquaintance of Stevenson, said:

He's physically a big, imposing man – good looking, well built, broad shoulders, clearly fit. He was usually in casual gear – sweatshirts, trackies – but it was always very clean, very neat. He had a feeling of sharpness about him. In person, he could be really amenable. It was like he knew the buttons to press to make people like him – like a conscious thing – but he could turn it off just as quickly.

One of his things is that, when he's talking to you, he locks right on to your eyes and stays there. He never looks away. It's like he's absolutely involved with your conversation. It can be disconcerting and intimidating but it's kind of flattering as well – that he seems so intent on what you've got to say. Of course, all the time that brain of his is taking what you're saying, computing it and working out all his angles.

He's certainly smart but then it wouldn't take much to be smarter than the halfwits and liabilities he started out in competition with. What he did show for those five years or so was that he was capable of taking his game up a league to do business with major criminals who were just as cute and just as ruthless.

But one criminologist, based at a Scottish university where he has studied the mechanics of organised crime, said it would be wrong to exaggerate the business skills of gangsters like Stevenson.

On one level, they are operating a multinational import business and making a huge amount of money. On another, they are criminals, operating outside of the law, paying no taxes, using violence to consolidate their position. They clearly have some of the skills of legitimate businessmen but it is dangerous to encourage this idea that, if they had only chosen another fork in the road, they would be Richard Branson. It's rubbish.

Most of these men – and they are invariably men – prosper in a life of crime because they are good at things abhorrent in the rest of society. They steal things and kill people. They should not be considered nominees for entrepreneur of the year.

Another investigator, with knowledge of the Folklore operation, agrees, saying:

Stevenson certainly had some attributes that might have secured a successful career in legitimate business but he enjoyed the game too much. He liked the excitement, the control, the reputation, the money. He's bright but not as clever as the guys like him who know when to step off the merry-go-round. They make their millions, launder their money and buy into legitimate business. They have made more money than they know how to spend and the choice is open to them to turn legit, to become businessmen instead of 'businessmen'.

A few manage to do it – the brightest ones – and it becomes harder to prove that drugs money helped launch their legit firms with every month that passes. Given their past, they may spend the rest of their lives looking over their shoulders but it won't be for the police.

The level Stevenson was operating at meant he had that choice and he decided to continue doing what he was doing. He enjoyed the life. He enjoyed being a criminal. He enjoyed the buzz. And he enjoyed taking on the police. He is an arrogant man. That arrogance was a big part of his character and a big part in what he achieved but it was to help bring him down.

27

Our Lost Boy

June Ross was talking on the phone with David, the eldest of her five children, around 9 p.m. on Friday, 16 March 2007, when an overdose of heroin killed him. She was sitting in the comfortable family home in the affluent village of Kilmacolm, Renfrewshire, where she and her husband Donald had raised David and his two brothers and two sisters.

David lived just along the road in the flat he shared with his girlfriend, who was away visiting her sister that weekend. When he was found two days later, his phone was still gripped in his lifeless hand.

June said:

> He had signed for a flat the Wednesday before he died and he started a job laying turf that week. Because he was paid cash at the end of each day, he was able to buy heroin. I had been speaking to him on the phone that Friday night and his speech was gradually getting slower and slower. I asked if he had taken Valium and he said he had so I just put it down to that. He then just stopped talking but the line was still open – he hadn't ended the call. I am now sure that was his last breath I heard on the phone.
>
> I work with heroin addicts and one of them said to me that what I heard on the phone was his death rattle. I at least knew that he wasn't on his own when he died even

though I was on the other end of the phone. Who wants
to die alone?

At the time, June thought that the heroin or the
tranquillising qualities of the Valium had taken effect and
David, thirty-six, was too out of it to continue the call. But,
when Saturday morning came, June's maternal instincts began
to gnaw away at her. Later that day, David had failed to keep
separate appointments – one with one of his brothers and the
other with a 'mentor' who was trying to help him break his
addiction.

On the Sunday, David's girlfriend phoned June to say
that she too was worried. It was unusual that David hadn't
answered any of her many phone calls or replied to the text
messages she'd sent him. She voiced her fears to June, saying,
'He might be lying blue-lipped in the flat.'

June said:

That just clarified in my mind that something was wrong
and, by the Sunday afternoon, I was sure he was lying up
there. I was feeling really uptight. Donald got hold of my
middle son who is very tall, over six foot four, to get him to
look in the window but the blinds were closed tight.

The key was on the inside of the lock so Donald and
my son went to get a wire coat hanger which they used to
unlock the door. When they got in, Donald went straight
through to the bedroom thinking that David would be
there.

My middle son went into the kitchen and found David
lying dead on the floor. He knew straight away that his
brother was dead and just closed the door.

Almost forty-eight hours after that final conversation
with his mum, David's phone remained in his hand, the many
texts and messages from his partner never to be answered.

When he died, he had been about to make a cup of tea as his mug, containing a teabag and sugar, was sitting beside the kettle.

Donald phoned the police and then returned home in order to confirm to his wife what she already sensed. June said:

> I knew anyway. I had a wee cry and said that I had to go and see him but the police could not let me in and said it was best to try and remember him as he was. I think that was good advice.

June finds solace in her Christian faith and believes that her troubled son is no longer suffering and that the torture that he and his family suffered for so many years is at an end. She also draws comfort in the fact that she was with him when he died, albeit at the end of the phone. She said, 'At least we know he is at peace now. We do have a faith in God and we believe that he is in heaven which is better than being here trying to get money for heroin.'

The couple carry themselves with great dignity in the wake of such a bitter loss which was compounded by an agonising wait for the release of his body by the authorities. On 8 May, more than seven weeks after his premature death, many hundreds of mourners crammed into a Port Glasgow church to celebrate David's troubled life. Those attending the service were given copies of a moving tribute about David which had been written by June. It read:

> My son David was the eldest of five children brought up in a Christian family, going to church as a baby then Sunday School as a young boy. Growing up, he was full of mischief, loved life, was always trying something exciting – skateboarding, BMX and skiing.
>
> As time went on, David got involved with friends who experimented with drugs and, like many young people,

experimented himself. This eventually led to a serious addiction to heroin.

David grew up in a time and place where most parents had a limited knowledge of drugs. Stories about cannabis being smoked in school playgrounds were enough to cause sleepless nights for many mums and dads. But, as the cancer of hard drugs began to creep across Scotland, Donald and June were well placed to understand it as they worked with a charity called Teen Challenge. This Christian group, founded in late 1950s New York and now operating in more than seventy countries, helps many young Scots battling with drug problems.

David was born nine days before Christmas in 1970 and over the next fourteen years his four siblings arrived into a loving family home filled with happiness. The first sign of a flirtation with any kind of substance came when David was thirteen years old. June had arrived home from a cash-and-carry with bulk supplies for her large family, including deodorant and hairspray. Donald said:

I remember hearing this aerosol noise in the bathroom and wondered what on earth he was up to in there. I shouted on him a couple of times but he didn't reply so I climbed in through the bathroom window. I found him lying semiconscious in the bath having inhaled this stuff. I dragged him out the bath and carried him outside to the fresh air where I made him walk round and round the fields to try and get it out of his system. It was only when I realised that he was OK that I got angry at him. It later came out that he had first done this on a school trip to Switzerland.

He was a bit of a character and a tearaway. He liked to be the class comedian at school and was very much a people person. From that moment, we began to get suspicious of everything that he got up to. At the age of fifteen or sixteen, he was away at a church summer camp and we think he was caught smoking hash which he was warned about but not sent home. When he was a bit older he was drinking and hanging around in bad company and we were suspicious of other things.

When he was eighteen, I had to give him three months notice to find somewhere else to live because he was going totally against what we as a family were prepared to accept. He was old enough to run his own affairs and we had to protect the other members of the family.

David moved out to stay with his then girlfriend and their parents in nearby Johnstone. His family don't know exactly when David first took heroin but, by the time he was twenty, they were certain he was doing so. June said:

Two of the counsellors who do voluntary work with Teen Challenge were round for supper and I was worried because I had heard nothing from David for five weeks, which was not like him. That night he appeared and, just from looking at him, I knew for sure that he was on heroin. We can't be certain when it started because, like all addicts, he became a very good liar. They develop a smokescreen.

Before their son became hooked, Donald and June helped set up The Haven, a residential centre in Kilmacolm which caters for up to a dozen people with drink and drugs problems. It was a place where David was to make some of his nine ultimately failed attempts at rehabilitation. The most successful of those was at a centre in Preston, in Lancashire, around three years before his death. He returned to the family home drug-free, confident and began attending a college course that would qualify him to help other addicts.

In Preston, he wrote and starred in a screenplay which was to be used to warn kids about the dangers of drugs. His mum occasionally watches the DVD to remember her son when he was happy. June said, 'He was doing so well but he then got involved with an old girlfriend and went back to Glasgow to live and that was it. It was the beginning of the end.'

After a spell at a London rehab clinic, he returned to Scotland at Christmas 2006, hoping to stay off the heroin, but it was yet another false dawn. June said:

> After he died, one of the counsellors from London wrote to me to say how he had told her that he wished he could be more like his brothers. He was striving to turn his back on it. He told me he wanted a normal life as he was almost forty. The desire to break free was there. He waited four months to get on that course in London, such was the high demand for places there but it didn't work out.
>
> He had been off drugs since Christmas 2006 but he had been gradually getting back into it.

David drifted between flats and partners in areas including Paisley, Gourock, Port Glasgow, Kilmacolm, Dumbarton and Glasgow's Pollok district. During much of that time, Stevenson's drugs network spread into many of those communities. His imported drugs were sold by his people to the massed ranks of faceless addicts. What is certain is that, if Stevenson's drugs business were a supermarket, people like David would be valued customers to be rewarded for their loyalty.

An addict can reasonably be expected to consume three tenner bags of heroin each day. Multiply this by David's sixteen years of addiction and those tenner bags would add up to a spend of £175,000. Over the years, David's various jobs included tyre-fitting and insurance sales but he never stayed at them for any length of time as, every time he seemed to be cleaning up, he would slide back into the chaotic, dangerous and dirty world of full-time heroin addiction.

He stole from shops to feed his habit and, before long, the mounting petty convictions resulted in a sheriff sending him to prison for the first of many times. June said:

> He appeared at various courts including Paisley, Greenock and Glasgow and was sent to Greenock and Low Moss Prisons several times. I went to visit him a few times and it was a whole new ball game. I just felt so sad and helpless.

One time, while living in Paisley, he was attacked with a golf club in an incident that his parents suspect may have been caused because he was then selling heroin to feed his own habit. Donald said:

> One night, someone kicked his car to set off the alarm and, when he ran out, he was smashed in the face with a golf club. It was serious – he had a plate put in his face, his jaw was broken and the whites of his eyes were red. The doctors thought he could lose his sight.
>
> Throughout all these years, there was the hassle that goes with it. We would be woken at 2 a.m. with phone calls from him asking for money or by the police telling us he was in custody. His girlfriend once phoned to ask me to come and help put the door back on as the police had raided the place. We only saw a fraction of what went on.

In the thirteen years between 1992 and 2005, a total of 3,945 drugs-related deaths were recorded in Scotland. In comparison, during the Troubles in Northern Ireland, between 1969 and 1999, bullets and bombs claimed around 3,500 lives and the 9/11 terrorist attacks of 2001 on America killed 3,016 people.

A report by the UK Drug Policy Commission published in April 2007, revealed that Scotland has 50,000 heroin addicts. The figure for England, with a population around ten times that of Scotland's, is 281,000 addicts. Experts fear for the 50,000 Scottish children currently being raised in homes where there are drug problems.

David's story is not unusual but it reminds people whose sense of shock and anger has been blunted by decades of drugs-death statistics about the human cost wreaked by heroin.

Donald understands that, with the money to be had in the drugs trade, there will always be willing criminals like Stevenson but June believes that those who make millions of pounds from dealing in death should face tougher justice. Donald said:

> If you take one out and shoot him, someone else will step into his place. They see the opportunity to make easy money and just go for it. There's no easy solution. Society can't even deal with the massive alcohol problem so what chance does it have with drugs?

June said, 'I know that David made the wrong choices in life but the big drug dealers should be put in jail and they should throw away the key. That's the way I see it.'

28
Folklore Begins

In the end, the decision was taken quickly. The meeting at the headquarters of the Scottish Crime and Drug Enforcement Agency (SCDEA) in March 2004 was, in itself, nothing special. The tasking and co-ordination committee met every month to review the progress of ongoing operations, to allocate resources and to choose the serious and organised criminals most deserving of the agency's special attention. The handful of senior detectives gathered around the conference table at the SCDEA's headquarters had read the intelligence dossier in front of them and the authors' analysis and recommendations were swiftly approved. They moved on to other business but the decision, taken in minutes but based on ten months of painstaking police work, was the most significant to be taken so far in the agency's short history.

The meeting launched a three-year crime-fighting offensive against some of the most ruthless and effective gangs in Scotland and it set the agency's sights squarely on one man – Scotland's biggest international drugs trafficker, Jamie Stevenson. From that point on, the Operation Folklore team was not gathering intelligence on Stevenson – they were trying to lock him up.

One SCDEA officer, with knowledge of the meeting, said:

There was no fanfare, no great excitement. There would have been a realisation that this was only the beginning of what, in all likelihood, was going to be a long, hard investigation into a criminal who had shown himself capable of avoiding conviction despite operating at a very high level for a very long time.

One of the agency's intelligence development teams had been working on nailing down the scale of the criminal operations of Stevenson and his close associate, Ayrshire drugs lord John 'Piddy' Gorman, since 20 May 2003. Confidential Folklore briefing documents, distributed on that day, could not have been clearer on the agency's remit. Its stated aim was to 'investigate the activities of a group of active criminals known to be involved in the large-scale importation of class A controlled drugs from mainland Europe into the UK for distribution throughout Scottish police force areas.'

The Folklore team of fifteen officers used all available methods of gathering intelligence on their targets, from undercover and electronic surveillance to forensic financial analysis of the accounts of front firms suspected of laundering their criminal fortunes. One source said:

> They're not just told to go off and come back in six months. Progress is looked at regularly and there has to be some encouragement, in terms of the inquiries pulling the right triggers.
>
> Of course, the likelihood of success comes into it. We have never not taken on a target because it looks too difficult but we have to be realistic. There are plenty of people with an awareness of Stevenson outside the agency who, if they had known we were looking at him, would have said we were wasting our time.
>
> The SCDEA has a specific remit to target certain categories of serious organised crime groups. But there

are so many, we have to apply a bit of science. We might know an individual well – know what they do and what they are capable of doing – but there has to be a system because investigation is an expensive and complicated process. There has to be a scientific approach to choosing targets.

The officers initially assessing Stevenson and Gorman as possible targets were not short of material. The source said:

At that point, Stevenson was already heavily involved in multinational drug trafficking along with the associated money laundering. He was willing to use extreme violence to protect his business.

He was in charge but had a very close relationship to Gorman, who basically had the drugs franchise from the southern edge of Glasgow, out through Paisley and Barrhead and down into Ayrshire. Stevenson dominated the drugs trade in Lanarkshire and south Glasgow but the quantity and range of class A drugs he was bringing in meant they were going all over Scotland.

Gorman had been a dealer for years and was a long-standing associate of Stevenson but their business relationship only started in earnest after Stevenson split from the McGoverns.

Neither of them had any serious form.

The data gathered by the intelligence development teams, month after painstaking month, is eventually put through a computer matrix, a Home Office process with fifteen points designed to grade and select criminal targets. Areas scrutinised include the criminal enterprise, associates, methods, damage inflicted on their communities through drugs or violence and the potential for successfully putting the criminals in the dock.

One officer said:

Basically, if these criminals are operating at a serious enough level of organised crime, we will take them on. If, after intelligence, the targets do not meet the grade for SCDEA, the case will be passed to the relevant local force. That's if we don't find what we are expecting to find.

It's like looking at any fairly substantial business to see what these people do and how they work. We get to understand them, their lifestyle, and develop an intimate knowledge of their habits.

In addition, there is a national flagging system in place. We put a flag on our targets which means that, if any police officer runs their details through the police national computer, we will be immediately notified. We can then go to the officer and ask why they did it and about the circumstances at the time.

After the meeting had rubber-stamped the targeting of Stevenson and Gorman by the Folklore team, another team of officers, led by a detective inspector, took over as Folklore – the codename randomly allocated from a centrally held Home Office register to avoid confusion with other crime-fighting operations – moved from intelligence gathering to evidence gathering.

The source continued:

The intelligence package came to the meeting in spring 2004 and Stevenson and Gorman ticked all of the boxes. It was very clear that they were involved in importation of huge quantities of drugs, including heroin, cocaine, amphetamine and cannabis. The recommendations hit the mark and, from then on, it was a criminal investigation like any other.

But, over the course of the three tortuous years ahead, Operation Folklore would become one of the most significant criminal investigations ever launched in Scotland. It would lead to the first conviction in Scotland of a serious and organised criminal based on the evidence gathered during a huge electronic surveillance offensive. It would signal a new determination and willingness of law enforcers to attack a criminal's ill-gotten fortune to put him in the dock. And it blazed a trail in the level of international co-operation with other forces as the Folklore team followed their target around the world and back to a nondescript flat in Burnside.

29
Boxed In

The truck carrying the forty kilos of heroin packed in two boxes and stowed in the driver's cabin had travelled across Europe, across the Channel and across Britain to Scotland – and it had been followed for every mile of its journey. The police swooped on an industrial estate in Dumfries as the boxes were being switched from the truck to a waiting car. They contained drugs that would have sold for almost £6 million on the streets of Scotland's towns and cities.

It was 27 June 2003 and the Scottish Crime and Drug Enforcement Agency's operation codenamed Folklore, still in its intelligence-gathering phase, had been underway for just five weeks.

In October, Robert McDowall, forty-eight, a driver for a Lisburn-based flower importer, and Francis Gallagher, thirty-nine, a career criminal from Springburn, Glasgow, appeared at the High Court in Kilmarnock to admit to being concerned in the supply of class A drugs.

SCDEA officers had trailed the lorry from Holland and tracked it 400 miles north after it was driven through Customs at the Harwich ferry terminal in Essex. They had been watching as McDowall met Gallagher, known as Frank, at a Little Chef restaurant on the M74 at Dumfries. They were watching as the men left and Gallagher drove to the deserted Lochside Industrial Estate with McDowall's truck following behind. And they were watching as Gallagher reversed up to the lorry trailer and the men started moving boxes from the truck to the car. Then they moved in and both men were arrested at the scene. Officers raiding Gallagher's house in Springburn found £26,000 in cash and a passport.

The court was told the SCDEA had been tipped off.

On 17 December, they were back in court for sentencing. Gallagher, who had a previous conviction for drug dealing, got twelve years and McDowall, an Irishman living in Ballantrae, Ayrshire, got ten. Jailing the pair, Lord Hardie told them:

> You are probably well aware of the consequences to the public and the misery [drugs] cause to addicts, their families and other members of society. It is often said that the drugs trade is an evil trade and I would endorse that sentiment.

To Gallagher, the judge said:

> I note you have a previous conviction for being involved in the supply of drugs and that will be reflected in your sentence. I take into account the nature and quantity of drugs with a street value of £5.85 million for which the maximum period I can impose is life imprisonment.
>
> I take into account also you are not at the top of the chain and I reserve a life sentence for those who are if they are ever brought to justice.

The judge was right. Gallagher was not the top man but he was at his right hand. For the first time, the police had got close to Stevenson. They had picked off one of his key lieutenants, a fixer feared for his capacity for violence. And their sights were now fixed squarely on his boss. And they had an ace up their sleeve. Stevenson had made a fundamental error. For once, he had got too close to the drugs. He had met McDowall to arrange the shipment of class A drugs.

And now Robert Henry McDowall was about to talk.

30
Burgers and Drugs

It was a bit early in the year to be sitting outside but the three men enjoying their burgers and chips around a table in the garden of the Queen's Hotel looked relaxed enough in the cold sunshine of spring 2003. One of them, Robert McDowall, a forty-eight-year-old Ulsterman, ran the small white-painted hotel with his wife Carol. It was sited on the main road running through the picturesque south Ayrshire village of Colmonell.

Much later, Carol would tell the police:

> It was a nice day. I was working at the hotel and Robert was there with me when the two guys arrived. It was afternoon time. Robert told me the two guys were lorry drivers. They had arrived together in what, I'm sure now, was a black car. I think it was an Audi – quite fancy looking.
>
> Robert and the two guys sat at a table out the back of the hotel talking. Robert asked if I could make them a couple of chicken burgers to eat. I remember Robert actually saying to me, 'Can you make Frank and the other guy a couple of chicken burgers?'
>
> I'm not sure what Robert called the other guy but I'm sure it was Jay or a name beginning with the letter J. I made the guys something to eat and they sat outside speaking to Robert.

They had a lot to discuss, McDowall and his new acquaintances from Glasgow. Within months, one of them, Frank Gallagher would be arrested alongside McDowall on a Dumfries industrial estate after taking delivery of two boxes each containing 20 kilos of heroin with an estimated street value of £6 million. The other man visiting Ayrshire that day was Jamie Stevenson.

The three men had met just once before, when they'd had a conversation in a car parked beside a Tesco supermarket, next to Ayr Racecourse, just before Christmas. A mutual associate from Northern Ireland had introduced them. The men discussed the possibility of McDowall earning a bit of extra money by adding drugs to his lorry's loads as he drove across the continent to Britain. They suggested he might find a job with a Northern Ireland-based flower importer. They told him there would be good money in it. He agreed.

Money had been tight since the McDowalls had taken over the hotel in the scenic village, tucked away in the rolling Ayrshire countryside, fourteen miles south of Girvan, four years earlier. Each month it had been a struggle to make ends meet – a struggle that became all the more difficult when McDowall suffered the stroke that had forced him off the road for a year.

Stevenson was usually too careful to be anywhere near the drugs he was pouring into Scotland. He was usually too careful to discuss those drugs with anyone apart from his tight and loyal inner circle. So why had he taken the risk of meeting a man he hardly knew to discuss, in incriminating detail, how he was regularly bringing class A drugs of every description into Scotland with the help of complicit HGV drivers and their trucks?

One associate remembers:

Stevenson was massively careful, verging on the paranoid. He had a few men whose judgement and abilities he

The New Morven pub in Glasgow. Gang boss Tony McGovern was gunned down in the pub's car park on 16 September 2000.

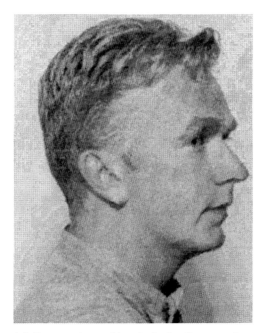

McGovern pictured in a leaked police mugshot. His family refused to release a picture to the police to help them in the hunt for his killer.

McGovern's wife, Jackie, right, leaves St Aloysius Church in Springburn, Glasgow, after her husband's funeral on 20 November 2000.

Jim Milligan, centre and wearing glasses, a McGovern business associate and the owner of the New Morven pub leaves the funeral. He would soon go into hiding as McGovern's brothers tried to track down a missing fortune.

Football-star-turned-TV-pundit Charlie Nicholas was formerly Milligan's business partner. Nicholas did not attend the funeral and would later accuse his former partner of forging his signature on legal documents.

Jamie 'The Iceman' Stevenson and his wife Caroline pictured before they married in 1998.

The McGoverns' brother-in-law, Russell Stirton, front, and Stirton's business partner Alexander Anderson leave the Court of Session in Edinburgh in 2004. Official asset-strippers claimed their business empire was built on dirty money.

The garage in Springburn, Glasgow, that Stirton and Anderson owned. Although it sold the cheapest petrol in Scotland, investigators found it hard to believe that the large sums it was banking every day in 2004 all came from fuel sales.

In October 2001, car thief John Hall was found shot dead in Lanarkshire. He had been bound, killed and then set alight.

The body of Hall's friend David McIntosh was found beside him. Detectives believe the double murder may have been linked to the killing of Tony McGovern thirteen months before.

The double murder bore striking similarities to the death of drug dealer John Nisbet, who had been shot and killed in 1999.

Nisbet's friend William Lindsay was murdered at the same time. The men had been tortured, shot and then set alight in Lanarkshire before their bodies were dumped over thirty miles away in East Lothian.

Some of the 8 tonnes of cannabis found on board the *Squilla* are unloaded on the dockside at Cadiz by Spanish police in June 2005. The converted trawler was seized at sea as part of Operation Folklore as it was sailing to Scotland.

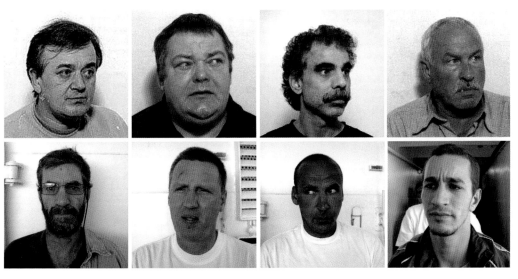

In April 2006, the *Squilla* ringleader and long-time Stevenson associate John 'Piddy' Gorman (top left) was jailed for twelve years. His gang included (clockwise from Gorman) William McDonald, Mushtaq Ahmed, James Lowrie, Sufian Mohammed Dris, Arno Podder, William Reid and Douglas Prince. Those in the top row were jailed in the UK while, in Madrid, the gang members pictured in the bottom row were also given prison terms.

Picture Ciaran Donnelly

Lorry driver Robert McDowall leaving the High Court in Edinburgh in February 2005 after having just £637 of his estimated £1 million assets seized. Politicians who criticised the deal were unaware that McDowall was to be the star witness against Stevenson.

This modest block of flats in Fishescoates Gardens, Burnside, near Glasgow, is where Jamie Stevenson lived quietly with his wife. From here, he ran Scotland's biggest international drugs trafficking operation.

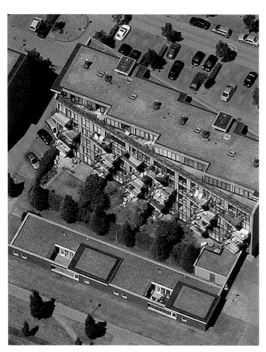

The apartment block in Nieuw Sloten, on the outskirts of Amsterdam, where Stevenson bolted in the summer of 2006. He and his wife Caroline lived in a flat, detached from the main block, on the bottom right.

Stevenson leaving Hamilton Sheriff Court in November 2005 after admitting a breach of the peace charge linked to his brawl with Robert 'Birdman' O'Hara in Shotts Prison. Until his conviction, this was the only contemporary picture of the gang leader.

Some of the fifty-five luxury watches that Stevenson had paid £307,087 for between 2003 and 2006. They included a Rolex Daytona worth £10,340 and a £30,000 Audemars Piguet.

Stevenson's wife, Caroline, leaves the High Court in Glasgow after an Operation Folklore hearing in February 2007.

Carbin's partner, Karen Maxwell, leaves the court after the same hearing. The charges against both women would later be dropped as part of the deal struck with the Crown.

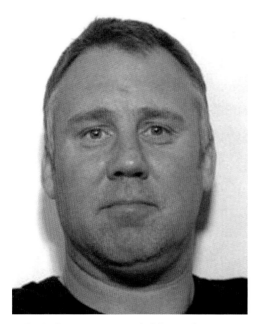

Jamie Stevenson was jailed for twelve years and nine months in April 2007 after being arrested in the Operation Folklore raids and admitting laundering more than £1 million of drugs money.

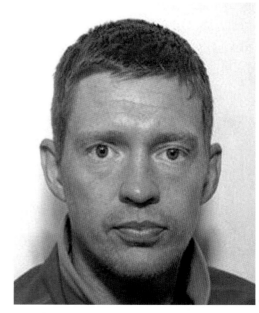

At the same time, Stevenson's stepson Gerry Carbin Jnr was jailed for a total of eleven years and nine months. His three sentences will run concurrently with the longest being five years and six months.

Derek Ogg, QC acted for Stevenson as his client reached agreement with the Crown to admit money laundering in return for the drugs charges against him disappearing.

Carbin's QC, Paul McBride, struck the deal that led to trafficking charges against his client being dropped at the High Court in Glasgow.

trusted completely and they would usually do any face-
to-face stuff. But he had to meet McDowall. The guy was
potentially going to be a big, big part of what they were
doing – a keystone. Stevenson had to see him for himself
– satisfy himself.

And it was almost the biggest mistake he ever made.

Stevenson and his henchmen now believe McDowall was
already working for the authorities when they enjoyed their
burgers al fresco. They suspect he had already been busted by
Customs at Dover as he brought in a load of drugs in January
2003. He had been allowed to drive away after agreeing to
help the authorities land the biggest fish in Scotland. They
believed it enough to take out a £10,000 contract on the
life of the suspected informer after he was jailed, along with
Gallagher, following a court case that was notable for being
the first time the SCDEA's Operation Folklore had ever been
mentioned in public.

What is not in doubt is that, within a year of the meeting
in Colmonell, McDowall had been stabbed in jail and told that
there was a price on his head. He had also asked for urgent
talks with detectives from the elite crime-fighting agency.
In a series of recorded conversations, he would lay bare the
astonishing scope of Stevenson's drug-smuggling operation.
He explained how the flower markets of Holland were being
used as cover for just some of the huge consignments of
heroin, cocaine, speed and Ecstasy being driven into Scotland
by HGV drivers on the gang's payroll.

He told of how the man he claimed to know only as
Jamie from Glasgow was said to be a killer who was armed
at all times; of how this man was the undisputed leader of
a gang that had been bringing huge consignments of drugs
into Scotland for years; of how his drugs money underwrote a
£36-million property spree on the Costa del Sol; and of how
guns – hard plastic pistols undetectable on Customs' X-ray

machines – were another profitable sideline for Stevenson's mob. And he explained how the operation did not depend on individual drivers because Stevenson had bought his own haulage firms, his own HGVs.

He told the police everything and, for the first time, detectives had found a witness to Stevenson's absolute immersion in the drugs trade. And, incredibly, the witness indicated that he could – and would – identify the Folklore team's number one target.

31
The J Fella

In May 2004, two officers from the Scottish Crime and Drug Enforcement Agency, a detective constable and a detective sergeant, interviewed Robert McDowall at Bowhouse Prison, in Kilmarnock. What follows is a transcript of their remarkable recorded conversation exposing the day-to-day business of smuggling drugs and guns across Europe.

> Police: *Can you tell us why we came to be here? Was that at your request?*
>
> McDowall: Yeah, it was at my request.
>
> *When did you first do that?*
>
> I spoke to my solicitor a couple of months back and asked him to contact the police due to the fact the people I worked for had taken a contract out on me.
>
> *Could you repeat that a wee bit louder, Robert?*
>
> The people I was working for in Glasgow – they've taken a contract out on me.
>
> *Your current status within the prison – would you like to explain it to us?*
>
> I'm a prisoner serving ten years for being concerned in the supply of forty kilos of heroin.
>
> *You're not on remand or anything? You're a convicted prisoner?*
>
> Yeah.

You said you spoke to your lawyer a couple of months ago. What's his name?

David Finnie of Walker & Sharpe in Dumfries.

What did you say to him?

I asked him if he would get in touch with the police as I might have some information – hopefully it would stem the flow of drugs coming into Glasgow.

Did you tell him what you were going to tell us?

I didn't tell him. I just gave him a brief outline of it and he said he would get in touch with the SDEA.

I've tried to speak to your lawyer earlier this week and left a message for him and he has not got back in touch with us so are you happy to continue?

Yeah, I'm happy to speak with yourselves.

We are just trying to get across that it was you who instigated us to come and speak to you.

Yes, it was at my instigation.

What would your reasons be for that?

I'm quite disgusted with the fact that it was heroin in the first place and by the fact that they are not prepared to let me just carry on doing my sentence.

Who's not?

The people I was working for in Glasgow.

Just so we are clear here. You were arrested bringing heroin into Scotland?

Yes, that's correct.

Was it on board a vehicle?

Yes, it was on the lorry, 27 June 2003, and I imported it from Holland.

So you are disgusted with the people who tasked you to do this – is this correct?

Yes, that's correct.

Who would that be?

My co-accused Frank . . . Francis Gallagher and the leader of the group, who I know as J or Jamie.

Are you saying Jimmy or Jamie?

Jamie – as in James.

What's his second name?

I don't know his second name.

Do you know anything else about him?

Apart from a rough description of him. He's pretty tall, six foot, very well built, slim build but muscular and any time I've saw him, he's always been wearing tracksuit types of things.

When did you first meet him?

I first met him in December of 2002.

How did that meeting come about?

It was arranged by a friend of mine in Ireland.

Do you want to give us his name?

No.

So what happened?

He had been in contact over the years and he asked me would I be interested in doing a wee bit extra and earning a few extra quid.

Were you going through a difficult time at that time?

Yes, I had the hotel down the road at the time and it had nearly gone bust and I needed money pretty fast. I'd been in for a couple of years. I had a stroke in November 2001 and was out of work until January 2003.

I appreciate you don't want to give his name if he's a friend of yours but what did he say to you exactly?

He said to me would I be interested in bringing in some gear from the continent if I started working for a continental firm.

A continental lorry firm?

A transport firm, yeah.

What firm would that be?

Kelly's Flowers, of Lisburn, Co. Antrim. [There is
    nothing to suggest the firm was aware of any
    illegal activity involving their vehicles.]

Northern Irish?

Northern Irish firm, yeah.

Did he tell you who you were doing that on behalf of if
    you decided to do it?

He basically offered me to meet the people up in
    Ayr in December.

Sorry. Did you say Ayr?

Yeah, Ayr in December 2002.

What was your understanding of what you were going
    to be doing when you were first asked?

My understanding was I would be bringing drugs
    in. I was under the impression it was soft drugs
    rather than heroin.

What happened?

I said I would go and meet the people and see what
    they think of it. If it was pretty good – talk
    business, nothing lost.

What happened thereafter?

He set the meeting up for me in December and I
    met the two guys at the racecourse car park in
    Ayr.

So who did you meet there?

Francis Gallagher, my co-accused, and the other guy,
    Jamie.

How did he introduce himself to you?

Just Frank and Jamie.

Was anyone else there?

My friend and myself.

How did Francis Gallagher and Jamie get there?

In a silver Mercedes – Y-reg.

Where exactly did the meeting take place?

At the side of Tesco's beside the racecourse.

What time of day, Robert?

It was about 11 p.m.

Who was doing the talking in this meeting?

We all sat in the Mercedes and spoke to the two guys and they told us roughly how the operation worked.

Who was doing the talking?

The J guy – Jamie.

Did you form an opinion?

He was the leader.

The leader?

I've no doubts about that – he was the man in charge.

What exactly did he say to you?

What he said was they use Kelly's Flowers lorries quite a lot to bring stuff from . . . he gave me the road number, the N11 in Holland and the name of the place was Rijnsburg.

Did he quiz you at all?

Yeah, he asked me if I had any previous convictions or if I had been done for anything?

Why do you think he was asking that question?

In case the police were following me or something. He was quite suspicious of me 'cos obviously they didn't know me.

OK. What else did he say? Did he talk about money?

Yeah. He said I'd be looked after. He never put an exact figure on it. He said it would be very, very good money in it for me.

So did he mention what type of drugs?

They said it would probably be Ecstasy, cannabis. I made it very clear to them that I wouldn't carry heroin. I'm very anti-drugs – particularly heroin. That's what makes it disgusting. That's what I got conned into bringing in for them.

Is there anything else about this guy J or Jamie that would help us identify him – anything about him at all?

I know for a fact that he's always in the gym of the Hilton Hotel, in East Kilbride.

How do you know that, Robert?

Frank Gallagher told me. I did a remand with him in Dumfries then I did a three-month remand with him here in Kilmarnock.

What else did you learn from Frank that might help us identify him? Did he say where he stays?

No. Obviously he's from Glasgow. He's a Glasgow boy. That's where he always contacts him by mobile phone.

That's how Frank communicates with him?

Yeah, that's how Frank communicated with him and how they communicated with me, with Vodafone throwaways.

Did he say anything about what this J guy's been involved in in the past?

He didn't. I've learned quite a bit about him from my friends. Last year, he bought a lot of properties in Spain. From what he said in multimillions – the property he bought. He's obviously a big player.

Any specific area in Spain?

Costa del Sol. The figure he mentioned was something like £36 million.

Did you learn anything else about this guy's criminal background? What he'd been involved in?

No. Apart from the fact that my mate told me that he's a killer – said he's killed people before and anyone who crosses him.

Did he mention any of the people?

No, he didn't mention any names.

OK. To go back slightly – is he asking you to do runs for him?

Yes. Just at that meeting in the car park. I said I had an old furniture van down at the hotel I had in Colmonell. I was wondering if it was suitable for transporting stuff for them. Him and Frank came down to have a look at it. The van was too old for them – too old, too conspicuous.

How did you get from that meeting to Colmonell. You and your unknown friend travel to Colmonell and did they come with you?

They followed us in the Mercedes.

And what happened during that meeting?

We went into the backyard of the hotel, showed them the lorry. They said, if I started working with Kelly's, they would throw a lot of money my way.

Anything else said about drugs or money at this point?

They just said the money would be very, very good. I'd be well looked after if I worked for them.

OK. What happened thereafter, Robert?

They stayed with me for about half an hour and that's the only time I ever seen J.

Half an hour is quite a long time. Is there anything else you can remember from that conversation that will help us identify him?

Just the fact that I would know him again. I will be able to recognise him by his mannerisms.

Any tattoos?

His arms were covered. Very, very clean and very sporty look about him. Muscular. I've learned since he's a fitness fanatic and he's always armed.

Did you see a weapon on him at all?

No.

You saw them for half an hour. Did you then make a decision?

I said I would be willing to work for them and, a couple of weeks later, they rang me and asked me to work for this guy Danny.

Who was it that rang you, Robert?

Frank . . . Frank Gallagher.

The number that Frank phoned you on – do you still have that number?

It might be on my mobile phone.

Were there mobile phones taken from you on your arrest?

Yeah. I don't know the phone itself. Do they have memories still in them?

Do you remember what date the call was made?

January 2003.

How many phones did you have?

Four. One belonged to Kelly's and three of my own.

Can you describe which phone?

I think it was a Siemens A55.

Can you remember what time of day that call came in?

Round about lunchtime. I couldn't honestly say.

What was the conversation about when he phoned you?

He asked me to go and drive for this guy, Danny [who ran a Dutch-registered transport company]. I was to meet him on the Saturday night at Larkhall. There's an industrial estate there, a fish processing place, fish wholesalers. Can't think of the name of the company and I went out that night to France, drove down to Poole and crossed on the ferry, dropped off the fish. I got stopped by Customs and Excise.

Can you remember what date that was?

Mid January.

*So, when you came back with this bona fide load, you get
stopped by Customs?*

Yes.

What happened?

They just checked the load – a lassie checked along the
top of the load – it was all frozen French bread.

What port?

Dover.

Who introduced you to Danny?

It was through Frank – Frank Gallagher.

Were you, Frank and Danny together?

No, I only met Danny that time up at the place in
Larkhall.

So what happened?

I done a couple of runs for him.

*Can you remember any of the other dates you were
stopped by Customs on bona fide runs?*

January 2003 as well.

*Can you remember the details of the vehicle you were
driving?*

It was a Dutch plate, Scania S40, two numbers and
thirty-four and another two numbers. A silver
Scania . . . sorry two letters, thirty-four and
then another two letters.

*How many times do you think you got stopped by the
Customs driving that vehicle?*

Three times altogether – twice at Dover and once at
Portsmouth.

*Were you stopped any other times by police officers on the
motorways or anything?*

No, I was never stopped by the police.

*So you've done a few bona fide runs for Danny, who
was introduced to you by Frank Gallagher. What
happened then?*

They decided I wasn't suitable for driving that lorry
'cos, every time I came back into the country,
Customs and Excise were taking it apart. They
didn't know if it was the lorry or myself but
they said they wouldn't give me any work.

Who told you this?

Frank told me this before. A couple of weeks after
that, Danny rang me to meet him at Carlisle
truck stop and asked me to go on a run with
him to Holland. When he got down to Carlisle
to meet me, he said he wasn't going to go. They
stopped him at Bothwell services.

Who stopped him?

Frank and the J fella. He actually said there were
four of them. They stopped him and put a gun
to him and told him, if I would be in his lorry,
they'd shoot him.

Danny told you about this?

Yes, he met me at the truck stop in Carlisle. He was
quite shaken.

Did he say who it was that put the gun to him?

He didn't say. He said there were four of them there
and they jumped into the cab with him.

*You don't recall who the antagonist was? Who was
taking the lead role?*

No, he didn't say. He just said the J guy was there,
Frank was there and two other thugs.

What happened thereafter?

That was the last time I heard of Danny. I done a
couple of weeks in early 2003 for a local firm in
Girvan. That was just local work – nothing to
do with drugs. I sold the hotel and then Kelly's
Flowers rang me and asked if I was interested
in doing a run with them.

Who was that from Kelly's Flowers, Robert?

Ken Munro, he's the transport manager. [There is nothing to suggest that Mr Munro was aware of McDowall's smuggling.]

Was that a bona fide run you were going to do?

Yes.

Where would Ken Munro have got your details from?

From my friend back in Ireland. I had done one run for them previous – just a one-off run for them.

For who?

For Kelly's.

A bona fide run?

A bona fide run, yes. A run over to the Breskens. A run over to the Breskens [a coastal town in Holland], drop it off and bring fruit back for them.

Can I just jump back slightly, Robert? The Danny guy – what do you know about his background?

What I know is Danny has, over a period, brought drugs into the country for this crowd.

For who?

For Jamie and Gallagher and they actually financed the purchase of the lorry.

The lorry that was used?

The Scania.

This being the same lorry that Danny was threatened in?

Yes.

So they financed that. How do you know that?

Danny told me.

What did he say?

Well, he'd actually gone bankrupt. He'd been in business and went bust and part of the deal was that he would bring some stuff in for them. They bought him . . . they actually had two lorries and bought him the two lorries and set him back up in business. It's an amalgamation of different transport companies operating under an operator's licence of a Dutch company, hence the Dutch registration.

So what you're saying is that Danny's brought drugs in for Jamie and Frank Gallagher and that it was Danny that told you that?

Yeah.

Was there ever any quantities involved?

He never mentioned any quantities but he said there were fantastic amounts of money for doing it and he also said he transported drugs from Spain up to Holland.

Did he ever mention what type of drugs?

No.

When you say fantastic amounts of money, did he ever actually give you a figure?

He was talking hundreds of thousands.

So Danny volunteered this information to you?

Yes, 'cos I went along on a couple of runs with him and he had told me. He also had another driver. He was sitting down in Valencia one time waiting to bring some stuff up and he kept him waiting there for a fortnight just so he could bring some drugs up from Spain to Holland for him. I've heard talking on the phone a couple of times and he said just hang out there for a few more days. Book yourself into a hotel or whatever and it will come up shortly.

Who do you think Danny was waiting instruction from?

I would say Jamie.

Did he tell you at any time he was waiting instruction from Jamie?

No. He said he was waiting on a load but no one

waits in Spain for a legitimate load. I mean, there's a big shortage of transport all around the continent and back and forth. You don't wait two weeks for anybody.

OK. Let's get back to yourself. You made a few genuine runs then the incident with Danny. What happened then?

I spoke to Danny that day – the day in the truck stop in Carlisle – and he said to me, 'Just let it go for a couple of weeks and I'll give you work over in the continent so you can bring stuff up from Spain to Holland for me. I do it all the time.'

You're talking about stuff there. You are talking about drugs?

Drugs, yes. We call it stuff, kit or gear.

Carry on, Robert.

That's the last I heard from Danny until I was working for the local firm in Girvan. He just rang me out of the blue and asked me if I could do a run that Saturday night for him.

Who rang you out of the blue?

Danny. He rang me on my mobile. He wanted me to do a fish run that Saturday night. It was a legitimate run.

What date?

Probably April or May 2003. I said no, I'm working and I'm away for two weeks. The way it worked, you go out for three weeks for them or six weeks and then take a fortnight off or something. They give you the time off when you're with the lorry. You get parked up for thirty-six hours or forty-eight hours or something but you're never back up in Scotland. It's always down in England and I said, 'Look, I'm here until they bring me back.' They had asked me to work full-time with them which I'm sorry I didn't do 'cos I would never have got involved in this. But that's water under the bridge.

So he's asked you to do one run and you've said no?

Yes. That was the last time I heard from Danny.

OK. What was your next communication with these individuals?

Right. Kelly's had rang me and I did a few legitimate runs for Kelly's. The way it worked with Kelly's was I went out every Saturday night, they sent the lorry over on the ferry from Belfast. I picked it up from Stranraer, drove on down to Dover, crossed over at Dover, up into Breskens in Holland, which is just at the Dutch/Belgian border, just over the border, dumped the fish off there and that was generally me finished until Monday. I'd collect flowers and fruit for Kelly's from three different pick-up points in Holland.

All bona fide stuff?

Yes, all bona fide stuff.

OK. What happened then?

There was one run . . . I was contacted by my friend in Ireland. He said would you be interested in bringing some of that stuff back. He gave me the details of where to meet and he said Frank or J would be in touch with me and on to Holland. He seemed to know where it was the whole time. When I got closer to Rijnsburg, they rang to see sort of what time I'd be.

Sorry to interrupt you – who rang you?

It was J. Mostly it was J who called me.

Can you tell us roughly what date that was?

First week in May 2003.

So we get this correct, your friend, who you don't want to name, phones you and tells you he wants you to bring some stuff back?

I was doing runs for the weeks before that and he knew I was going out on the Saturday night.

What vehicle were you in then?

In the DAF – Kelly's DAF. Can't think of the registration number. It was a DAF. It's the only DAF that Kelly's have.

So you don't know the registration?

If I could get back to my tachos sometime, I could dig the number out. It wouldn't be hard to find the number. It's the only DAF Kelly's have.

So your friend – what details did he give you?

He just told me to carry on with the run and I'd be contacted when I was in Holland. They had a rough idea what times I'd be 'cos he had worked for Kelly's before.

So you were doing a bona fide run at that time?

Yes. I dropped the fish in Breskens. I had some more to drop off but, Jesus Christ, I can't remember the names of these places in Holland. I had another drop-off to do and I went over to Rijnsburg and that's when they put the stuff on before I started loading the fruit.

Who told you to go to Rijnsburg?

My mate from Ireland.

And were you communicated by people when you were over there?

Yes.

What phone did they phone you on?

They phoned me on the Siemens A55.

Always?

Yes. That was the number I had at the time that had the chip in it.

So who phoned you?

J.

Where was he phoning you from?

Scotland.

You sure about that?

Nearly sure – I couldn't say 100 per cent.

So the number he phoned you on will be on your phone somewhere possibly?

If the chip . . . the telephone has a memory. I've changed the chip since. Actually changed the chip on the way home that time.

You changed the SIM card so, unless it's on the memory, it's gone?

Yes.

So what did he say to you on the phone?

He just said what time will you be at Rijnsburg at? I told him the time and it was the Sunday. I wasn't starting to load the fruit until Monday. So I went up and sat on the road from the garage, filled up with fuel. And the guy pulled up in a Golf GTi with Dutch plates on.

Where exactly were you sitting?

I was sitting on the main road into the village of Rijnsburg.

Who directed you to that position?

Right, I knew where it was. I knew what the position was 'cos it had been explained to me before and it was close to where Kelly's Flowers is in Rijnsburg.

How far from Kelly's is it?

Quarter of a mile.

So it's actually a road. You sat on the road?

Yes, a main road.

What I'm trying to get to is who told you to go to that specific location?

J.

He phoned you and told you to go there?

Well, he phoned and said, 'Do you know exactly where you're going?' I said, 'Yes in Rijnsburg.'

Did he tell you what time to be there at?

I told him what time I'd be there at and he said just park there and there will be someone along in a few minutes of you arriving, which there was.

What time was that at? Was it night?

No. It was a Sunday afternoon.

So you park up. J told you there would be someone there in a few minutes?

Yes.

What happens?

A Golf GTi, black with Dutch plates, pulled in and a coloured guy – I've actually remembered his name, the nickname. It was Tony the Moroccan – that's what his name was. He handed the five boxes into me and I kept them in the cab of the DAF.

In the cab?

Yeah.

How long did this exchange take? Minutes?

Seconds.

So did you look in the boxes?

No.

And he just drove away?

He just drove away.

Can you give us an age for him?

Mid to late twenties.

What happened?

I loaded the fruit not far from Rijnsburg, maybe twenty minutes or so. Started loading the fruit there and I loaded some more on the way down the road and then went down to Belgium and loaded the lorry more.

It's fair to say the rest of your load was bona fide?

Yes. It was all fruits and loaded right to the top. I had intended to put the boxes in among the load but I'd that much fruit, I kept them in the cab.

How many boxes?

Five.

How would you describe the boxes?

About three-foot, taped-up cardboard boxes with parcel tape.

What colour of tape?

Brown.

Were they heavy?

Reasonably heavy, yeah.

So then what happened?

I load the fruit, head down for the train [the Eurotunnel freight service] at Calais.

Did you receive any other communication?

He rang me a few times en route to see that everything was OK.

When you were coming back?

Yeah. I was on the way down from Holland down into Belgium.

After you collected the boxes?

Yeah.

Who phoned you?

J.

What did he ask you?

Just asked if everything was OK.

This J on the phone is the same J that you met face-to-face?

Yeah.

Definitely the same J?

Yeah.

So he phoned you a few times?

Yeah. I went down for the train and I was waved through the X-ray machine to check for immigrants and things like that. Drove on in and I was coming down towards the British Customs. The lassie said to go over to the tent on the right-hand side which I thought was Customs but it turned out was Immigration. They closed the doors behind me and put sensors on the lorry and the sensors showed a pulse so they opened the lorry and the guy said there was no way anybody's in there, it's full to the roof with fruit. So they closed it up and one of the other guys checked the cab but he was more interested in the fact that I was from Ireland 'cos he had been stationed there when he was in the army. He was more interested in talking about Ireland than checking the thing. I can say I was quite relieved.

You must have been a worried man?

I was. I was touching cloth.

What was the date of that?

That was the first weekend in May of 2003.

What happened after you got clear of your wee scare?

I got on the train and got off and drove up towards Dumfries which would have run me into late on Monday night.

What happened?

I'd been in touch with Frank Gallagher.

You'd been in touch with him?

Yeah. He'd been in touch with me, sorry. He rang me, asked me what time I'd be round about Dumfries and he arranged to meet me at the Shell services just at the Dumfries roundabout there. But when I got there, there were three lorries parked so we couldn't change anything over . . . So I followed him. He was driving a black Audi at the time and every lay-by we came to someone was parked in it. So we were two or three miles up the road and I pulled into a lay-by, left enough space for him to drive the car up the inside of the lorry and I just handed the boxes from the lorry to him. He threw them into the car and disappeared.

Did he say anything?

He said, 'You OK?'

That was it?

That was it. That was the last time I heard for six weeks. I just carried on working for Kelly's. Obviously I got paid, arranged by my mate in Ireland to collect the money for me.

What money was that?

£20,000.

You got paid £20,000 for that run? That one run for those boxes?

Yeah.

How did you come into possession of that money?

I went to Ireland and collected it.

Was it cash?

It was cash.

What did you do with the money?

Paid quite a few bills of the hotel and sort of got myself out of debt. Made the hotel reasonably presentable for selling.

What was the name of the hotel again?

Queen's Hotel, Colmonell.

Where did that £20,000 come from?

It came from J and Frank Gallagher.

How do you know that?

'Cos my mate told me it came from him. He went

and collected it from him.

Did you know where he went to collect it?

Glasgow.

Were you with him?

No.

So that's done and dusted now, long gone. What happened then?

I just carried on working for Kelly's for the next few weeks. I took two weeks off 'cos we had sold the hotel and I got a wee flat in Ballantrae and I wasn't due to start back with Kelly's until Saturday 28 June. But on the Monday I received a call from Kelly's. I never done a midweek run for Kelly's before. On the Monday I received a call from Kelly's asking me if I could take some prawns to Le Havre in France on the Tuesday. He said, if I got myself down to Stranraer for the 5.15 ferry on Tuesday morning, I would go across with Ken, the transport manager. So I agreed to do that and, while I was away, my mate from Ireland rang me and asked me to do the run for Kelly's first thing on Tuesday and he said would I be interested in bringing some drugs back – 'Would you be interested in bringing some stuff back?'

For him?

For the boys in Glasgow.

Did he mention the boys in Glasgow?

Aye.

What names?

J and Frank.

So he's acting as a sort of . . .

Go-between.

Was this guy [Ken] Munro still with you at this stage?

No.

So you then travelled abroad with these prawns?

Yeah. I drove down to Newhaven in Sussex and got the 5.15 ferry over to Dieppe from Newhaven.

Was there any reason for you going to Newhaven?

It was just where Kelly's told me to go.

When did you get this phone call from your friend?

On the Monday.

What day is this we're talking about now?

Wednesday, late Tuesday evening, arrived in Dieppe on Wednesday night. I rang Kelly's. They told me to go up to Rijnsburg to load flowers. So I drove up more or less non-stop, apart from a break for tea and statutory breaks and things like that. More or less just drove straight . . . well I did stop, not too far from Rijnsburg and collected five trolleys there. That's where my problems really started 'cos four trolleys fit across the fridge together, the fifth trolley was rolling about. I tried to secure the trolley and J rang me to see what was keeping me. I said I would be at Rijnsburg about 10 o'clock or so. And it was midnight and I was still trying to get the load secure. I said, 'Look, I really think you should cancel this load.' He said, 'The guy is sitting there waiting for you. It has to come.'

So why did you want to cancel it?

'Cos everything was going wrong. I had an awful bad feeling about it, which turned out to be correct. This was Thursday 26 June.

Did he put any pressure on you to go through with it?

He said you're going to cause a hell of a lot of trouble for me, which means a hell of a lot of trouble for yourself, if you don't go ahead with it.

Do you remember what time that call came into your phone?

Midnight.

What phone?

The Siemens. I managed to tie the loose trolley, just
to get me over to Rijnsburg and I parked on
the road into Rijnsburg.

Same place as before?

Yes. Same place and the guy pulled up. This time in
a black Mercedes.

The same person?

The same person. Dutch plates again. And he
handed me the two boxes which I kept in the
cab with me overnight. I had to go and park at
Kelly's place in Rijnsburg and wait for the guy
to load me out with flowers so he loaded me
out and I went to collect more trolleys to load
me out completely. I loaded them. I was late for
the ferry. I had to get the ferry from the Hook
into Harwich and by the time I got the load, it
was about ten to seven. I was starting to panic
as I had these two boxes. I was driving the
wee Mann lorry with these two boxes sitting
conspicuously in the cab.

What lorry was that you were in?

The Mann, the one I was arrested in.

You were not happy with the boxes?

No. I wanted to put them into the load so, after I
loaded, I went round to the fruit market and
parked there. I put two boxes in amongst the
flowers. I got to the ferry about twenty past
seven and it was still standing there. I got off at
Harwich about half ten.

*So was there any communication after you took possession
of the boxes?*

Not until I got to England.

What was it?

When I got off the ferry, I was last off and Customs
and Excise were standing checking some other
lorries. They had the big X-ray machine as well.
But they just ignored me completely and waved
me on. On the ferry, I destroyed the SIM card
of my phone.

Why did you do that?

In case something happened.

Did somebody tell you to do that?

No. It was just a thing I done and, on the way up,
I rang Frank. I had taken a note of Frank's
number from him ringing me. I rang Frank to
say I was through Customs and I was on my
way up the road. Little did I know I was getting followed by the Regional Crime. And I told
him roughly what time I'd be at Dumfries. So I
drove up and stopped at Ferry-bridge Services
[near Leeds], had a bite to eat and a cup of tea.
I then rang Frank and I said it's usually about
three hours from here to Dumfries. We got
in touch back and forward. He rang me and I
rang him.

*So most of the communication that day was just you and
Frank?*

Yeah. I pulled into the services, the Shell services
at Dumfries. He said he would come down
there to meet me and take me to the industrial
estate 'cos I'd never been there before. At the
roundabout at the services, I went in convoy
with him into the industrial estate and then we
handed over. Then all hell broke loose.

*It's fair to say to those who will be listening to this
tape that that's the stage when you and Francis
Gallagher were apprehended?*

Yeah.

So have they ever asked you to bring anything else into the country?

Yes. At one time I took a lorry up to Kilsyth. It was just a unit, no cab and left it up there. Frank picked me up to run me back to Ayr. He dropped me back at Ayr.

Can you remember what date?

Mid June. Shortly before I got arrested. Maybe two weeks before that on a Friday about lunchtime. There was a wee burger van outside and I was starving. I had a wee burger while I was waiting on him coming.

What vehicle did he pick you up in?

An Audi – a black Audi.

What happened after that?

He asked me would I be interested in bringing some guns in, handguns. Just one box. He mentioned the figure £10,000 for bringing the box in.

Was this for him?

For him and J. He said J asked me to ask you would you be interested in bringing some guns in?

What was your response to that?

An Irishman with guns just doesn't really mix. If I was caught with guns, it's immediately regarded as a terrorist offence rather than a civil offence. But I said I would probably have a think about it.

Did he say this to you in the vehicle?

Yeah – in the car.

Did he say if he was going back to report to anybody?

He said he'd get back to J and let him know what the score is and we could talk about it again. Maybe up the price if I was prepared to do it.

Is it your understanding that he was acting as a go-

181

between for J?

From what I can gather, Frank and J were more or
    less on a par with each other.

Did he say they grew up together?

No. He just said they'd been friends for quite a while.
    He said J is the man with the overall power
    but he's his lieutenant type of thing – his right-
    hand man. He said they were like brothers.

So it was not only drugs they asked you to bring in?
They also asked you to bring in firearms?

Firearms, also. I mean that's a dodgy deal.

Is there anything else you can think of? We were here
earlier on today and I think you mentioned that
Jamie was involved with the McGoverns?

Yeah. I've heard the name McGovern mentioned by
    Gallagher a couple of times.

What do you know about that?

Very little. I know the McGoverns are big-time
    criminals from Glasgow and I've a feeling that
    they are directly or indirectly involved with
    them. One thing I do know is that most of
    the drugs in Glasgow and the Central Belt are
    controlled by this Jamie.

What makes you say that?

It's what Frank told me when we were on remand.

Did he say that as a generalisation?

Aye. We were talking about different things and he
    said anything that comes into Glasgow or the
    Central Belt has to go through him first . . .

This interview was instigated by whom?

By myself.

You're quite happy there was no lawyer present?

No problem. Quite happy.

And your reasons for providing us with this information
are what?

The J guy has authorised a contract on me. I've already been stabbed in the prison here.

When?

Third of March this year.

Has that been investigated?

The police interviewed me and took a brief statement and that's the last I heard about it.

How do you know it's this J guy that's taken out this contract?

In January, I was supposed to go to the National Induction Centre in Shotts [Prison], Frank Gallagher and myself were supposed to go there the same day. I was over in A-Wing at the prison here. I'd everything packed up and ready to go and a guy from the wing who I'd never spoken to before said to me, 'Do you know there's a contract out on you?' I was amazed. He said, 'Frank Gallagher has taken a contract out on you 'cos you set the whole lot up with Customs and Excise for him to get arrested.'

I said it'd be pretty poor to get myself ten years as well.

32
Identity Crisis

No one is eager to talk about Robert McDowall, whose current whereabouts are unknown, or the murky nexus where informers and law enforcers meet. This is for the most obvious reason – police waging war against serious and organised crime will not discuss their methods in detail. They do not disclose the day-to-day work that edges them closer to their targets – the surveillance, the bugs, the undercover agents . . . and their criminal informers.

When McDowall started working for the police may never be admitted. What can be established is that, within seventeen months of being sentenced to ten years in prison for smuggling £6 million of heroin into Scotland, McDowall was a free man. What can be said is that the police swoop to arrest McDowall and Frank Gallagher on the industrial estate on the outskirts of Dumfries in June 2003 was part of Operation Folklore. What can be noted is that Jamie Stevenson and his thuggish henchmen believe McDowall was a supergrass who was secretly working with the police.

In January 2005, McDowall had his sentence cut from ten years to five on appeal. The following month, a bid to seize around £1 million of his assets ended with the Crown recovering just £637. At the High Court in Edinburgh, the judge, Lord Penrose, said the cost of McDowall's legal aid would have 'far exceeded' what was recovered by the Crown while the SNP's then Shadow Justice Minister, now the

Cabinet Secretary for Justice, Kenny MacAskill, voiced his disappointment saying:

> The whole point of the Proceeds of Crime Act was to demonstrate that crime does not pay. This paltry figure does little to reinforce this message. I think the Crown should review what has taken place in this case to ensure it does not happen again.

But sources close to Stevenson say the Crown already knew exactly what happened and that is why McDowall was freed so early with a ludicrously light financial sanction. One said:

> Dumfries was a set-up and McDowall had to be involved. Nothing else makes sense. Stevenson believes McDowall had been turned in the January after getting caught coming through Dover in an apparently empty truck that was actually carrying heroin, speed, Ecstasy and cocaine. From there, he's allowed to go on condition he passes on information about big runs to Scotland. You'll never get any admission of that. The first acknowledged discussions between McDowall and the SCDEA come in Kilmarnock jail, after his conviction, when he's in fear for his life.
>
> McDowall had his sentence halved on appeal. His co-accused Gallagher went down from twelve to ten. So the big question remains – how did McDowall, a drugs smuggler caught with forty kilos of heroin and originally sentenced to ten years, get out in seventeen months? That's the question. But there'll be no answers.

Whatever McDowall's status within Folklore, the Ulsterman was out of jail by August 2006 as the SCDEA command were plotting the raids that it was hoped would end Stevenson's underworld reign. Interviewed again, McDowall told detectives that he could identify the man he knew as

Jamie – the man who had asked him to ferry drugs and guns across Europe to the Central Belt of Scotland.

On 27 September, exactly a week after the Folklore busts, an identity parade at the high-security police station in Govan's Helen Street gave McDowall the chance. And, in the viewing room of the station's parade suite, looking carefully at the seven innocent men and Jamie Stevenson lined up on the other side of the one-way glass, McDowall's memory failed him.

He picked Number Three. Jamie Stevenson stood at position Number Five. In the parade suite's dismissal room, McDowall suggested he might have made a mistake – that perhaps Number One was a familiar face. He told officers that he had been trying to recognise another member of the gang, not Stevenson. He said maybe Number Five looked like a man he remembered. It was all too late.

The one witness capable of placing the gang boss known as The Iceman at the very heart of Scotland's biggest drugs trafficking operation had failed to identify him. One source remembers:

> The cops were in a stone-cold fury but what could they do? They had placed huge reliance on McDowall. During the interviews, he had picked Stevenson out from a bunch of pictures. McDowall told them he could definitely identify him again. And then, after all those months, they get Stevenson into a line-up and their number one witness suffers a memory lapse. It happens of course but it can't help when you and your wife are living in some safe house in Ireland in a state of abject terror. Your memory might falter when you've already been stabbed in jail, heard there's £10,000 on offer for your life and know the man you are going to help put away for life is said to have shot men for a lot less. I guess that kind of pressure can help your memory play tricks.

33
No Limits

At first, the newspaper reporter thought his contact was joking. 'What do I tell him? I've got to phone him in half-an-hour or you will be getting shot.' But the journalist from the *Sunday Mail* realised from the sweat across the man's brow and the tone of his voice that he was deadly serious as he raised the phone, looking for instructions on what he should tell the person waiting for his call. The person awaiting a call from the man in the Counting House pub at Glasgow's George Square that Thursday afternoon in late January 2004 was Jamie Stevenson who was sitting in an Amsterdam apartment.

Stevenson had learned that the reporter had been sniffing about his affairs. Stevenson accepted that newspapers would take an interest in him – after all, he was the alleged killer of his former best pal Tony McGovern and had now become Scotland's major drugs smuggler – but, this particular week, for some reason, publicity would be catastrophic.

The contact explained, 'You can write anything you want about him next week or next month but not this Sunday. Something's going down and it could damage that.'

The veteran reporter shrugged his shoulders and agreed that nothing would be published that Sunday – not because of Stevenson's bizarre combination of plea and threat but because he had no story to write. The grateful contact made the call to Stevenson.

The supposed criminal code of honour which protects 'non-combatants' from being caught up in gangland violence does not exist and never did. Many criminals do not recognise a dividing line between 'legitimate' targets and the rest. Their wrath can be unleashed on anyone that might get in their way, including those in the media.

Eight days after the shooting threat, management at the *Sunday Mail* were told by the police about non-specific threats against its staff. The threats were understood to have come from Stevenson's gang. The fact that Stevenson was willing to consider such intimidation may have been the kind of ruthless tactic that he learned from his former partners-in-crime, the McGoverns.

A *Daily Record* reporter had received a warning that she was a potential target of McGovern violence because of a report she had written about Tony McGovern's funeral in November 2000.

Four months later, Serious Crime Squad officers summoned another *Sunday Mail* reporter to Helen Street police office in Govan to warn about a potential plot against him from the McGovern camp for exposing the family's criminal and business affairs.

But it's not just the media who are the targets. As far back as 1987, when Tony and Tommy were taking a few ounces of smack from Arthur Thompson, there was niggling between them and local police. The young McGoverns made a bold move – one that truly crossed the line. An officer, who had been giving the young drugs gang on his patch a hard time, arrived home one day to find every single window of his family home in the southside of Glasgow had been smashed. One colleague from those days said:

> The McGovern boys were bold and reckless on the way up and didn't care much for any so-called rules. One police officer was a real thorn in their sides. He was always giving

them a hard time. To smash his house windows was a very big statement for them to make. They were saying that they were big enough to take on the police. I'm not saying that it was connected but, within a week, every single window in their HQ at Thomson's bar had been put in.

Thirteen years after making a personal attack on a police officer's home, the McGoverns showed their willingness to push the boundaries again. This time the target was the elderly and much-admired parish priest for Springburn. In the view of some family members, Father Noel Murray had failed to properly praise Tony McGovern during his funeral service. At least, on this occasion, windows were spared and the priest just received a direct reproach from disgruntled female McGoverns rather than a warning from the Serious Crime Squad that somebody had been making death threats towards him.

34
Welcome to The Hague

Stevenson may not have known any language apart from Glaswegian but he could speak cash on delivery, which was the only language that mattered when he was making wholesale purchases of huge quantities of drugs across the northern rim of mainland Europe. Even the Folklore team, who were well aware of his capabilities in pioneering new sources and supply routes into Scotland, were stunned as they uncovered his business associations across Europe and beyond.

The team building their case in the shadow of Glasgow's international airport suspected Stevenson's cross-border operations may have already been registered by their colleagues abroad. In 2004, they called on the continent's biggest bank of criminal intelligence, Europol. The 500 staff and ninety liaison officers based at the European Police Office in The Hague are not a police force. Their agents will not be bursting through traffickers' doors in early-morning raids. But the information held on their massive databases of intelligence may have helped the forces of the then twenty-five members of the European Union find those doors.

Dr Martin Elvins, of the University of Dundee, has spent years studying the institutions of transnational crime-fighting and is not surprised the Folklore team visited Europol as they followed the chain of Stevenson's supply routes as it snaked through one country after another. He said:

Today's organised criminals are using many of the techniques of multinational corporations. The people getting away with a life of crime for the longest periods are demonstrating a high level of strategic thinking. The European Union is designed to encourage trade but, if you want to grow economies, if you want to encourage import/export, then there can be no surprise when 'bads' as well as 'goods' are also being traded. The law enforcement agencies have had to learn new tricks.

These people are resident in one country but making their money and spending their money in a number of other countries. They are well aware of being watched and well aware that they have to conceal their money. Their methods for doing that are in a constant process of adaptation.

They are aware they need to have access to the legitimate economy. That is the great unspoken truth at the heart of criminal enterprise – to do what they do, to conceal what they conceal, they must have access to corrupt people in the legitimate economy. These men are not islands.

Europol was launched under the Maastricht Treaty of 1992 as the Europol Drugs Unit, a force dedicated to gathering intelligence on the organised criminal trade in narcotics. Its remit was extended through the following decade until, by the start of 2002, the agency was working to combat all serious forms of international crime, from gun-running and human trafficking to terrorism and money laundering. The Europol Computer System (TECS) underpins the agency's work. Capable of the collection and intricate cross-analysis of huge amounts of intelligence submitted by law enforcement agencies and working twenty-four hours a day, Europol can offer multilingual assistance to officers trailing suspects across borders.

Dr Elvins says police have to overcome a territorial inclination and inherent reluctance to share information so painstakingly amassed if Europol is to help.

It is a fishing expedition, a game of show-and-tell. You offer something – you hope to get something back. Europol is most basically a silo of information based on the new reality of databases increasingly capable of holding and processing complex information. It is a conduit, a way of facilitating the sharing of information.

You're looking at a man who keeps flying down to Malaga, perhaps the Spanish police have been wondering who this Scots guy is that keeps meeting one of their suspects. You don't know until you ask.

The liaison officers are crucial. Seconded from forces in the member states, they are the channel of communication between the forces and Europol. Europol can also facilitate joint investigation teams. It provides a platform to set up an operation implemented by local forces in different member states which can have a number of different fronts.

A coordinated response can help ensure that one force is not tugging at a thread that is unravelling a case thousands of miles away. It is common-sense policing.

As Stevenson's deals stretched across borders, the Folklore team tracking him did not only visit Europol agents. The issues raised by cross-border jurisdiction meant talks at Eurojust were also on their itinerary. Based beside Europol, Eurojust was launched in 2002. Bringing senior prosecutors and judges from the European Union members together, it stages multilingual meetings with law enforcement agencies to discuss individual investigations of serious cross-border crime. The intention is to advise and to ease international legal cooperation although even the EU's Commissioner for Justice, Freedom and Security Franco Frattini admits it is meeting some resistance from crime-fighters across the continent.

Despite his dream of a single European prosecutor to oversee cross-border investigations into serious and organised crime and despite advising on 1,000 investigations involving the smuggling of arms, drugs, and humans a year, Eurojust remains a marginal influence. In April 2007, Frattini said, 'Eurojust should be made stronger. Our message to members is to make better use of joint investigation teams and make Eurojust involved.'

Dr Elvins, who researches cross-border police cooperation against transnational organised crime, says the international nature of the drugs trade will increasingly force the partnership of different governments and their law enforcers. He said:

Once you are building a case against these types of criminal, you very quickly hit the problem of cross-border jurisdiction. That is where Eurojust comes in. The drugs trade is a supply chain and it is not vertically integrated. At every level, it is an individual dealing with an individual. They might be dealing in container ships or a few condoms full of cocaine. The question for law enforcers is where to break the link most effectively. If someone linked to someone linked to someone you are looking at is buying a consignment in Morocco, is that going to help you put them away in the UK? Is it going to stick?

Europol and Eurojust are not well-known institutions. The public's idea that Europol is a police force, for example, is just wrong. It is a knowledge bank. Whatever intelligence, guidance and practical support they can offer, the real nitty-gritty, the building of the case, is still down to the quality of the police work on the ground – the prioritising of targets and resources, the analysis of surveillance, making the connections, the kind of work that police officers do day in and day out.

The police attempts to stop criminals [have] always been a game of cat and mouse. There may be different institutions, different techniques but the game remains the same.

THE ICEMAN

In Europol's 2005 annual report, director Max-Peter Ratzel was to highlight a dramatic seizure of drugs that illustrated the new way forward for crime-busters co-operating across borders. His report included a Europol bulletin issued on 7 June 2005:

> Close cooperation between British and Spanish authorities [has] resulted in the seizure of eight tonnes of cannabis destined for the British market. The crew on board the fishing boat *Squilla* – two Britons, one Estonian and one Spaniard – were taken by surprise when they were confronted and arrested by police officers in open waters off the coast of Spain. The police officers belonged to 'Grupo de Respuesta Especial contra el Crimen Organizado' (GRECO) and the 'Unidad contra la Droga y el Crimen Organizado' (UDYCO).
>
> The drugs traffickers had been under investigation for a longer period and the arrests made on early Sunday morning were the culmination of several months of analysis, investigation, expertise and liaison between the involved Member States and Europol.
>
> At the same time, three more persons suspected of having arranged the shipment of cannabis from Morocco were arrested in Glasgow, Scotland.
>
> As a law enforcement officer, it is always a pleasure when seizures and arrests such as this one are successful since they prove the value of a close and trustful cooperation between several different law enforcement entities.
>
> The investigation is ongoing and more arrests are expected.

35
All at Sea

A storm was looming and the MV *Squilla* was already struggling as it churned north out of the Mediterranean into the deep waters of the Atlantic. Loaded to its limit, with the cargo lashed to the deck, the British-registered trawler was dangerously unstable. Its cargo, transferred ship-to-ship off the coast of Morocco the day before, was not one recorded on any ship's manifest – a cargo of eight tonnes of cannabis worth £24 million on the streets of Scotland.

Dawn was yet to break on Sunday, 5 June 2005 but, when it did, the police moved in. The four crew on board put up no struggle as the Spanish cutter stopped the *Squilla* dead in the water. One source said:

> A decision had been taken that it was too risky to allow the
> vessel to run with the drugs back to Britain. The trawler
> was really well down in the water when she was stopped.
> She was loaded to the absolute limit.

The dramatic raid in international waters, 100 miles west of Lisbon, may have been code-named Operation Bouzas after the Spanish port where the fishing boat had anchored before sailing to its Moroccan rendezvous. It may have involved Spanish police and Customs, the National Crime Squad and Europol. It may have enlisted the Spanish air force and navy to track the boat's progress across the Med. But the operation

195

had been masterminded and co-ordinated by the detectives leading the Folkore offensive against Jamie Stevenson and his key lieutenant John 'Piddy' Gorman.

The *Squilla* was towed to Cadiz by the Spanish authorities and the crew were led in handcuffs down the gangway to face justice. They included Billy Reid, who had, since the 1990s, been a key member of the Tartan Mafia of the Costa del Sol, a fluid coalition of Caledonian gangsters who were making millions smuggling hash from Morocco. Reid had briefly done business with Gerry Carbin Snr, another Scot willing to exploit the criminal opportunities of the Costas and he was close to Walter Douglas. The elusive Douglas, known as the Tartan Pimpernel, was the most notorious of the Costa's Scots mobsters. Reid was flash – a big-spender who loved the high life – but he retained a reputation for professionalism, for doing his job. One source said, 'He was a well-organised man and made sure all the bits were fitting together. He was doing it for years and was seen as someone who could be relied on.'

The Folklore police team were delighted to have bagged Glasgow-born Reid, a major international drugs smuggler, but they had set their sights higher. The multimillion-pound drugs operation of Gorman, who, along with long-time cohort Stevenson, had spent £5 million bankrolling the *Squilla's* drug run, was about to be dismantled as the Folklore team edged ever closer to their number-one target.

Gorman, forty-nine, of Irvine in Ayrshire, was a career criminal who had graduated from street dealing to international drug trafficking. He was responsible for bringing tonnes of hash and class A drugs into Scotland. He was one of the very, very few associates Stevenson trusted and they often worked together. The Ayrshire man had offered Stevenson safe haven in his villas and apartments around the resort of Fuengirola when the Glasgow mobster was lying low after the McGovern murder. They spent much of that year immersed in the mechanics of the hash trade – the boats, cars and adapted trucks bringing cannabis resin from Morocco across the Straits of Gibraltar to the southern coast of Spain and onwards by road to Scotland.

In 2004, the SCDEA surveillance teams, who had been watching Gorman since the launch of Folklore, were looking on as he met Douglas Price, the skipper of the *Squilla*, in the Spanish port of Cadiz where the converted trawler was anchored. When it became clear the men were planning a huge cannabis shipment, the SCDEA alerted colleagues in Spain, who began their own surveillance on Price in March 2005 and monitored the *Squilla* as it was refitted in readiness for its drugs run. The international surveillance operation had also monitored meetings at the luxury apartment block in the millionaires' playground of Marbella where Stevenson had one of his many homes on the Costa del Sol.

One of his neighbours in the apartments on Avenida del Prado, in the heart of the chic Nueva Andalucia neighbourhood, was a millionaire Irish Republican and major cocaine smuggler. Vastly experienced in specially adapting boats to carry drugs and the techniques needed to transfer contraband ship-to-ship while at sea, detectives believe he, along with Stevenson and Gorman, was a key player in the *Squilla* plot.

On 26 April 2006, Gorman, Reid and the rest were jailed at court hearings held simultaneously in Scotland and Spain. At the end of an eight-week trial, Gorman got twelve years at the High Court in Glasgow after being convicted of drug running and money laundering. He was never convicted over the *Squilla* bust but, after Crown prosecutors focused on the Scottish end of his operation, Gorman was jailed over £360,000 worth of drugs and laundering £178,000 of drugs money. Gorman, a self-styled builder who rarely visited a site, had claimed the cash was for trading in tobacco and fireworks – a sideline in pyrotechnics that seemed to surprise his accountant when he was called to give evidence. The judge,

Lord Bracadale, told Gorman, 'The evidence showed you were the likely organiser and manager who arranged deals. The profits were high and so were the risks.'

Money launderers William McDonald, forty-four, from Glasgow, James Lowrie, sixty, from Liverpool, Bradford-based Mushtaq Ahmed, fifty-one, and cannabis dealer Robert Thomson, twenty-seven, from Irvine, shared sentences totalling sixteen and a half years.

Meanwhile, in Madrid, the *Squilla* smugglers were also being sentenced. Douglas Price, fifty, from Kilwinning in Gorman's Ayrshire heartlands, got four years. Reid, forty-four, Arno Podder, thirty-eight, from Estonia, the boat's mechanic, and Moroccan fixer Sufian Mohammed Dris, twenty-two, were jailed for three years each.

Afterwards, the SCDEA's director, Graeme Pearson, told reporters:

> There is not a village or town in the West of Scotland that has not been impacted by Gorman and his trade. Thousands of ghosts created by drugs who are today wandering the streets have him to thank for their plight. What astounds me is that he could still manage to live within the very communities that he has blighted.
>
> It must be like the man who invented the iPod walking around and being proud seeing everyone using his product. Gorman must have been the same in some Ayrshire villages.
>
> How does he cope with knowing there is a family down the street whose kids have not been fed because their parents are addicted to his drugs – or knowing that some parents are wondering why they failed their kids because they end up being hooked?
>
> Gorman and his associates funded comfortable lifestyles on the backs of many thousands of people stricken by the scourge of drug abuse.

And Pearson had only one man in mind when he delivered a final and pointed message to Gorman's associates still at large – 'We will not forget about you.'

36
Birdman

Coke often causes violence between criminals but usually Colombia's biggest export is behind it rather than the best-selling cola. However, anyone who was in the visiting room of maximum-security Shotts Prison one evening in July 2005 would have learned that is not always the case.

The niggling had started outside in the car park. Jamie Stevenson and his stepson Gerry Carbin Jnr had been striding to the entrance of the Lanarkshire jail when words were exchanged with another group of visitors. Prison officers quickly extinguished the row.

Wives, partners, mums, dads and kids filed slowly into the large visiting room. Prisoners sat at the bolted-down plastic tables, holding hands with loved ones, under the poker faces of the prison officers. They talked about family, friends, old times – anything that gave a temporary escape from their surroundings. A few children amused themselves in the play area.

Suddenly, the low murmur of conversation was shattered when a full can of Coke was hurled with great force towards the head of Stevenson. The bright red missile rocketed through the air before smashing squarely off his temple. Stevenson barely paused under the blow, hurling himself across the visiting room towards an old adversary four seats along – Robert 'Birdman' O'Hara. Bedlam ensued as the pair traded blows. They were joined by Carbin along with another prisoner and O'Hara's female visitor. Prison officers waded in to break it up and, within moments, peace returned.

For many years, no one in Scotland's criminal underworld was either brave enough or stupid enough to cross Stevenson. Even people like the members of the Daniel family, who shared his untouchable reputation, would back away from conflict with him. His notoriety was justified. Enemies were dealt with directly and forcefully. It would take a very brave, dangerous or reckless man to have a go. Enter O'Hara.

Then aged just twenty-eight but serving a jail sentence that will not see him freed until at least 2025, his reputation was almost as ugly as Stevenson's. O'Hara grew up on the tough streets of Possilpark, an area bordering the McGovern family's Springburn base. From an early age, his ability to dish out violence was noted by the family in much the same way a schoolboy footballer's skill may catch the eye of a big club's scout. Indeed, his 'natural ability' reminded some of Stevenson when he was a young man.

From 2000 onwards, O'Hara went from a nasty nuisance in Possil to the head of a drugs operation turning over £2 million a year, with direct links to the McGoverns. He drove a £65,000 Audi and lived in a £400,000 penthouse flat in a sophisticated city-centre apartment block. His gang's drugs profits, mainly from heroin and cannabis, were laundered through a couple of car washes.

His gang was hated and feared in equal measure. During the summer of 2004, O'Hara and his crew were at their most dangerous with a similar reputation for violence as that which had once been carved out by the young McGovern brothers. Paul McDowall, no relation to Robert McDowall, was to become the latest casualty in the city's drugs wars when O'Hara ordered one of his cronies to kill him. The twenty-five-year-old victim was an associate of a rival dealer and O'Hara wanted to show his power. The price for McDowall's murder was the £2,000 worth of drugs which the knifeman owed O'Hara.

Killer Colin McKay, who shares his name with another McGovern associate linked to earlier gangland killings, phoned O'Hara afterwards to tell him the job was done. His call was not necessary as CCTV cameras had actually seen O'Hara and his right-hand man, Robert Murray, edging close enough to view the imminent knife attack outside the Saracen pub. They were like two spectators at a sporting event.

In another parallel with the McGoverns, the O'Hara mob knew that all the evidence in the world meant nothing if the witnesses could be got at. When he was arrested after arriving back in Scotland from a luxury holiday in Mexico, he casually insisted that he would get someone else to take the fall but his confidence was misplaced and his next holiday was not going to be as exotic as the last one.

Soon after the murder, police found evidence of attempts to threaten and bribe those who were to give evidence. O'Hara's girlfriend stood trial for offering £10,000 to the sister of a key witness but the case against her was found not proven. One witness fled Scotland while two others who did give evidence remain under official protection provided by the authorities.

Raids linked to the murder investigation yielded a huge and terrifying arsenal of guns including a MAC-11 sub-machine gun, which spits out ten deadly rounds per second – that is 600 per minute. It was the first time such a weapon had been found in Scotland and O'Hara's gang were the last people that should have had it.

The trial was switched from Glasgow to a High Court sitting in Dunfermline to give armed police an extra edge in the containment and monitoring of the convoy of thugs making the daily journey from Possil to Fife. On this occasion, despite his bold prediction that he would walk free, the system won and the man who terrorised large areas of north Glasgow was jailed. As he was sent down, his moronic foot soldiers clapped defiantly from the public gallery.

One figure who was occasionally present during the trial was Paul McGovern. Although the McGoverns valued having O'Hara on their side, they knew he was volatile figure who could have turned on them in a flash so, despite losing money tied up in Birdman's drugs business, there was an almost palpable sense of relief that he had gone. He was a terrifying man with the unpredictable capability of bringing down enemies and allies alike.

He and three associates got a total of fifty-six years in May 2005. Just a few weeks before, the most deadly weapon O'Hara could aim at Stevenson was the can of Coca-Cola. One associate said:

> O'Hara was loyal to the McGoverns and had been making it clear for long enough what he thought of Stevenson and what he intended to do to him. If it was a square go, Stevenson would have torn him apart but had they both stayed out of jail with weapons, money and contacts, anything could have happened.

Following the Coke-can attack, Stevenson, who was seething with rage, and Carbin were bundled into a police van and carted off to a cell for the night before appearing the next morning at Hamilton Sheriff Court. The charge against Carbin was later dropped but Stevenson, appearing at the same court in November 2005, admitted a breach of the peace charge. It is the most common non-motoring charge brought in Scotland and one which requires the accused to 'cause fear and alarm'. He was admonished – the least serious sentence that could have been given and the legal equivalent of a slap on the wrist.

Fiscal Depute Ian McCann told the court:

The whole incident was sparked when Robert O'Hara threw a can of juice at Mr Stevenson. A fight occurred and, by his plea of guilty, Mr Stevenson admits he was involved in it. The police were called and Mr Stevenson was arrested.

For a man linked with a series of murders and who headed an international drugs and money laundering network, it was a bizarre first criminal conviction. The news agency photographer who snapped Stevenson as he left court that day secured the first contemporary image of Scotland's number one criminal.

As Stevenson emerged into the winter chill from the court, he had no idea the Folklore team were in the process of assembling their own album of secret snapshots.

37
On the Run Again

'Have you counted it yet? Why not? Well, gonnae do it right now? Every bundle. I want an exact figure. Is it all right where it is? That safe . . . is it big enough to hold all that?'

It was Friday, 26 May 2006 and Jamie Stevenson had a cash problem – he had too much to hide. He unwittingly shared his storage difficulty with the surveillance officers bugging his home but one detective said that the almost-daily collection of thousands of pounds in used notes was a logistical headache for the drugs gang.

> Everyone talks about money laundering and all the ways the cash is whitened up but, way before it becomes a line buried in some company's accounts or a digitised electronic transfer, drugs money is literally dirty – thousands and thousands of used notes, sometimes rolled into £5,000 bundles, sometimes just lying loose like confetti and stuffed into bags and cases. We're not talking about a cheque that can be slipped into a top pocket. These guys get paid in cash money and lots of it. It's big and it's bulky. Every day, they face the problem of hiding it until they can get rid of it safely.
>
> Stevenson could stay away from the drugs but he had to get close to the money. That was his Achilles heel and, in the end, that's how we got him.

At the premises of one of Stevenson's taxi firms, in the south-east of Glasgow, not far from his home, there was a large, reinforced-steel safe set into its foundations and, two days after that conversation, on the last Sunday in May, Stevenson headed there. He was tailed by undercover officers, who watched as he entered the building, talked with two associates and left twenty minutes later. The other two men left minutes after their boss.

The police already suspected the capacious under-floor safe was a regular hiding place for Stevenson's dirty money on the way to the laundry. Months before, when Stevenson had discussed the size, security status and location of a large sum of money, they had been listening. They had heard him tell his associate, 'No, it's under the ground . . . in a safe under the ground.'

When the two men left Stevenson's firm, they were followed by another surveillance team as they drove to a house five minutes away. The officers already knew it was the location for the stash of money because Stevenson had been heard discussing it two days earlier. His associates were only in the house a matter of minutes before they left, wheeling a very large and heavy suitcase behind them. Hefting it into the boot of their car, they drove off. They did not get far before police swooped. Inside the case, they found £389,035 in used notes. Stevenson would at least get an exact figure.

He was back home at Fishescoates Gardens when he took a telephone call fifteen minutes after the police bust. Hanging up, he told his wife, 'Got taken out. Christ, we'll need to go intae his house.'

Within minutes, he had driven back to the premises of his taxi firm but, after spotting surveillance teams on the ground, he did not stop. Hours later, he was gone – away from Glasgow and out of Scotland.

The Folklore tapes recorded his fears that the men caught with the money might talk and forge a deal where his arrest would be exchanged for their freedom. He was not prepared to take that chance. Like he had done after Tony McGovern was murdered, like he did whenever police attention seemed to be drawing uncomfortably close, Stevenson simply vanished.

Reaching for his passport, possibly his own or perhaps his counterfeit documents in the name of Jeremiah Dooley, Stevenson left for the airport.

This time, though, the police were ready.

38
We're Listening

The halogen glare of a street light outside the apartment complex at 133 Berlaarstraat looks like any other. The lamp post in the suburb of Nieuw Sloten on the outskirts of Amsterdam lights a quiet patch of street outside the entrance to a nondescript block but this was the block where Jamie Stevenson lived for three months during the summer of 2006.

The light illuminated the visitors arriving at the Iceman's Dutch bolthole after dark and it improved the quality of the video being shot by the tiny camera hidden inside the casing of the lamp post. For months, the Amsterdam police had been secretly recording everyone coming and going from Stevenson's apartment, which was tucked in behind the main block.

One criminal justice source in Holland said:

On any job like this, you study the location, the terrain, and use what is there. There was a streetlight outside his flat and the police simply took the whole thing away and put in a replacement – identical apart from the small camera filming everybody coming and going. They bugged his phone too. He got a lawyer to apply for the transcripts through the courts here but, by then, it was all too late for Mr Stevenson.

The Dutch authorities had been alerted to Stevenson's presence in the city by SCDEA detectives who had covertly followed the criminal as he fled Scotland in the wake of the cash seizure in May 2006. He would not return to Scotland until August of that year.

Even if Stevenson did not have a history of fleeing Scotland for extended periods whenever his finely tuned antenna for police interest began to twitch, the agency would have been watching him anyway. The officers who tailed him and his wife to Glasgow Airport were unaware of his secret Dutch bolthole until he flew to Amsterdam where the couple were immediately picked up and followed.

One Scot who visited the couple recalls:

> I don't know if it was their flat or if it belonged to someone else – one of Jamie's friends or business contacts. He always hated being away from home but he quite liked the hustle and bustle in Amsterdam. It was no luxury penthouse or anything. You can see the flats from the train going through the outskirts. To be honest, the neighbourhood reminded me of Springburn. Maybe that's why Jamie liked it.
>
> He had people there to do business with but he just did his thing – no great fuss. And, unlike when he went on the run after the McGovern murder, Caroline was with him which made him happier. They lived the same kind of life that they were living in Burnside – quiet, going for a drink, a meal.
>
> Folk would go out and see them. They had visitors. Obviously, they didn't know they were appearing on *Candid Camera*.

The techniques deployed to gather intelligence on Stevenson's Dutch-based friends and business associates may have been particularly ingenious but they were only an extension of the massive surveillance offensive already underway against Stevenson and his gang by the police trailing him around the world.

The arsenal of covert and electronic surveillance techniques available to modern law-enforcers was targeted on Stevenson. For very obvious reasons, the SCDEA refuse to discuss any operational aspects of their surveillance campaign against Stevenson but sources describe the phenomenal array of methods used to gather intelligence on the gang, their operations and their associates.

Across the West of Scotland, covert surveillance was taking place as officers, hidden from view, passing in cars, cleaning windows, repairing potholes and mending phone lines, watched and listened. They monitored the homes of Stevenson, Carbin, and the other gang leaders. They followed them on foot, on the road, in the air. They trailed them to the gym, to the shops, to their meetings.

Six months before his arrest, detectives became aware of an imminent sit-down with Stevenson and two key associates, Anthony Burnette and Willie Cross. At lunchtime on Wednesday, 15 March 2006, plainclothes officers followed Stevenson to the Holiday Inn, in Stewartfield, East Kilbride. According to one source:

> They basically tailed him there and the three of them are sitting down in the hotel, discussing deals or whatever and never even look twice at a couple at the next table who are all lovey-dovey, hugging and winching. They were cops and they sat listening as the three of them talked about buying this, buying that, pulling out architectural plans, moving money about, the lot.
>
> That's how tight they were on him and they were on him for months and months.

But the physical surveillance teams of officers on the ground were only a small part of the monitoring operation that would ultimately pull Stevenson's operation apart. Electronic bugs and tags were being used in the coordinated intelligence-gathering onslaught, certainly the biggest ever launched by a Scots police force. The SCDEA began intrusive surveillance against Stevenson and his gang at the launch of Folklore in May 2003. Intrusive surveillance, giving police powers to break into private homes and cars and use undercover officers as spies, can only be authorised if a subsequent conviction could carry a sentence of at least three years. The police later requested, and received, authority to plant hidden listening devices capable of monitoring conversations in the homes of both Stevenson and Carbin.

One legal source, with knowledge of the evidence ultimately ranged against Stevenson and his cohorts, said the electronic surveillance operation was huge.

> They had bugs in their homes, in their cars. Their phones were being tracked. They were basically in the cross hairs all day, every day, for years. The bugs at the homes were absolutely the latest technology – fibre-optic stuff. I was told NASA had helped develop them. They were remote control and would be turned on and off depending on what was happening. Basically, if the police saw somebody interesting arriving at the houses or if somebody's phone rang, the tapes were on and every word was recorded then transcribed. When the bug's off, it won't show even if the rooms are being swept. I don't know where the bugs were hidden but the police don't even have to get into the house they're targeting. They can come in through the walls, through the ceiling, below the floor, wherever.
>
> God knows how many thousands of hours were recorded. I know they put about 3,500 hours in as evidence and that was only a small part of it. They will still be picking the bones out of the transcripts. The intelligence picked up by those mics could be the starting gun for all sorts of investigations.

The cost of the four-year operation is huge but, so far, undisclosed with the thousands and thousands of hours of surveillance driving costs ever upward. One officer, who was not involved in Folklore but has years of experience in surveillance work, said:

> The cost would have been huge but electronics used with a bit of gumption can cut down the number of officers you need on the ground and the number of times you need them. You can track their cars. You can track their mobile phones as they pass different masts and you can track their associates' cars and phones in the same way. Before, you would need big teams on the ground watching all these guys every minute, every day. Now, you can watch them moving about, see where they're going, see who they're meeting and send the teams straight there.
>
> You just need to be nimble – to move quickly when you have to.

The SCDEA were certainly nimble just before 7 p.m. on the night of Saturday, 21 January 2006, when they listened in as a man delivered a holdall to Gerry Carbin's home in East Kilbride. The figure 'two-oh-four' was mentioned before Carbin tried to stash the bulging bag in various hiding places around the house. At 5 a.m. the next morning, the police were at his door. 'You would think the penny might drop at that point, wouldn't you?' asks one observer. He continued:

> The cops come in, go straight to the bag filled with £204,000 and Gerry doesn't twig that they might have had a wee clue. He gets taken to Hamilton police station and, as soon as he gets out that morning, hotfoots it over to Stevenson's flat in Burnside to have a blether about it. Of course, the cops are sitting listening into all of this as well. These guys are wide but not always smart.

Some associates say Stevenson was aware that he was being watched by police for most of the duration of Folklore. They said he even used to go out of his home to wave at suspected surveillance teams but he didn't realise the extent of the intelligence-gathering operation. One said:

Jamie and his senior people have been around the block a million times. He was careful. I know that, at one meeting, he told the guys there to get their shirts off to make sure they were not wearing wires and these were his own men not strangers. They were obviously super-careful about talking on their phones. It's all throwaway, pay-as-you-go phones and they'll have umpteen on the go at once. It's all in code. They'll say to someone, 'I'll take fifty engines off you.' And 'Have you got oil for them?' Or it'll be 'Have you got two hits on the thingwy?' Hits will be kilos and the thingwy could be a car, a truck, anything. They speak it and the cops know they're speaking it but the hard bit is deciphering it to put them close to specific shipments. They're cute. It's not easy.

There was a lot of that kind of talk in the tapes from Stevenson's house but not nearly as much as you would expect. He can say what he likes now but he clearly did not know he was being bugged. Really unguarded and clearly talking about drugs, about business, about property deals, about money, about millions and millions of pounds. The transcripts are astonishing – really astonishing.

39
Talking Business

A transcript of a conversation between Jamie Stevenson and his business associate Anthony Burnette at Stevenson's home in Fishescoates Gardens reveals the astonishing extent of the business empire he'd designed to launder his criminal fortune. During the discussion, secretly being recorded by the police, the pair discuss deals worth millions. They casually discuss buying and selling land, homes and businesses as if they were playing Monopoly. However, the money was real. They talk about merging three firms into a single business worth £1 million to increase their leverage with mortgage lenders. They discuss shares, property portfolios and new business opportunities in their conversation beginning at 9.29 p.m. on Thursday, 2 March 2006, and ending twenty-four minutes later. The transcript offers a unique insight into how Stevenson legitimised his dirty fortune.

> *Anthony Burnette: They were supposed to come to you the following day to report progress.*
> Jamie Stevenson: They didn't. He's still to get back to me on that one.

This is followed by the sound of a telephone keypad being pressed and then Stevenson begins talking on the phone.

> JS: Willie, I'm with Tony the now. Did we ever get

any thingwy on the site in Motherwell? Did it not? All right, no bother. I'm at the other place tomorrow. What time do you want to go down at? Aye, OK. No bother. Cheerio.

Here, Stevenson terminates the call and addresses Burnette again.

JS: No, nothing came of it. But what he says to me there . . . do you want to take a run? There's a place down near Helensburgh where Walter Smith . . . it's a hotel but it went into liquidation and Walter says to Willie it would be ideal for youse to get in and build flats in it, he says.

AB: *Walter Smith, the football manager?*

JS: Aye.

AB: *Willie knows him, does he?*

JS: Aye.

AB: *I didn't know that.*

JS: It's his partner Paul, aye. He's known him for thirteen years on and off. I don't know how close he is but he's pally with him anyway because he goes to Willie's house and that for fireworks and things like that. They're pals – put it that way. Paul is friendly with Willie, very friendly with Willie. Willie's sister runs one of Walter's and his partner's pubs and has done for five, six years and they pay her for holidays and all that because she doesn't steal. She's just a straight goer. Obviously that's why they've got in tow with Willie through his sister.

'Why don't we take a run down and see that place?' he says because Walter says it would be stunning for flats – absolutely stunning. So I says to Willie the-night, 'Let's get all the

money in place because if I wanted to buy that place we would need to put it in the now.' The money we generated, the income from the garage, would hopefully pay the loan for this place or whatever – if we could get planning permission.
Willie says to me that Walter says to him, 'Listen, buy that – it's going into liquidation and it's a going concern.' That's what he said to me there. 'Why don't we take a run down and see that?' he says. He says you need to go and see it during the day. You want to take a run down at the weekend or if you wanted to take a run down with him tomorrow then you could do that. See what it's like. Just got to keep looking.

AB: *Well, I could run down with him tomorrow because you're going to be tied up all day and I've got . . .*

Here the men begin discussing one of their petrol stations where the leaseholder is apparently obstructing their plans to sell.

JS: He knows, he knows. He'll phone him tomorrow.

AB: *I'll just go. I'll go and nudge them around tomorrow.*

JS: I don't think he's there much. I've never seen him the last couple of weeks.

AB: *I think he just goes in very early and gets out, doesn't he? He didn't do us any favours with the surveyor on getting the re-valuation done. He was talking it down, saying it's garbage, shite takings – this, that and the other. Basically, the guy rang me. I*

216

said, 'Listen, he's at it because he wanted to get his hands on the place and that's not going to happen.' So I sent him a copy of the lease and he's talked his figures down for gas sales and that. We've got the valuations coming in at three-twenty [£320,000] as it is.

JS: Fuck him.

AB: *He's no' getting . . .*

JS: He's not getting it anyway. He's fucked himself. He's just blew himself out of the water. He's just a stupid wee man.

AB: *Greedy.*

JS: He'll just need to pay through – pay the money he owes and pay the next couple of years.

AB: *His rent goes up again in June.*

JS: Aye, well, just speak to him.

AB: *And the lease has got another two years to run. He told me he was looking for a five-year lease 'cos he wanted to put a spa in there.*

JS: Just give him a fuckin' five-year lease.

AB: *He hasn't come back to me with a proposal. These are the things I said to him in an e-mail. Y'know, come back to me with a proposal and tell me about the Shell station 'cos he seemed to be in the know about it. 'Cos I can't . . . I've been all over Shell's website and I can't get any information about even where to look about their properties.*

The men then discuss difficulties in locating a Shell station that they have been told is up for sale in Glasgow. They go on to discuss more property deals and the merging of three firms into one business worth £1 million. Stevenson reveals he plans to start buying property in Edinburgh.

JS: It'll be in one of they thingwies.

AB: *What the agents?*

JS: Aye.

AB: *I was just on the Shell site. That's all I've been on.*

JS: Naw, they won't tell you.

AB: *Well, they don't even have a page to go to on their estates or anything – properties . . .*

JS: Do you not put it in under petrol stations for sale in the UK – Glasgow area?

AB: *Looked into everything. I've looked into everything.*

JS: Maybe he's just talking a lot of shite.

AB: *See we could turn that Viking round as well and make that start earning money.*

JS: First you need to get a valuation on it. 'Cos it's not worth anything as a business.

AB: *The only way we can do this merger is on a property valuation.*

JS: Aye, aye.

AB: *That's the only way it can be done. It can be done by the issuing of shares and credits with directors' loan accounts so that you don't attract any tax – capital gains tax. You know it's just a property transaction but we still need to do it. We got to generate income so I mean the garage is generating income – that's got to generate income for the group.*
So that means we have to get a hold of the business and turn it around, let the property, sort the vans out and everything. But that's not hard. Well, I won't bore you with all that tonight. Shall I ring Willie in the morning and arrange to go down to Helensburgh and look at that flat?

JS: Aye

AB: *I've got my camera with me so I can take a few snaps. It's closed down now, has it?*

JS: I don't know, Tony. It was Willie that came up

with it.

AB: *Does he do training in the morning?*

JS: Aye, have you got his number?

AB: *Well, I haven't got my phones with me. If you see him, ask him what time he'll be available. He'll probably be in his bed now, won't he? Watching telly.*

JS: It'll be the afternoon he'll go down. Take his number.

AB: *I'll give him a ring tomorrow, then go down and look at that. I've got to see the auditors and the accountants 'cos they've got some of the paperwork that you and I need to go over together. I'm meeting them on Tuesday. Also their tax consultant, who's given me the formula to put all this together. Between them, they're saying we should set up a holding company. That's got to be done. There'll be some tax to pay on shares, share transfers, and their fees will come to about three and a half grand to do it all, put it all in place, which is not a lot. What about Ronnie's house? Do you want me to get a mortgage for that?*

JS: Aye, we'll need to, won't we?

AB: *Yeah.*

They begin to talk about buying flats and then Stevenson is told the seller of one property is reluctant.

JS: What about that one next door?

AB: *I haven't even started on that yet. I want to get that one first. You're probably looking at about two-twenty to two-twenty-five [£225,000] for that plus costs.*

JS: If he doesn't sell it? Well, he will sell it. He'll sell it all right or we'll start pouring paint over it, spray-paint the windows. It'll be the worst mistake if he doesn't sell it. There's nothing worse than getting your wee windows smashed now and again. Or a big window smashed. I'm looking for somewhere, anyway. What do you think?

AB: *What I was going to suggest is we lease that. Lease it, you know, all proper and kosher. And I'll lease this one off you.*

JS: Aye.

AB: *You know, pay you rent for this one 'cos you don't want to get rid of this do you?*

There is the sound of a dog panting.

JS: I'm trying to get it out of her name, actually.

AB: *Is it hard?*

JS: Naw, there's a few probs. There's a few down the stairs for sale.

AB: *I see there's a sold sign downstairs.*

JS: Aye that sold in a day.

AB *(to the dog): You're in a bad way. You're in a bad way, mate.*

JS: I'm actually waiting on a price for six flats up in East Kilbride but they've no' got back to us. Need to get back to the boy. Apparently he's making about twenty grand off each of them – it's a fuckin' steal.

AB: *So, with the fusion, the merger of all three different assets, you've got about one-point-one million [£1.1 million] there.*

JS: Aye, easy.

AB: *Bought and paid for. It's a good lever.*

JS: For what?

AB: *You've got the asset value there so you'd be able to*

raise mortgage finance no problem at all.

JS: Oh, fuck, aye. No problem, no bother what-
soever. I'll tell you one thing. See that fuckin'
Edinburgh, on that Leith waterfront. When
that development finishes . . . absolutely
frightening.

AB: Is it? Have you been down and had a look?

JS: Aye, spent a day in Edinburgh. I didn't
know what like the market was but there's
Barratt doing a two-bedroom at one-eight-
five [£185,000]. Trinity . . . where's Trinity in
Edinburgh? Anyway the boy's got a meeting
with Barratt who does a lot of business with
him and I told him twenty – twenty per cent.
I don't want anything less than twenty per cent
off the market value of the house. So I reckon,
when the development's finished, that's when
we should cash them in. The people would be
selling if you get thirty grand off each unit.
For talking's sake, if you bought three off that
development, three in that, four in that – so, if
the house is on at one-eight-five, Barratt give
you the cash back at one-twenty.

Say we use a hundred grand for the four properties,
twenty-five on each property. The properties are
one-eight-five so you've got a mortgage of one-
sixty but Barratt actually give you back thirty
or forty grand so you can either leave it in the
property equity or you can take it out, so you've
no' put anything in but it still looks as if you're
still paying the one-eight-five. So when you
go to sell it at a later date, you've no' paid like
you've got thirty grand off it. You've no' paid
one-fifty on paper – you've paid one-eight-five
or whatever it was.

AB: You pay the taxes on one-eight-five?

JS: Aye, so at the end of the day when you go to sell it when the development's finished, then you've fuckin' won a watch, haven't you?

AB: Aye.

JS: It was the boy that was explaining 'cos that's all he does, see – he goes and buys twenty and thirty at a time so I've been firing him up there 'cos he says there's six in East Kilbride at the corner of the Whirlies [a roundabout] and they're doing one-three-two [£132,000]. He says, 'Jamie, if I can get something off them, then I think, in hindsight, go for the six of them.' Then 'Wait,' he says, 'and wait 'cos I've went in and they're really good value for money.'

AB: Where's that? In East Kilbride?

JS: Just at the Whirlies. Good renting potential as well. Just need to get a good rent, a good agent.

AB: There's plenty of good agents around at the moment.

JS: Naw, letting agents.

AB: We could do our own factoring, couldn't we?

JS: Aye, no bother. There's four flats – I've gied them away there to Gerard [Carbin] in Castlemilk. Four flats in the centre of Castlemilk. Three of them are leased out – two-seventy, two-seventy, three hundred [£270 and £300 per month]. The other one wasn't leased 'cos the people got put out. It's cost eighty grand for the four of them. Eighty thousand. The guy's taking fifteen under the table which made them sixty-five. It's got rental income of fucking twelve hundred quid or something. Fuck's sake, you couldn't whack that.

AB: *I must say that's a pretty good return.*

JS: That's good. Fuck's sake, five year and you're getting your money back. The social would fill them with people. You'd get three hundred quid off the social, two-seventy for one bedroom, three hundred for two.

AB: *Guaranteed.*

JS: It's just actually going out and looking – finding it.

AB: *Have you got furnishings?*

JS: What?

AB: *Have you got furnishings as well or will the tenants get their own furniture?*

JS: I don't know. I think there's furniture in them. Fuck, it doesn't take much to furnish a house now. A furnished flat is just a . . .

AB: *A grand to furnish a flat – carpets, bed.*

JS: Get carpets. Jim's got all that wood.

AB: *I've been trying to sell that for him but he won't come back to me with details. Harry wants to buy that off him.*

JS: I seen the wood in Focus for twenty pound. I think he's just trying to get his money back. Stupid-looking twat.

AB: *Yeah but he's got some partner or other that's involved and he's got it all stashed somewhere, hasn't he?*

JS: I don't know. I knew he was trying to sell it. Somebody was wanting it at fourteen quid a square metre.

AB: *He'll be doing well to get that. He'll be doing very well to get that off Harry. Harry will probably pay him a tenner. I've knocked back that Rockwood offer. They've come back with an offer.*

JS: For what?

AB: *Troon. Four-twenty [£420,000].*

JS: Which has planning?

AB: *Yeah so I just said your offer has no merit – forget it. I spoke to Wallace about it – he reckoned he'd have to pay us between six-fifty and eight hundred [£650,000–£800,000] for that to make it worth our while so I just knocked him back.*

JS: I think we paid too much for that.

AB: *Things all stack up. Figures all stack up. We're getting a good wage out of that.*

JS: Aye, I reckon I'll get fuckin' one-six-five [£165,000] anyway.

AB: *Well, it's two years ago. Local estate agent priced those at one-five-six [£156,000] – small two-beds, one-five-six each – two years ago. Probably value's gone up in that area – probably fifteen per cent in that intervening period. They only got two penthouses on top.*

JS: Two-twenty [£220,000], you'd get for them. So we've done all right.

AB: *I'm going to get down the road. I'll ring Willie tomorrow.*

JS: I'll get you down. Fuckin' like an oven in here.

There's the sound of a door closing and a TV in the background.

40
Doing Time

'Anyone with money can appreciate jewels and gemstones; it takes someone with refinement to appreciate a fine timepiece.' This is an old saying of Asian watch collectors. While the refinement of gang boss Stevenson is arguable, there can be no debate that, for a few years, he was among Scotland's most extravagant and discerning horologists. Officers searching his home and the homes of others that were raided in the Folklore busts of September 2006 found more than forty luxury watches. In fact, he had bought a dozen more and his collection, which included many of the rarest and most prestigious models on the market, was scattered around his safe houses. In total, they would be valued at more than £307,000.

One detective recalling the scramble of organised criminals to clamber through loopholes in the Proceeds of Crime Act (PoCA) says many invested in high-end jewellery and watches as a way of hiding and washing their dirty money.

> For a time, it was thought to be one way of doing it. Going into a jewellers and buying watches that would maintain or increase in value over the years seemed a relatively safe and straightforward way of getting rid of the banknotes while keeping the investment.
>
> Stevenson was already trading in jewels and watches through Amsterdam to help clean his money but you have

to remember that, when the Proceeds of Crime Act came in, these guys basically went out and got a copy. They knew what it was meant to do but knew laws have loopholes and they were going to find them. The run on luxury watches was part of that process.

These men have not managed to do what they do over a sustained period of time without adapting to changing circumstances. It is part of their business, part of what they do. They are constantly aware of new opportunities, new ways of sourcing their drugs, new ways of hiding their money. PoCA meant there was an urgency but most of them were confident there would be ways around it and made it their priority to find them. They did not believe for a moment, the game was up.

Criminals at Stevenson's level will never go near their drugs. You wouldn't expect the chief executive of Nike to be loading trainers on to the back of a van. But, while they can stay at arm's length from the product, they have to get close to the profit – literally piles and piles of notes. Their big challenge is how to spend that money safely. And that's where PoCA comes in.

The millionaire gangsters, who were splashing out £23.60 for a copy of the act from Her Majesty's Stationary Office, also had expert help in locating possible loopholes from their legal and financial advisers. A senior police officer, with years of experience investigating organised crime, said:

> They have lawyers and accountants who are aware of what they are and where their money is coming from. They don't ask because they don't need to and don't want to hear the answer. But they will also have been asked to look at PoCA and offer their hypothetical advice to a hypothetical client who may or may not have an interest in concealing the proceeds of crime.

They have tried a number of things to wash their money. Cash businesses with a high turnover of small cash transactions is one. The watches were another.

The market in luxury watches has boomed in the last two decades. In 2006, a rose gold Patek Philippe sold at Sotheby's in New York for £500,000. The world record was set at the same auction house in 1999 when a Patek Philippe watch, commissioned by financier Henry Graves Jnr, went for £6 million.

For decades, pocket watches were the only ones worth collecting but the auction houses and dealers have seen prices climb dramatically for post-war wristwatches made by the world's most famous brands. The big three – Audemars Piguet, Patek Philippe and Vacheron Constantin – continue to command the highest prices but buyers of Breguet, Rolex, and Cartier have also seen their investment in chronometry soar in value.

Stevenson and Carbin showed good taste or had good advice in amassing a collection that featured watches made by Audemars Piguet, Rolex, Dior and Cartier. Often buying from their favourite jewellers, Mappin & Webb in Glasgow's Buchanan Street and Strang's, in the affluent southside suburb of Newton Mearns, their shopping spree between December 2003 and September 2006 would include some of the most famous and expensive timepieces ever made.

The Rolex Daytona, one of the models seized by officers in Stevenson's home, is one of the world's most sought-after watches. Worn by Hollywood celebrities and racing drivers, the watch is one of the ultimate and hard-to-find status symbols. Stevenson paid £10,340 but the Daytona's value, in the soaring market in watches, was unlikely to decrease.

An Audemars Piguet watch, also found in Fishescoates Gardens, was valued at £30,000. The model had been painstakingly constructed in the company's workshops in the village of Le Brassus in the Jura region of Switzerland where the watchmakers Jules-Louis Audemars and Edward-Auguste Piguet had founded their prestigious business in 1875.

Fine watches were not the only jewellery bought and sold by Stevenson as he cleaned his fortune. Officers in the Folklore busts recovered diamond-encrusted rings, bracelets and pendants and police familiar with his career say Stevenson had long-standing links with diamond merchants in Amsterdam. One said:

> When he came back to Glasgow full-time after the McGovern charges were dropped, he started trading in jewellery on the back of his drugs money. It was an easy way of churning his money around while also offering convenient cover for dealing with some very important business associates in Holland.

Stevenson had a very close relationship with one particular diamond merchant, as an associate revealed:

> There was a businessman in Amsterdam, a Serb who runs a diamond firm, who Stevenson had a lot of dealing with. He is a serious man involved in many different businesses with a very interesting contacts book. He doesn't waste his time doing business with anyone apart from Europe's wealthiest criminals.

41
Laundry Business

Legend has it that American mob bosses, who were raking in a fortune during Prohibition in the 1920s, literally invented money laundering. Keen to conceal and legitimise the takings from their illegal trade in outlawed alcohol, they are said to have filtered the cash through apparently legitimate businesses with a high turnover in cash. Laundromats were a favourite.

Whether this is true or not, the downfall of Al Capone, who was jailed for tax evasion in 1931, sharpened gangsters' focus on the need for financial finesse. Over seventy-five years later, the process of money laundering remains the same – only the sums involved are very different. George P. Schultz, the former United States Secretary of State, was not mistaken when he noted, 'Today's criminals make the Capone crowd and the old Mafia look like small-time crooks.'

Money laundering, like the crime that feeds it, is now a global business. Dirty money floods out of Scotland every day and, on its way, it crosses paths with the millions of recycled and rinsed pounds returning to the country's criminals.

The fortune made and laundered by Stevenson in his years as the biggest drugs trafficker Scotland has ever seen will never be quantified. Even he probably could not put a figure on the many, many millions that have been sent abroad or cleansed through front businesses and property deals in Scotland. One source, with an awareness of the scale of his operation, says the sums involved are almost unimaginable. He commented:

> Nobody knows basically but you can start with the Home Office saying criminal profits in Britain are a little over £5 billion a year – that's profit, not turnover. The usual rule of thumb would make that £500 million of profits being shared by gangsters in Scotland every year – most of it drugs money. Add in that, for at least five years, Stevenson was bringing in the vast majority of those drugs and you're in the ballpark.
>
> A cop I know told me that, over the twenty years Stevenson was doing it and particularly in the last five, he could have brought in drugs worth £2 billion on the street. He was selling wholesale but was still making £15,000 or so for every kilo of heroin or coke. Given that one of his shipments could be 100, 150 kilos and he was bringing in hundreds and hundreds of kilos every year, then he's not going to be short for a pint of milk. That's about all he could openly buy, though – anything bigger and the cops would be all over it.

And he did not discount the claims of Frank Gallagher, one of Stevenson's key men, that his boss spent £36 million on a property spree on the Costa del Sol.

> It sounds high even for a guy like Stevenson but, for people with no knowledge of the money being made from drugs, the sums involved are unimaginable. Put it this way, I would be very surprised if Stevenson does not have at least £20 million in clean cash and assets.

The process of turning Stevenson's dirty millions into an apparently legitimate fortune involved a morass of cash transfers, dubious import/export activity, property deals and front firms. But the aim of obscuring his wealth and its source remained constant. Like the Mafia's laundries, businesses dealing in a large number of transactions each involving a small amount of cash are a popular way of rinsing money for Stevenson and other Scots gangsters. Legitimate front men, ideally with no serious criminal record and of no particular interest to the police, would be installed to run the firms. Some of the businesses may have been bought with dirty money but operated legitimately. Others were relentlessly used to launder drugs profits.

Pubs, security firms, scrapyards, sunbed parlours, nail bars and hairdressers have all got their fans among Scottish criminals but taxi firms have remained the enduring favourite. Fleets of minicabs each making a series of short trips are an almost impossible target for official scrutiny. Many, if not most, of the taxi firms advertising for business in the West of Scotland and through West Lothian to Edinburgh are fronts for organised crime clans. Thousands of phantom fares inflate the accounts covering for the injection of drugs money while drivers can make special tips from their bosses by criss-crossing the city carrying contraband. Some firms have been bought by gangsters while others have been specially created. Stevenson did both and, at the time of his arrest, had a con-trolling interest in one medium-sized firm, was in the process of setting up another and was busy taking over a third.

The Folklore tapes were running as Stevenson discussed the launch of a new firm, CS Cars – named after and ostensibly run by his wife Caroline. The couple spent almost £100,000 on a fleet of ten Skoda Octavias but, on 29 March 2006, Stevenson was secretly recorded detailing exactly how the cars would help launder his money. He was heard telling his wife:

> This is what we're gonnae do with the taxis. There'll be twelve hundred pound going in your bank but I'm going

to put twenty-four hundred [£2,400] in every week and say I double shift the motors . . . over a year that will be £100,000 minus tax.

Taxi drivers were frequent customers at a service station near Stevenson's home in Burnside where the fuel prices were usually the lowest around. Stevenson would also fill up at the garage but he might not even have paid the bargain prices since he was its secret owner. The garage was one of several Stevenson enterprises to be looked after by one of his key business associates, Anthony Burnette, the business fixer who appeared on the Folklore tapes discussing commercial opportunities with Stevenson, including the purchase of other forecourt garages.

But taxis and petrol stations were not Stevenson's only involvement in the motor trade. Unlike many gangsters, he did not buy and sell cars frequently to wash some cash. Instead of selling cars, Stevenson cleaned them.

One officer said:

A lot of these guys started car washes to launder their money but then the latest trend became mobile valets. Stevenson was one of the first. He had some guy running about in a van cleaning cars. He must have done a right good job because, to make what he was meant to be earning, he would have needed to have been polishing every car in the southside.

He also had put money in car showrooms and haulage firms. The gang boss, nicknamed The Iceman, was not known for his sense of irony but he also had a stake in a fleet of ice-cream vans selling sweets around the schemes of Glasgow. Dirty money launched each of his businesses but many were not subsequently used to launder drugs cash. Rather, they were straightforward investments gaining a layer of legitimacy with every year that passed. The service stations, for example, would be rented to leaseholders who were often unaware of the true identity or business of the owner.

Stevenson also had extensive property interests. He bought scores of flats and houses in Scotland and around the world, with a portfolio that included homes in Spain, Holland and Eastern Europe. He leased out many, some were bought at the development stage and off-loaded when built and others would simply lie empty until it was a convenient time to sell them.

Of course, Stevenson's sideline of trading in gems and luxury watches was another convenient cover for moving his money. A £10,000 watch or jewel-encrusted necklace bought in Scotland could be sold to an amenable Amsterdam gem trader for a tenth of that before being sold again for the full market value and the proceeds returned to Stevenson fully cleansed minus a cut for his contact.

The *halawar* money transfers from Makkah Travel and other agencies in England also sent millions abroad. Some was laundered and some would be used to pay for more drug shipments. And, despite his aversion to unnecessary risk, police believe that Stevenson, his stepson Carbin and other members of their outfit got directly involved in the most basic mechanics for transferring money abroad. One officer said:

> They were never caught so it is impossible to say for sure but I have absolutely no doubt they carted hundreds and thousands of pounds through Glasgow Airport in their hand luggage. They were flying to Spain, Amsterdam and Dubai – all over the place – and I don't think they could resist the opportunity to get some cash out of the road. What's the worst thing that could have happened? They could lose a bagful of cash at check-in – a bad day at the office, that's all.

One source, who was involved in an investigation into Stevenson before the launch of Folklore, said:

> Cleaning their money and keeping track of their investments is a full-time job for Stevenson and criminals like him. Of course, they will not be burdened with the paperwork but have to instruct their people organising that, keep briefed on their investments, and, most importantly, keep an eye out for new opportunities. That's the key to it. The volume of notes coming in has to be moved quickly or you literally run out of places to hide them. You need a range of options, a number of different channels to get rid of it, so that, if one is closed, you can try another. Stevenson knew that. He wouldn't drive past a For Sale sign without thinking about it. He was always looking for things to do with his money.
>
> He might have the ideas but he still needed help to legitimise his money. And he got that help from legitimate people. Lots of very legitimate people.

42

The Money Detectives

A recent recruit to the elite agency targeting Scotland's serious and organised criminals will never make an arrest, interview a suspect, or take a fingerprint. A forensic accountant started work at the Scottish Crime and Drug Enforcement Agency in May 2007, signalling a new front in the war against gangsters. The £60,000-a-year accountant joined the agency's money-laundering unit after the capture and conviction of Jamie Stevenson but he will help to track the money trail of Scotland's other gangland leaders.

Ken Milliken, who leads the Scottish forensic team for international accountancy giants KPMG, believes the appointment only underlines the increasing focus on the finances of modern criminals. The expertise and experience that a forensic accountant can bring to bear on suspected criminal assets are vital as millionaire gangsters increasingly blend dirty money with legitimate income in a diverse portfolio of firms and property. Milliken said:

> Typically, they will have a number of businesses. Some may operate entirely legitimately after being bought or launched with criminal proceeds. Some firms may be laundering money. Some may be supplying services and goods to others owned by the same people. The aim is simply to create as complex a web of income, transactions and investments as possible – to build a shell of transactions

coming and going to make it more difficult to identify and follow the criminal money.

Using dirty money to secure legitimate loans is one method of obscuring the source of the start-up capital. Banks are in the business of encouraging enterprise and, if people come to them with proof of identity and an acceptable level of apparently legitimate income, then there will be nothing to suggest that those loans should not be given. If you are apparently in a small start-up situation and you say, 'I am employed as such and such and here's some bank statements showing my income and this is my house and some proof that I own it.', then banks cannot really be expected to question that.

Of course, the legislation now means you do not have to prove assets were bought with criminal funds to seize them. You must only prove that Mr X spent so many hundreds of thousands of pounds and then prove that his income is, or was, less than that. Years may have passed but the paperwork will still be there. It will be a case of rewinding backwards to the start and then looking at the conveyancing records, seeing where the money came from. The difficulty is that, once you have a range of businesses and they are buying and selling to each other or merging with each other, the money is being mixed up and the web is becoming more complex.

Milliken believes that police intelligence is the key to focusing attention on suspect individuals and businesses. He said:

It has to be driven by intelligence. Once they are looking at a particular person, then the flags can go up at the banks, the tax authorities, wherever. Once an individual's business is being investigated, then there is work that can be done without alerting them. The police can get warrants to access the bank accounts to look at the cash coming in and going out. They can look at Revenue and Customs records, look at VAT returns, look at staff numbers and wages through PAYE and National Insurance.

Police surveillance can test things like staff numbers and the number of customers going through a shop's door, for example, but, eventually, you will come to a point where you need to see the books. There will be a raid and the accounts will be seized.

It is at that point, Milliken believes, that the specialist expertise of forensic accountants can be vital. He said:

They can look at those books for the things that don't fit in. There may be unusual patterns of transactions. One part of the accounts might not fit with another. They look at the cash flow, the receipts, the VAT records. They scrutinise all the pieces of information that make up the financial profile of a firm and then identify where there are possible mismatches, where the financial information is not fitting together as smoothly as it should.

Comparisons will also be made to other similar-sized businesses within the same industry to compare those key elements.

This experienced accountant, who has led a series of major fraud investigations, believes that businesses involving a large number of cash transactions are popular with criminals for very obvious reasons. He said:

The ease with which the cash takings of taxi firms, for example, can be falsely inflated and the difficulties proving that make them attractive for money laundering. Criminals will pay tax on those earnings, of course, but they will see that as commission. They will get back eighty pence in the pound or whatever the tax rate may be.

Of course, buying property as an investment may well return more than that. They may easily recoup more than a pound for every pound invested.

There has been a growing awareness among law enforcement agencies that, if you can prove that an individual's money has not come from legitimate services, then that money can be attacked. Businesses launched with or laundering criminal money are no different to a legitimate business. They will employ people, they will have managers, finance officers, accountants. There are records. There are accounts. If you can take away the finance, you are disrupting them. You are moving them on.

He thinks the Proceeds of Crime Act and related legislation has helped close a number of routes previously open to criminals seeking to legitimise their profits. He said:

Ultimately, money laundering is a very simple concept. What are you going to do with that £1,000 or £100,000 that you have earned from drugs, human trafficking or whatever? How do you turn that money into legitimate money, money you can spend? You can't put it into a bank because they will report it. Lawyers and accountants are under a similar obligation to report suspect transactions.

If you go to a lawyer with £20,000 in cash as a down payment on a flat and they are unclear where that money came from, then their report may soon be with the police. You can buy some big cash purchases but the car showrooms, the jewellers and the rest have also been ordered to be vigilant and report any suspicious cash payments. Of course, you will always have lawyers, accountants and traders willing to turn a blind eye – there will always be a small proportion of people prepared to take the money without question.

There is no doubt that very many criminals have the highest quality of legal and financial advice. There is the possibility that the police could build a case against their advisers for money laundering or that they might be struck off by their professional bodies. However, that will not necessarily remove them from their advisory role. It does not stop them having that expertise.

Milliken is not surprised that the SCDEA and Strathclyde Police have now employed their own forensic accountants in-house.

It would appear to make perfect sense. The costs involved in this kind of financial investigation are considerable and clearly the police are working under the constraints of their budgets. They must decide if £30,000 spent paying a forensic accountant to carry out a complicated investigation would, for example, be better spent putting another officer on the beat.

The workload is such that I would very much doubt they will be able to take on all the forensic accountancy previously contracted out. They will presumably act as filters. They will have the expertise to identify those investigations where there is the realistic prospect of identifying discrepancies capable of being taken to court. Ultimately, it has to be driven by the police and focused by their intelligence.

The skilled fraud investigator said that the Proceeds of Crime Act has already had a substantial impact on the money-laundering systems being put in place but warned that budgetary constraints could undermine the financial offensive against crime gangs. He said:

The fact that these guys have got copies of the act on their coffee tables suggests it's working. The difficulties are twofold. One is to keep up with the new methods that criminals will find to move money around and out of Britain's jurisdiction. The other is to ensure resources are there to fund these investigations as they increasingly become an integral part of criminal investigation. There are clearly budgetary limits for this kind of work. There is also a need to capture the knowledge – for all the expertise being gained by all the different agencies to be pooled.

In England, an 'incentivisation' programme means fifty per cent of the money seized under PoCA is handed back to the police to bolster and extend their financial investigation units. The Metropolitan Police, for example, were given £7.9 million in 2006, with the Home Office recommending that the money should be spent on more financial investigators, training and specialist teams. In Scotland, seized money returned to the police is dedicated to more general initiatives, such as Crimestoppers, which has a free-to-call number for people to pass on information anonymously.

Milliken said:

In England and Wales, there is a greater emphasis on funding financial investigation and the sequence is clear – the more you do, the more you can do. There is a snowball effect. That does not seem to be happening in Scotland. The other factor giving financial investigation fresh momentum is advancing technology. Previously, if you were given a hundred pages of bank statements, involving thousands of deposits and withdrawals, you would have had to input them manually to create a spreadsheet. That is a time-consuming process. There are now computer programmes that can scan those statements and create a spreadsheet capable of being analysed for certain patterns or anomalies.

But, despite advancing technology, the expertise and experience of the forensic accountant cannot be replaced. According to Milliken:

> The skills and experience of the accountant looking at that spreadsheet and knowing what doesn't look right and knowing where to start unpicking the threads are the key – in the same way, an experienced detective will look at a piece of intelligence and have a hunch that something doesn't fit, that there is something not right. Everything rests on that expertise.

43
We Take Cash

It was the nightlife that attracted Cory Kerr to Aberdeen, allegedly. According to the unemployed mechanic, he and his two pals had driven 400 miles north from their homes in the Black Country for a good night out.

Back at home in Wolverhampton, Kerr told reporters the Granite City's clubland had prompted the trip. He said:

> It was an adventure, a trip. We wanted to go to a different place. If it was drugs money, where were the drugs? Where was the evidence of drugs? What did they find in my pockets connected to drugs? They found money. Money can come from thousands of places rather than drugs. You can find money like that. People find money in bushes and all kind of stuff.

Kerr and his friends had just made Scottish legal history as the first suspected drug dealers to be stripped of their profits without ever being charged, never mind convicted. It was their misfortune to be stopped by police just after midnight on 8 January 2003 – eight days after some of the powers of the Proceeds of Crime Act came into force. Officers searching Kerr's Audi found three holdalls packed with just over £2,000 and another £11,700 hidden in the lining of the car's boot.

An application to Stonehaven Sheriff Court summarised police suspicions that they had been ferrying drugs from the Midlands to Aberdeen dealers. It noted that 'the sum of £11,500 to £12,500 is a reasonable wholesale price for half a kilo of cocaine or heroin. There is an established trade route for illicit drugs between the Midlands, and in particular Wolverhampton, and Aberdeen'. The legal papers also reveal how Kerr and his associates refused to explain where the money had come from or why it was in Scottish banknotes.

At the court on Thursday, 1 May 2003, John Keir, a lawyer with the Crown Office's new Civil Recovery Unit (CRU), told Sheriff Alexander Jessop, 'This is a minute for the application of forfeiture of the sum of money seized by Grampian Police.'

In the trio's absence, the sheriff took less than a minute to grant the order and usher in a new era for law enforcers working to dismantle the apparatus of Scotland's crime barons. They could not claim they had not been warned.

In 1998, Scotland's mob bosses continued to scan the property pages for the perfect sandstone mansion, discreetly hidden behind the trees, hedges and high fences of the city's exclusive suburbs. They may also have been skimming through the glossy property schedules for villas in Marbella and luxury condos in Florida. But, that summer, only one property deal mattered to the most astute of the criminals putting Scotland's drug-ravaged neighbourhoods through the wringer and squeezing out multimillion-pound fortunes. And, when the auctioneer brought down his hammer to sell a small pub on Ireland's west coast to businessman Patrick Humphries, he set off alarm bells throughout Scotland's underworld.

The Paradise Bar looked like an ordinary bar but the previous owner of the green-and-white bedecked Celtic pub was no ordinary publican. He was called Tam McGraw and soon to become the best-known gangster in Scotland. His pub in Donegal had laundered hundreds of thousands of pounds since he'd bought it in 1996 but it was only one of countless businesses rinsing the multimillionaire's drugs-contaminated cash. His name was nowhere on the paperwork, of course, but that did not matter to the officers of Ireland's Criminal Assets Bureau (CAB) who seized the pub in March 1998 and sold it two months later. They had been told by colleagues in Strathclyde that McGraw was a suspected drug trafficker and that was good enough for them.

And, by the time, McGraw's defence lawyer, Donald Findlay QC, had delivered a bravura display to win him a not proven verdict on the drugs charges, his Irish operation was already in the hands of the police.

The gangster, known as 'The Licensee', walked free from the High Court in Glasgow after being cleared of funding a hash-smuggling run from Spain in July 1998 but his pub was gone along with the £177,000 frozen in its account at the Allied Irish Bank in the town of Donegal. A further £255,000 in another account was also seized, never to be reclaimed.

The money meant little to this career criminal with more cash than he could count. The gangster, who died of a heart attack in 2007, had enjoyed visiting the Donegal pub but the loss of a front firm could be shrugged off. It was the Irish authorities' gung-ho attitude towards his dirty fortune which was more worrying, particularly if ordinary Scots began to ask why the men wreaking havoc in their communities seemed immune to the asset stripping that was inflicting financial pain on their counterparts in Ireland. The CAB had won international attention for its impact since being launched in the wake of crime reporter Veronica Guerin's murder in June 1996 by a Dublin drugs baron.

Short-sighted rivals may have smirked when they heard of McGraw's misfortune but the smart ones made appointments with their lawyers to discuss their own financial arrangements. The sudden success of the CAB team and their pre-emptory seizure of cash and property from anyone just suspected of a crime – never mind convicted – could not be ignored.

It would be almost five years after McGraw lost his pub before Scotland got its own asset strippers, a move inspired by the Irish template. Colin Boyd, then Lord Advocate in charge of Scotland's prosecutions, said:

> It will make sure, as far as we can, that people don't benefit from crime. Crime will not pay. Criminals commit crime to make money. Take the money away and it no longer pays. People go to prison and know the nest egg is still there. Take away the nest egg and it's not worth doing the prison time.

The CRU, led by experienced lawyer Lorna Harris, scrutinised how the ownership of the mansions, speedboats and Mercedes could be justified on what suspected gangsters claimed to earn. Her team worked in tandem with the Criminal Confiscation Unit – later renamed the Financial Crime Unit (FCU) – also scouring criminals' financial backgrounds but their targets, unlike those of the CRU, had to have been convicted before being stripped of their ill-gotten assets.

Harris did not underestimate the wealth flooding through Scotland's underworld or how ruthlessly it would be protected. She refused to be photographed in order to protect her identity and, in her first interview, said only a fool would not be aware of the capabilities of her intended targets. She said:

> I'm not going to be these people's best friend. It goes with the territory. I'm not paranoid about security but I don't want to be unduly vulnerable. The idea is to hit them where it hurts and that is in the pocket.

She led a team of a dozen expert investigators. Based in Edinburgh, they had been recruited from prosecutors, police and Customs. Until 2003, the law in the UK meant prosecutors had to prove 'beyond reasonable doubt' that money and assets were a result of crime but PoCA changed the level of proof to 'on the balance of probability'.

Harris, who returned to Scotland after twenty years in London as a career civil servant, said:

> Police and Customs have always had power to seize cash at borders if it related to drug trafficking but they can now seize cash if someone is walking down Sauchiehall Street. Any money on the move is vulnerable. We're not going to launch a hundred cases but we will go slowly and test out all our new powers carefully – to make sure we get it right.

Four years later, in her office at the Crown Office, Harris believes the work of her twelve-strong team of underworld asset-strippers has sent a powerful message to Scotland's criminals. Armed with PoCA, the Civil Recovery Unit and the Financial Crime Unit – now part of the National Casework Division – they have, between them, seized cash and assets worth £15.5 million from criminals since 2003.

Harris said:

> Our purpose is to deter and to disrupt criminals and we are succeeding. Crime is a business and, if you remove money from that business, there will be a level of disruption. That money is working capital. They've got it from their last drug deal or whatever and it is going to help pay for the next one. Taking that away will cause them problems.
>
> We target the lifestyle criminals themselves and we help ensure they are no longer role models for others. Without the money, without the profit motive, why commit the crime?
>
> These are the men who seemingly live on air. If they are not paying tax and not claiming benefit, then how can

they afford to service their £150,000 mortgage. There is a mismatch there – a black hole.

The FCU now routinely freeze a suspected criminal's recoverable assets as soon as the police launch an investigation. This gives them no time to hide or transfer their fortune. After a conviction, the Crown Office team will ask for a confiscation order to seize those assets permanently. Harris explained that the CRU only target suspects when a criminal prosecution is impossible or has failed to win a conviction. She described a typical example of a criminal's move up the property ladder, starting when he buys a council house for £20,000 in 1999. She said:

> His house rises in price so, in 2002, he sells it for £80,000 and uses that to help get a mortgage on a £250,000 house in 2002 that, in 2007, is worth £420,000. So what we are now asking is where the £20,000 came from in 1999. He was not convicted for drugs but maybe there was police intelligence that he was a well-kent thief, who went about with drug dealers. Has he any employment record? Has he ever paid tax or claimed benefits? We build up the circumstantial case and then we ask how can he can afford the plasma TV, the holidays, the house.
>
> It is not just the original dirty slug of £20,000 – it is the dirty slug of £80,000 that was then used to commit mortgage fraud. We will target the property, not the individual. They do not like losing their house.

However, Harris insists the priority remains the criminal prosecution of Scotland's gangsters. Only when that is impossible, will her team get involved. She said:

> We are distinct from the Crown Office because we are not a prosecuting agency – all of our cases will have previously

been looked at by the police or the Crown before being passed to us. The prosecution of crime is the overarching priority. We will take on a case only when, for whatever reason, there is no prosecution or when a prosecution has not led to a conviction.

Stevenson and others like him now knew that not only their freedom but also their fortune could be snatched from them. The rules had changed.

44
Outlaw In-Law

Louise Rivers was attracting keen interest from those making money in the criminal economies of Glasgow and Belfast. She was an accountant appointed by the courts to investigate wealthy individuals with no apparent explanation for their fortunes. Armed with the new Proceeds of Crime laws, Louise terrified her targets. She could strip them of their ill-gotten gains – the suburban mansions, the prestige cars with vanity registrations, the trust funds and the shares.

For these men, it was not a threat to be taken lying down but all that they knew about Louise was that she worked for a company called Mallard Associates from Suite 210, 34 Buckingham Palace Road in London. This address sounds impressive but it is merely an anonymous mail drop – the type of address used by the conmen behind bogus lotteries, miracle medical cures and other postal rackets. More investigation failed to find Louise on the internet where there were no professional qualifications, company directorships or reports of previous inquiries. There seemed to be no record of her or her employers. They were ghosts.

Russell Stirton was among those most keen to know who Louise was and where she might be contacted. By then, she had been appointed to lead several high-profile criminal asset seizure cases in Scotland and Northern Ireland – including his own. Former soldier Stirton, who friends say was a member of the 4th Battalion of the Parachute Regiment which forms part of the Territorial Army, is married to Jackie, the sister of the McGovern brothers. There may have been some advantage for an ambitious criminal in having such family connections but Stirton also possesses a sharp mind.

During one 1987 court case, he was described as 'an alleged drugs dealer and a dangerous criminal who could carry and use guns'. Almost two decades later, he became the first high-profile Scottish casualty of the biting new laws which were designed to bankrupt wealthy organised crime bosses across Britain.

Strathclyde Police invited a band of TV crews and press photographers to accompany them on a series of dawn raids on 14 January 2004. The police wanted the world to see Operation Maple unfolding in Scotland's living rooms on that evening's news bulletins. Stirton was not at home as police piled into his mansion that winter's morning, the yellow fluorescent jackets of the raiding party reflecting back the glare of the BBC lights. His non-appearance was later attributed to advanced warning from a contact inside the force.

By March 2003, the Proceeds of Crime Act 2002 had come fully into play and ten months later, Stirton, 'a builder and property developer', became its biggest target in Scotland. He and business partner Alex Anderson owned a service station and car wash in Springburn which had been the subject of six separate reports from banks who suspected it was laundering money. The garage was hit by police at 6.30 a.m. but they did not find a cache of .38 calibre revolvers that detectives had been told were being sold from the premises.

At exactly the same time, police descended on Stirton's mansion, The Limes, in the affluent village of Mugdock to the north of Glasgow. Jackie, who has criminal convictions for dishonesty, reluctantly allowed officers to enter through the electronic gates and they spent the day searching her home. Neighbours, who had long resented Stirton in their rural idyll, were horrified at the presence of armed policemen. It had been bad enough when he chopped down trees without permission. When Stirton arrived at The Limes, he glowered at the media pack who were camped outside but he remained calm towards the police as they swarmed through his home.

At least ten other addresses, including homes and three law firms were paid a visit. One business raided was the Springburn HQ of Network Private Hire, Scotland's second-largest taxi firm which was known to have McGovern links. One of the hundreds of drivers for the firm was later revealed as the councillor for Springburn, Baillie Jim Todd.

Thomson's bar, the McGovern's symbolic haunt and unofficial base of many years, was also paid a visit. It had, until 2001, been part of the chain owned, at least on paper, by Charlie Nicholas and the fugitive Jim Milligan.

Operation Maple was a large operation involving officers from two police forces, Customs and Excise and the then SDEA. If it was designed to cause panic inside other major Scottish crime groups, then it worked.

By the end of this long Wednesday, the pub and the service station were amongst the businesses frozen by the tough new legislation. Also restrained by the authorities were cars, bank accounts, cash and several homes including Stirton's. The Crown Office alleged that Stirton had even laundered dirty money through bank accounts held in the names of five of his six children plus the three children of his murdered brother-in-law Tony McGovern. They claimed that Stirton was 'reasonably believed to have been involved in the supply of controlled drugs since at least 1983' and revealed details of police surveillance operations.

One case monitored Stirton and an Alex Hughson in 1997 on a ferry travelling from Calais to Dover. Also on the ferry was HGV driver Mark Haig, whose truck was carrying kilos of cannabis, amphetamines and a handgun. Once at

Dover, the three men met up at a motorway service station and later, during a search in Uddingston, Lanarkshire, the truck yielded its illicit cargo. This resulted in Haig – who was deemed to be the mule – being convicted along with a fourth man who had also previously been spotted with Stirton.

The books of Stirton's mail-order pornography business Love Boat showed strong profits but the accountant who was supposed to have prepared this healthy balance sheet denied having done so. These accounts could have helped secure a mortgage for Stirton's Mugdock home. Police long suspected the porn business was just an early vehicle for laundering cash.

Janice Leonard confessed to the police that she had used bogus accounts to obtain a mortgage for her Uddingston home when the cash to pay the loan had actually come from her boyfriend Anderson, Stirton's business partner.

The most recent figure to be put on the total value of that day's haul is £5.6 million. Police hailed Operation Maple as a huge success but it was a long way from over.

The new Proceeds of Crime laws were different to conventional criminal laws. In theory, the crooks need to illustrate that their wealth is legitimate. It was a major legal shift and people like Stirton were squirming. The well-spoken fitness fanatic and marathon runner hired Richard Keen, one of Scotland's most skilled QCs, to fight his corner.

During the first court hearing weeks later, it emerged that the seized Shell garage of Stirton and Anderson had an annual turnover of £12 million, with £6 million of that coming by way of cash. Despite selling some of the cheapest fuel in Britain, it seemed hard to explain how almost £16,500 in banknotes passed through the till every single day of the year. Crown lawyers told how they would have to keep the identities of witnesses secret for fear of retribution were they to be unmasked while Stirton's legal team attacked 'the flagrant disregard' of their human rights. Following lunch, it was agreed that the garage and the pub would be returned to the pair under strict conditions.

In March, Stirton was arrested in Edinburgh after flying in from a trip to London. He and Anderson appeared in court on criminal charges of extortion and money laundering but they were later dropped, a development which was a sign of things to come as the early confidence of the police began to ebb away.

Stirton and Anderson's legal team got to work. The first blow for the Crown case was the revelation that criminal convictions, which they had attributed to Anderson, did not exist. The pair's costly legal team then set about the task of unpicking Operation Maple as Scotland's flagship Proceeds of Crime case became bogged down in a legal quagmire.

More than four years after those triumphant raids, the case against Stirton and his finances continues to limp through the legal system. Since the raids, Stirton has fallen out with the McGovern brothers over their suspicions that he had ripped them off. This sparked a bitter feud that still threatens violence. He and Anderson have already rejected an offer to settle the case by jointly handing over just £175,000 on the condition that they would not be able to sue over the process. Critics fear the case, which was meant to highlight the new legislation's sweeping powers, has only exposed its inadequacies. In recent years, there has been greater emphasis on confiscating the fortunes of convicted criminals rather than attempting to seize assets from those only suspected of crime.

Another issue that Stirton's lawyers pounced upon relates to the true identity of 'Louise Rivers', which was discovered to be a pseudonym – something that had not been declared to the court at the outset. The Crown lawyers said that this had been an 'innocent oversight' and the reasons for anonymity were that 'it would put at risk her own safety and that of her staff if she practised under her own name'. Stirton's lawyers were to withdraw attempts to establish her real identity perhaps because, by then, there was no need.

Away from the Court of Session in Edinburgh and unknown to the legal team, a plot to unmask the enigmatic accountant had already been hatched. In order to find out who she was or, at the very least, the name and location of her true employers, an apparently ordinary package was sent to her through the post from Scotland. Contained within the parcel was an electronic tracking device. As that day's post was collected from the branch of Mail Boxes Etc. in Buckingham Palace Road, the transmitter was sending its signal. Someone in Scotland was determined to find out who she was and they had gone to extraordinary lengths to locate her.

Her pursuers' audacious scheme to track down the mysterious accountant failed after the bug was intercepted before reaching her workplace and a senior judge, Lord Macfadyen, has since ruled that it would be a criminal offence to reveal her – or his – identity. Louise will continue her work of asset stripping Scotland's untouchables without fear of reprisals.

45
Jamie Soprano

The surveillance officers tailing Jamie Stevenson in the summer of 2003 did not instantly recognise his route as he left home heading into the city. Folklore's surveillance offensive against the gang boss had only been launched a few weeks earlier and Stevenson's regular haunts and habits were still uncharted. Their target picked his way through the lunchtime traffic into Glasgow's southside before turning into Mansionhouse Road, a tree-lined avenue in the Langside neighbourhood.

The tailing officers speculated that he was perhaps heading to the popular Boswell Hotel for a meeting but, on reaching the hotel, Stevenson did not turn left into the car park but instead turned right into the drive of the imposing sandstone mansion opposite. The handsome, discreetly extended building was the Priory Hospital, the only private clinic in Scotland specialising in the treatment and management of acute psychiatric disorders. Stevenson was going to see his therapist.

The Scots gang boss had started going to the Priory a year before in the summer of 2002 to discuss a range of mental health issues with the hospital's expert counsellors. This imposing man was feared throughout the underworld, he was suspected of a series of murders and he was leading an intricate and international drugs-trafficking network. Yet behind this most serious and organised criminal lay a troubled mind. One source, aware of his treatment, said, 'He had anxiety issues, anger-management issues, some problems sleeping, a little paranoia. Let's face it – he was Tony Soprano.'

The police team tracking Stevenson to his regular sessions at the Priory in the years that followed were also not slow to compare the Scots crime boss with the head of the famous but fictional crime family. The relationship between Soprano and his psychotherapist has been at the heart of the acclaimed US television crime drama since the first episode screened in 1999. Soprano, played by actor James Gandolfini, loves his wife, is devoted to his children and is a loyal friend. He's a charismatic leader, a skilled manager and a brutish thug capable of barbaric violence. He leads an effective organised crime gang, lives under constant FBI surveillance and suffers panic attacks, anxiety and depression.

A source with knowledge of Stevenson's business and health issues says the comparisons between the TV mobster and the Scot are inescapable. He said:

> Jamie had little option but to seek professional help. The alternative would have been to give up what he was doing and I don't believe he ever considered that. Given what he had been doing every day for twenty years, it's no great surprise that he was anxious, angry and insomniac. And you've got to think Stevenson being paranoid was understandable. He wasn't imagining it. People really were out to get him. They really were watching him.
>
> The sleep thing was a problem. He had a lot of trouble sleeping, particularly when he was away from home. That's not great given the amount of travelling he was doing. He hated going away. He hated being far from his home. He knew he had to do it but he hated it. And I think that got worse as time went on.

Another associate says it was not surprising that the pressures of Stevenson's lifestyle took a toll on his health.

He had a handful of guys who were trusted to do stuff but basically he was directing traffic across the board. Like his boy Gerry – he just didn't have the mental furniture without Stevenson there in the morning to tell him to do this, go there, do that. Stevenson was like Alan Sugar in *The Apprentice*.

In addition to all the stuff Stevenson was doing himself, people would be coming to him with their problems all the time. You see it in the transcripts of the Folklore tapes, guys are round his flat looking for favours, asking him to intercede in this or that and, more often than not, he would get involved. He took a lot on.

Stevenson was right at the top, pulling the strings of these guys working for him but a lot of them would be doing their own things as well and he didn't necessarily know what.

Speaking to him, you would never have known because he seemed so confident and on top of things but, years of doing what he did, must have been taking its toll.

Professor David Cooke, a forensic clinical psychologist at Glasgow Caledonian University, has spent years analysing the mental health of Scottish criminals and believes many suffer personality disorders. For one of his research projects, he studied hundreds of prisoners at the city's Barlinnie Prison and concluded that between fifty and sixty per cent of them had psychological issues. He said:

There is a high correlation between crime and personality disorders and a lot of work has been done on the reasons for that. Are there influences in their childhood or even before they are born which lead people to a life of crime? There is not a crime gene but there are genetic factors at play along with biological influences, sociological influences – the influence of parents and peers and so on. You can see how people accumulate risk factors through their lives.

Professor Cooke believes antisocial personality disorders are common among criminals who are incapable of an emotional response to their actions but he also suspects that major criminals who have been breaking the law over many years do not share the personality traits that often help to end other criminals' careers far earlier. He said:

> To be a good career criminal, you need to be organised. Many criminals are not. They might be impulsive and reckless – might like to boast about their achievements, drive fast cars and spend all their money. In short, they get caught.
>
> Career criminals operating over a period of time may be able to maintain a flatness of emotion. They will do things that would cause most people to feel guilt or remorse but will have no emotional reaction to their actions. This lack of emotionality may make them more immune to stresses and strains of life.
>
> While there are personality disorders that are common in criminals, it is far more difficult to identify the development of common psychological traits as criminal careers progress. There may be clear evidence of disorder way before they get into a life of crime but, equally, a long career in crime may generate forces and influences of its own.

At the Priory, part of the chain of clinics famous for offering a haven for celebrities in rehab, Stevenson took part in group therapy and one-to-one sessions. Like Tony Soprano, whose sessions with Dr Jennifer Melfi are a vital part of the TV drama, Stevenson's therapist was a woman.

Renowned psychiatrist Glen Gabbard wrote a book, *The Psychology of the Sopranos*, after becoming a fan of the Mafia drama and, in it, he discusses the criminal's psychological symptoms. He concludes that 'Tony Soprano is split down the middle' – vertically split, according to the textbooks. The division allows the two parts of his character – the doting dad and family man and the lying, violent criminal – to remain in separate mental compartments. Dr Gabbard writes:

> Keeping the impulsive or violent behaviour disconnected is an automatic response that helps preserve a stable sense of integrity. Splitting is a method of avoiding internal conflict, especially moral conflict about the consequences of our behaviour.
>
> The wall between Tony's two lives has begun to crumble when he first seeks out psychiatric treatment.

However, in his 2002 book, Houston-based Gabbard decides Tony Soprano is not a psychopath despite his capacity for lying and violence.

> In the latter half of the twentieth century, the term 'psychopath' fell out of favour. 'Antisocial personality disorder' became the preferred diagnostic label for corrupt people who had no regard for the laws of civilisation. This terminology has been widely criticised, however, because it casts too broad a net. Because of these criticisms, the term 'psychopath' is currently making a comeback. It now refers to a person prone to criminal behaviour who has a sadomasochistic style of interacting with others based on power and a total absence of remorse for any harm he does. In fact, a psychopath enjoys the suffering. He is not capable of loyalty and loving emotional attachments.
>
> Only their own needs matter to them. They are profoundly detached from all human relationships and from emotional experience in general. A psychopath would not do well in Tony Soprano's Mob family. Loyalty to others and a deep

bond of attachment are absolutely necessary to survive in that family.

46
In the Dock

The day after the Folklore raids, on 21 September 2006, Stevenson and Carbin joined six others in the dock of Glasgow Sheriff Court to face charges including accusations of heroin trafficking and money laundering. They included Stevenson's wife Caroline, forty-eight, Carbin's partner Karen Maxwell, thirty, William Cross, forty-five, and three others. All would eventually be granted bail apart from Stevenson, who was held on remand at Edinburgh's Saughton Prison.

By the time the indictment was formally heard at a preliminary hearing in January 2007, now at the High Court in Glasgow, the eight accused had been joined by two others and they faced a total of twenty-two charges. The most serious alleged they plotted to import heroin and cocaine and tried to launder the proceeds of crime. Additional charges alleged that Stevenson had a forged passport and that Carbin had had small amounts of cocaine and cannabis in his home when it was raided a year earlier.

Stevenson and his nine alleged accomplices arrived for the next hearing in February knowing that his legal team had all but secured a deal. Both sides, for different but equally compelling reasons, wanted to avoid what was certain to become one of the longest and most expensive trials ever staged in a Scottish court.

The Crown, faced with a trial lasting months, a large number of accused, a complex mass of evidence and an unpredictable jury, were keen to settle – provided a deal could be forged that would seem like a fitting end to a flagship police operation. In addition, the public airing of the covert techniques used to amass the piles of secretly recorded transcripts was to be avoided if possible.

Meanwhile, Stevenson's legal team were privately acknowledging the welter of evidence that their client was a major drugs trafficker and so were equally keen to prevent a jury hearing the damning, secretly taped conversations. Stevenson and Carbin were insistent that any deal would rest on the dropping of all charges against their partners, Caroline and Karen. Putting the women in the dock had been a priority for the Folklore team. The police knew that, according to the rules of underworld chivalry, the men would never allow their partners to be convicted. It was a powerful bargaining chip for the prosecutors.

Just before Christmas, Derek Ogg QC for Stevenson and Carbin's counsel Paul McBride had opened talks with experienced Crown prosecutor Sean Murphy to propose a package deal for both men. They suggested that, in return for dropping all the drugs charges and the allegations against their partners, the pair would admit the money-laundering charges. To their surprise, the leading lawyers were told within days that the offer, their first, was broadly acceptable.

One senior source at the High Court said:

> There seems to have been no fight, no bluffing and very little negotiation. The offer was made and it was more or less accepted straight off the bat. Given what the Crown had in terms of evidence, that was surprising. If you were representing those two you would not be looking forward to taking them in front of a jury.

Exactly where do you start trying to explain where they got these huge sums of money from? Where they got £400,000 of luxury watches? Why they were all over the world meeting criminals? And, most of all, why they were on tape, in their own homes, talking about importing tonnes and tonnes of class A drugs? Good luck.

At more meetings through January the detailed wording of the charges to be admitted was ground out and, by the end of the month, Murphy, an experienced advocate depute, was confident of striking a settlement capable of being justified to his bosses and the public. Convincing the detectives, who had spent four years building a case against Scotland's biggest-ever drugs cartel, would prove more difficult.

Another lawyer with knowledge of the case said Murphy made the right decision to drop the drugs in return for making the jailing of Stevenson and Carbin a certainty. He said:

> There was definitely evidence the defence teams would have struggled to explain. The case that these guys were major drugs traffickers was there but it was a way off being bombproof. They weren't caught next to drugs. And nobody could place them next to drugs. That's a problem.
>
> The lorry driver Robert McDowall was a big part of it and, even if he hadn't had his memory problem at the line-up, he would have been a gamble for the Crown. You've got problems when your star witness is a drugs smuggler, a gunrunner and whatever else.
>
> There would have been a lot of questions about who was pulling his strings, about when and how the police got involved with him, about whether he was an agent provocateur. It would have been a long, complicated trial and juries get tired. Good defence lawyers – and these guys had *very* good defence lawyers – would undoubtedly

have done some serious damage but whether they would manage to get them off . . . Who knows?

It definitely wasn't a certainty for the prosecution and Sean Murphy knew that. He was happy to get them on the money, leave the drugs and put them away for a stretch.

A pretrial hearing on Monday, 12 February saw the gang arrive, two and three at a time, at the High Court in Glasgow, a modern, marbled complex cut into a sandstone spur off the city's Briggait. Caroline Stevenson, sunbed brown, bleached blonde and dressed in black apart from her purple high heels, arrived at court with her son, Stevenson's co-accused Gerry Carbin Jnr. He was dressed in a fur-trimmed leather jacket and designer jeans and was accompanied by another blonde, his partner Karen Maxwell. Her family were no strangers to the High Court complex. Her father Robert Maxwell had appeared there a year earlier to receive a five-year jail sentence for dealing in heroin. It was his third long-term sentence for drugs. A drug-dealing dad was something she and her partner had in common. Carbin peered at the electronic information board designating the courts where the different cases were to be heard before heading to the canteen to wait. The co-accused, apart from one, joined them there.

Stevenson, himself, was the only one not to come through the court's airport-style security gates shortly before 10 a.m. He was the sole suspect of the ten now charged to remain in custody awaiting trial and, shortly after 11 a.m., he was led from a holding cell beneath the North Court flanked by a male and female security guard. They remained silent and straight-faced – in contrast to their prisoner. A deal had been struck and Stevenson, wearing black trousers and a black zipped cardigan, had every reason to smile. He knew the drugs charges had disappeared. He would not be tried for smuggling heroin and cocaine. He was no longer facing the threat of spending decades behind bars.

One source, aware of the legal negotiations, said:

Stevenson was happy enough. If the drugs charges had stood up, he'd have been looking at twenty-five to thirty years. With them gone, it was down to the money laundering and a maximum of fourteen years and the hope of seven or eight.

The number of suspects meant the court's dock was too small to accommodate them all and they would need to take their place in the benched box usually used by the jury. As he was led to the back row of the jury box, Stevenson, recognising familiar faces in the gallery, pointed and smiled. After being ushered into the back row of the jury box, Stevenson, leaning backwards, sat with his legs splayed and mouthed jokes to his supporters. As his guards sat staring straight ahead, Stevenson, ostensibly in the dock to face charges that could propel him behind bars for the next thirty years, was enjoying himself – he was, quite literally, playing to the gallery. Pulling faces and grinning while miming making a call on a mobile phone, he told one supporter that he'd call later – presumably from his cell in the remand wing of Edinburgh's Saughton jail.

When the rest of his gang were called and led to the two benches in front of him, he acknowledged each with a smile and a nod, as if they had just bumped into each other in the street. He grinned at his wife and stepson as they edged into the row directly in front. And, as he leaned over to whisper to them both in turn, the smile never left his face.

Outside in the air-conditioned, black-and-white tiled hallway beside the North Court, the mood seemed equally relaxed, as the defence teams chatted in groups before entering the courtroom through a side door. There was no sense of urgency or of last-minute negotiation. When the QCs crammed around the table before the bench with the ten accused packing the jury box, the court was about to hear public confirmation of what was already clear – a deal was all but done.

When asked if their clients were ready for trial, each QC, in turn, referred to McBride, who was acting for Carbin. Eventually, he rose to his feet to inform the court that his client was very close to reaching an agreement with the Crown. Ogg, representing Stevenson, stood next and he stated that the man accused of leading such a brutally effective and massively lucrative criminal enterprise had already reached an agreement with the Crown. That agreement, Ogg revealed, was capable of 'radically transforming' the indictment facing his client and the rest of the accused but, he insisted, that agreement would collapse if Carbin's legal team failed to find common ground with prosecutors as they edged towards agreement. No one in court – from the QCs to the alleged drug traffickers and money launderers looking bored in the dock – seemed to think that was likely.

After a hearing lasting no more than ten minutes, another was set for three weeks and one thing seemed certain – Stevenson would never face a jury. There would be no trial.

When they returned to court on Friday, 9 March, the men's lawyers had sealed the plea deal with prosecutors. Stevenson sat at the end of the dock, Carbin on his right, then Caroline and Karen. The other six men accused with them filled the row. At 2.30 p.m., the judge, Lord Hodge, formerly Patrick Hodge, a graduate of the Universities of Cambridge and Edinburgh, was told that Stevenson was pleading guilty to five charges of money laundering while Carbin admitted three charges.

As agreed, the two women were allowed to walk free while the six other men were also released but warned that they faced possible future prosecution. Even though Carbin was now facing a jail term, he was allowed to remain on bail to enjoy thirty precious days of freedom. His QC McBride stated:

He's twenty-seven with no previous convictions of any kind. He's never served any time in custody. He must sign in at a police station every day which he has done without fail. He has a fixed address, a partner of ten years and two young children, aged six years old and twenty months.

He and Stevenson were back in court on Thursday, 5 April, sitting together in the dock while their eight former co-accused sat in separate groups in the public gallery.

Murphy presented the Crown's case against the men, summarising the evidence that led to their guilty pleas. They were due to be sentenced that day but background reports to be presented to the judge were still not ready.

During this hearing, Carbin's QC McBride urged the judge to be lenient when sentencing his client in five days' time. He highlighted the recent seven-year sentence of Terry Adams – 'described in the popular press as a Godfather figure for what that is worth'. He also reminded the judge that the early guilty pleas had avoided a trial lasting several months, which would have cost 'millions of pounds'.

At the end of the short hearing, Stevenson hugged Carbin and smiled and winked at his wife and friends in the gallery before being led downstairs to the holding cells beneath the court.

When Stevenson left court after being sentenced five days later, on Tuesday, 10 April, the grin had been wiped from his face.

47
Different Country, Same Story

There was only a clutch of British gangsters whose operation and ambition outstripped Jamie Stevenson's. Terry Adams was undoubtedly one. It was coincidence that, in the spring of 2007, their falls coincided but the similarity in techniques deployed by the forces pursuing them was no accident. While the Met in London launched a covert, electronic surveillance offensive against Adams in a determined bid to follow his dirty money and find a weakness in his defences, their colleagues 400 miles north in Glasgow were using identical tactics against Stevenson.

The almost simultaneous convictions of two of Britain's biggest gangsters, who had, up until then, avoided serious prosecution, defined the modern battleground where police are waging war against the country's organised criminals.

Adams, fifty-two, was sentenced to seven years for laundering £1million – 'the tip of the iceberg', according to prosecutors – at the Old Bailey on 9 March 2007 almost exactly a month before Stevenson appeared in the dock at the High Court in Glasgow.

Both men had been the top-priority targets of detectives dedicated to investigating serious and organised criminals. Both believed themselves to be untouchable. Both would finally face justice over money-laundering charges after protracted police investigations – inquiries that, in Adams' case, had lasted ten years and, in Stevenson's, almost four. Both were convicted largely on the evidence contained in hundreds of hours of secretly recorded conversations. Both their wives were originally charged alongside them. Both wives were to walk free as part of their husbands' deals with prosecutors.

The Londoner was the leader of the Adams family, the managing director of a family crime firm known as the A Team and linked to more than thirty gangland murders. He and his brothers, Tommy and Patsy, had amassed an estimated fortune of £100 million in lifelong criminal careers that were founded on extortion, armed robbery, drugs trafficking and violence.

In 1998, Tommy was convicted of arranging an £8-million hash-smuggling operation and sentenced to seven years. At his sentencing, after being told he would face another five years if he did not hand over some of his dirty money, his wife turned up at court with a suitcase holding £1 million in cash. Four years later, and out of jail, Tommy was to bizarrely accompany ex-footballer Kenny Dalglish to a meeting when one of the Scotland legend's business associates would dispute the future contract of rising star Wayne Rooney with a rival agent. Dalglish has never explained Tommy Adams' invitation to the business meeting. Following Tommy's release, Patsy and Tommy moved to southern Spain where they both now live.

The police investigating their big brother Terry called on the surveillance expertise of MI5 and, for two years, sophisticated listening devices, including one buried deep in a sofa, transmitted conversations from Terry's cars and inside his fortified mansion in Finchley, north London, where he lived with his wife Ruth. They were able to pick up conversations that revealed Adams' capacity for violence and the problems he had in justifying his massive criminal fortune. In one conversation, he tells an associate of an encounter over a disputed debt.

A hundred grand it was, Dan, or eighty grand. And I went 'crack'. On my baby's life, Dan, his kneecap came right out there ... all white, Dan, all bone and white.

When I hit someone I do them damage.

After the Inland Revenue begin asking difficult questions of the millionaire, who was apparently jobless and paid no tax or National Insurance, his financial adviser Solly Nahome is heard telling him that the priority is to legitimise his fortune. 'We've got to think of a way of koshering you up,' says Nahome, who was shot dead outside his home in the same street as Terry Adams' mansion in a gangland hit in 1998. The method of execution, a motorcycle drive-by, had been adopted by a rival crime gang after it had been pioneered by Patsy Adams.

Like Stevenson, Adams created sham businesses to justify his income and used jewellery to launder some of his money through Nahome, who also traded in London's diamond quarter, Hatton Garden.

Like the car-valeting, jewellery-trading Stevenson, he had various attempts at convincing the authorities of his occupation. In another covertly taped conversation, Adams told a pal, 'I'm a consultant, Tone. I consult about anything you want me to consult about.'

When police finally raided the Adams' home, they found £500,000 of antiques and paintings – many of them stolen – £48,000 of jewellery and a shoebox in the attic stuffed with £60,000 'spending money'.

Adams was originally charged in 2003 but dragged the proceedings out for four more years. One delaying tactic was to sack his legal team. Another was to demand that twenty-one months of largely irrelevant bugged conversations should be transcribed at a cost to taxpayers of £2.7 million.

Sentencing him, Judge Timothy Pontius said he had 'a fertile, cunning and imaginative mind, capable of sophisticated complex and dishonest financial manipulation'.

Andrew Mitchell QC for the prosecution told the Old Bailey, 'It is suggested that Terence Adams was one of the country's most feared and revered organised criminals. He comes with pedigree, as one of a family whose name had a currency all of its own in the underworld.'

In spring 2007, the conviction of a third major criminal, Brian Wright, secured more headlines as law enforcers took on the underworld's untouchables. Within weeks of Adams and Stevenson appearing in the dock, Wright, reputedly Britain's richest criminal, was convicted after police dismantled one of the world's biggest cocaine-trafficking operations. Nicknamed 'The Milkman' because he always delivered, Wright amassed a £500-million fortune through using luxury yachts to ferry tonnes of drugs to Europe from Venezuela through the Caribbean.

Irish-born Wright, sixty, a notorious punter and fixer of horse races, had escaped justice in 2003 when he fled to Turkish northern Cyprus, where he was safe from extradition. But, in 2005, he returned to his villa – called 'El Lechero' – in Malaga, on the Costa del Sol, where he was arrested by British Customs officers who were armed with one of the recently introduced European warrants.

The arrogant Godfather told one officer, 'I bet you £1 of your money against £1 million of mine that I will never stand trial.'

He lost his bet at Woolwich Crown Court in early April 2007 when he was jailed for thirty years.

As his lawyer was pleading for a lighter sentence, Wright interrupted him and addressed Judge Peter Moss, saying, 'Excuse me, your honour, there is no mitigation.'

Stevenson was the next to fall. It was to complete a remarkable hat-trick for Britain's law enforcers.

48
Frozen Out

Almost four years after Operation Folklore was launched, under the strictest secrecy, against him, Jamie Stevenson faced a very public day of reckoning. He stood in the dock of the High Court in Glasgow on Tuesday, 10 April 2007, waiting to be sentenced. Looking smart in a blue pinstripe suit and open-necked pink shirt, he appeared ready for business. Worryingly for him, so did the judge, Lord Hodge. He listened intently as Crown prosecutor Sean Murphy summarised the evidence against Stevenson and his stepson Carbin, who was wearing a grey suit and white shirt.

The lawyers had done the deal. Stevenson and Carbin admitted laundering more than £1 million of drugs money. In return, the charges detailing their cocaine and heroin smuggling and Stevenson's false passport would be dropped. Their partners, Caroline and Karen, had already walked free.

The judge was told how Stevenson and Carbin were in court to admit 'laundering substantial proceeds from drugs trafficking, including trafficking in class A drugs'. He heard how the surveillance operation against the pair was authorised in May 2003 as part of the SCDEA's 'extensive undercover operation' and how, by autumn 2005, electronic listening devices had been hidden in both their homes. Much of the case against them, the judge heard, rested on conversations recorded by those bugs.

The prosecutor took the judge through each of the five charges that had been brought under the Proceeds of Crime Act 2002 and which one or both of the men were admitting. Most related to Section 327 of the Act, which makes it illegal to hide, disguise, transfer or remove criminal assets.

They both admitted the first charge of hiding £204,510 of dirty money. This sum had been found by police searching Carbin's house in Campsie Road, East Kilbride. Murphy told how a man, identified only as 'Kevin', came to the home of Carbin and his partner Karen Maxwell looking for Stevenson on Saturday, 21 January 2006. He arrived at 6.40 p.m. carrying a large holdall and he was heard being told that Stevenson was out for a meal with his wife. He was only there for ten minutes but, in that time, he mentioned a figure 'two-o-four' and, when he departed, he left behind the bag. Murphy said:

> Once he had gone, it is apparent from the conversation that Gerard Carbin attempted unsuccessfully to place the holdall within a cupboard in the house, after which he placed it in the corner of a room and pushed a chair up against it.
>
> Police officers suspected that a large quantity of cash had been delivered and a warrant to search the house was obtained. Officers attended in the early hours of Sunday, 22 January 2006, and were admitted by Gerard Carbin. On being asked if there was any money in the house, Carbin replied, '£10,000 or something like that. Aye, let's go.'

He led officers to a white polythene bag in a kitchen cupboard. It held £9,550 and the bundles of cash were secured by elastic bands. In the study next to the kitchen, the recently delivered holdall was found and it contained £204,510. Murphy continued:

Carbin was asked to whom it belonged and he answered, 'No comment.' He then became agitated and shouted and swore at the officers. A further £400 was found in the pocket of a jacket in an upstairs cupboard and Carbin directed the police to a second bundle of notes making up another £400 in a bedroom unit. It was noted that there were a number of high-value watches within a bedroom but these were not seized at that time.

At the conclusion of the search, Gerard Carbin was taken to Hamilton police station where he was interviewed on tape. He made no comment throughout the interview.

After being released without charge, Carbin went to Stevenson's home in Burnside. During Carbin's visit, his stepfather described the cash as 'our money' and repeatedly said that he would tell the police it was his profits from selling cars and jewellery. He told Carbin, as police eavesdroppers listened in, 'I never have any money in the house.'

Stevenson alone admitted the second charge of using £98,605 of drugs money to buy ten Skoda Octavias for a taxi business called CS Cars. The firm was licensed in the name of his wife Caroline Stevenson and registered at the couple's home in Burnside. The prosecutor said Stevenson had bought the Octavia saloons from a Hamilton showroom in February 2006, paying for them with four cheques and a £10,105 cash payment.

Glasgow City Council awarded taxi licences to the firm meant to be run by Caroline but Murphy added: 'It is clear from overheard and monitored conversations that [Stevenson] himself was the guiding hand behind the operation. It is equally clear that the entire operation was designed to launder criminal proceeds.'

The third charge involved the attempted concealment of £389,035 of drugs money and this too was admitted by Stevenson alone. He had been recorded in conversation at his home on 16 May 2006 discussing a 'large and bulky' stash of money in a safe at another house. He asked his associate if it had been counted and 'if the safe had been big enough to contain it all'. Two days after the conversation, two men were followed by surveillance officers to the house where the money was hidden. The men came out carrying a large suitcase that they put in their boot. Stopped by police, the case was opened and £389,035 was found inside. Within fifteen minutes, a call to Burnside had delivered the bad news to Stevenson. Murphy told the court, 'Later that night, the police monitored a conversation at James Stevenson's home in which he expressed concern over the possibility of those who had been stopped talking to the police about his involvement.' He would be on his way to Amsterdam within hours.

Carbin admitted the fourth and penultimate charge summarised by the prosecutor that he was holding £7,820 of drugs money found by officers raiding his home in the Folklore busts. The prosecutor explained:

> On 20 September 2006, police officers moved to detain and arrest a number of persons to draw the operation to a conclusion. Officers in possession of a search warrant attended at Gerard Carbin's home address where entry was forced when no one answered the door. On searching the premises, the officers found cash within a box and two envelopes which were beside each other in a cupboard in the kitchen. The amounts were subsequently found to total £7,820. Gerard Carbin and his wife were detained and removed to Govan police station.

Finally, Stevenson and Carbin jointly admitted a fifth charge of spending £307,087 of dirty money on fifty-five luxury watches between December 2003 and September 2006. Forty-four of the watches – all of them luxury brands, including Rolex, Cartier, Dior and a £30,000 Audemars Piguet

– had been found in the homes searched by police in the early morning raids that brought Folklore to its conclusion.

The prosecutor said:

> It became clear to the police, from a number of the monitored conversations, that the accused had disposed of cash assets by purchasing a number of watches of very high value. The police learned that Carbin and Stevenson had bought these principally through Mappin & Webb, jewellers in Glasgow, and Strang's, a jewellers in Newton Mearns, on the southern outskirts of Glasgow. Stevenson, in particular had bought a number of watches for cash. Other rare examples and collectors' items had been ordered by him and some very high-price examples had been reserved and paid for in cash instalments over periods of months.

On 17 December 2005, officers overheard Carbin discussing his stepfather's Christmas present, a £3,500 Breitling watch. He had bought him a £9,000 Rolex Daytona the year before. He, in turn, had received a handsome Jacobs watch as a festive token from his stepfather.

Murphy went on to give further details of the conversation between the men in the hours after the bag containing drugs cash had been seized in Carbin's home, saying:

> In the course of the meeting at James Stevenson's house on the afternoon after the police had recovered £204,000 from a holdall in Gerard Carbin's house, a discussion took place involving both accused in which it was noted that the police had filmed a number of high-value watches within 44 Campsie Road in the course of the search. Thereafter, these were removed from Carbin's house and passed to Stevenson for safekeeping.

Inquiries were made of the various jewellers who had been involved in the sale of the watches with the result that the police were able to establish that the two accused between them appeared to have purchased a total of fifty-five watches with a total value of £307,087 over the period between December 2003 and September 2006.

In short, Stevenson and Carbin admitted laundering over £1-million profits from drugs trafficking over the four years of Operation Folklore.

The judge told Carbin, 'It is clear from the Crown narrative that you had a significant role in the money-laundering group in which your stepfather was the head. You are described as one of his senior associates.'

He sentenced Carbin to a total of eleven years and nine months for the three charges that he admitted. Crucially, they were to run concurrently meaning the longest single sentence – five years and six months – would be used to calculate how long he should spend behind bars. With parole, he could hope to be free in just over three. Carbin, fearing a longer sentence, had fittingly just 'won a watch', as they say in the West of Scotland.

Stevenson was the biggest criminal to face money-laundering charges since Scots prosecutors began chasing their dirty fortunes; the first to be hemmed into the dock by the weight of thousands of hours of evidence amassed through electronic surveillance and painstakingly transcribed; and the biggest scalp possible for Scotland's law enforcers.

Stevenson was hoping for seven years, maybe eight. Lord Hodge had other ideas. Sentencing him to nine years and nine months for the charges involving the cash and watches and a further three years for the taxi firm launched with dirty money, the judge said Stevenson had been caught as his criminal operations were 'developing and expanding'. He said:

It is clear that your illegal activities were developing over time. You had also two large sums of money, which were the proceeds of crime. This also confirms your position at a very high level in the criminal hierarchy. The charges to which you have pleaded guilty represent a high level of criminality. This must be reflected in the sentence.

The judge acknowledged the police assault on the underworld's financial systems because money laundering 'went hand in hand with the drugs trade and contributed materially to its profitability. Operation Folklore was a big success because, all too frequently, it is the small players who are detected and punished.'

Stevenson, in court the day before his forty-second birthday, listened impassively. He gave a thumbs-up to the gallery as he was taken down to the holding cells below the court to begin his sentence. Despite his bluff show of defiance, the sentence was several years longer than he had prepared for. The Iceman had been frozen out. In Springburn, where the McGoverns were still a force, a few glasses were raised by his enemies to toast Stevenson's fall.

Afterwards, Detective Superintendent Stephen Ward, the SCDEA's crime co-ordinator, noted that the capture of Stevenson, the elite agency's number one target, was a signal to the others. He said:

> Stevenson considered himself untouchable. I think today's outcome very clearly indicates that any individual or group involved in serious organised crime in Scotland cannot consider themselves untouchable.
>
> We've worked very closely with colleagues all over the world. Every part of the agency has been touched by this operation from surveillance units to technical support. This type of activity, law enforcement, is the way we conduct our operations. We target the very top people involved

in serious organised crime in Scotland and that's why operations like this can take years. We will use every lawful tool in the box to bring these individuals to the courts. We did use sophisticated listening devices in Stevenson's home address and that technique is one of the lawful tools in the box.

Organised crime is led by ruthless and dangerous individuals who seek to make profit from the pain and suffering of the most vulnerable people in our communities. The public expect our response to be tough. I promise those involved in this evil organised crime that this agency will remove them from their positions of influence and confiscate their money, jewellery, cars and houses.

49
Only the Start

Graeme Pearson enjoyed the moment. Word had come through from the High Court that Scotland's most serious and organised criminal was going to jail thanks to a four-year operation mounted by the Scottish Crime and Drug Enforcement Agency. The targeting of Stevenson by the agency almost exactly coincided with Pearson's arrival as its director and he was quietly satisfied that his team had succeeded in putting the man, who had been their priority target for years, behind bars.

The policeman then in charge of an annual £23-million budget to battle Scotland's most serious criminals believes Folklore revealed how even self-styled untouchables like Stevenson can be put in the dock and taken off the streets of Scotland. Before Pearson stood down from the SCDEA in late 2007, he sat in his first-floor office at the agency's fortress-like headquarters minutes from Glasgow Airport and reviewed the tortuous progress of Folklore and the far-reaching consequences of the operation's success. He said:

> Looking back, you see all those years of effort on behalf of hundreds of people in constructing the evidence possible to convict someone like Stevenson. It is amazing the sheer effort and professionalism of so many people across so many specialisms, from the intelligence teams through to investigation and surveillance. It is a remarkable feat. The impact of Stevenson and Carbin is that they made

millions of pounds for Organised Crime Plc and it was highly disciplined in the way that it was run.

I think it was a major coup for the agency. It has sent a message to others who may have regarded him as a role model, as someone to emulate. He probably regarded himself as untouchable. Other criminals certainly regarded him as untouchable and were genuinely surprised that he was even arrested, never mind convicted.

People said throughout the period when he was on remand that he would get out. That was the belief so, when he was convicted, it caused a real sensation amongst fellow criminals. They knew that, if we could do Stevenson, then we could do them.

Pearson, fifty-eight, explained that Stevenson had been vigilant and careful and had encouraged his gang to share his caution.

His advice to his group was to stay four or five steps away from the business, from the product. Our job was to close those steps. The closer you get to the main players, the less product you get. It's the couriers, the minions that get caught. It's always going to be the worker bees that are connected to seizures. If you are biding your time waiting for their bosses to come into a room with contraband, then you will be waiting for a long time. Someone might be stopped on the motorway at 2 a.m. with 100 kilos of heroin but Stevenson will be miles away, tucked up in bed.

Pearson admits there was some frustration at the agency when news came through that the drugs charges against Stevenson had been dropped but he added:

I think it was realistic. With hindsight, it was a professional decision. In my career, the Stevenson case has probably been the most challenging in terms of organisation and professionalism and how they went about their business but it was never a personal issue for me – if it becomes personal, it's because they make it personal.

What it's about is Folklore. There should be more Folklores and whether it's Stevenson or anyone else does not matter.

It was part of our lives here for almost four years. We remained committed to it. It would have been easy to walk away and just gone after the shipments and the people at the bottom. Personally, I think that is wrong – we need to go for those at the top level of the tree and crush the branches.

It seems that Pearson was destined to take charge of the SCDEA. He even shares his birthday – April Fools' Day – with the date the agency was inaugurated. When the then SDEA came into being on 1 April 2001, Pearson was an assistant chief constable with Strathclyde Police. In March 2004, he was recruited to take charge of the agency. He led a team of 197 officers and seventy-seven civilians that has, since its launch, arrested 1284 people and seized almost 20 tonnes of drugs with an estimated street value of £206 million.

Even early in his career, the University of Glasgow graduate's raw enthusiasm for jailing criminals impressed his more experienced colleagues and he never lost his passion for catching wrongdoers. He believes their removal from the streets makes communities better places to live. He questions claims that a 'war on drugs' is unwinnable because other gangsters will quickly move in to take over the trade of jailed rivals. He said:

The bottom line is [that] what we did with Stevenson and what we do with others like him is worth it. I was speaking to some prisoners at Polmont Young Offenders Institution a couple of months back not long after we seized the *Squilla* in Spain. They were saying to me as the director general of SCDEA that they could not get cannabis and none of their friends on the outside could either. There was a dearth of cannabis for some time. I don't think it's true that there is no impact in what we do. I know that there was a dearth of heroin for some time.

There is a constant movement of supply and demand and other people will move in but they won't replicate Stevenson's organisation very quickly. Given the complexity of what he was doing, you cannot take part of his organisation and copy it within a week.

Folklore's other legacy will be a database of priceless intelligence about Stevenson's wholesaling of drugs to other Scottish gangs. Pearson said:

The impact will continue. There are lots of bits of evidence lying about that will continue to be used – like time-delay explosions, they will keep going off over the months and years to come. A piece of evidence from Folklore could lie dormant and then something else happens and suddenly that matches up with it.

None of these criminal groups operate in isolation. There are other groups in Scotland who are very sensitive just now because they had contact right into the heart of Stevenson's organisation. They all know that they have been linked to the Stevenson bust and they know this information is lying there waiting to fall into place.

Pearson estimates that Scotland is home to around 150 people, possibly even more, who are millionaires as a result of crime. His greatest fear is that the dirty millions generated from drugs, prostitution, fraud and other organised crime will seep into the fabric of Scottish society. Councillors, MSPs and officials are groomed by mobsters as useful friends with power and influence. Like legitimate businessmen, criminals will attend black-tie charity dinners to entertain powerful guests and make influential contacts. The point where business ends and corruption begins shades into grey.

High-profile examples of the nexus between crime and politics were the three Scottish Labour Party fund-raising Red Rose Dinners staged at Dalziel Park Golf and Country Club in Lanarkshire. The then First Minister, Jack McConnell, the MP, Frank Roy, and the then Northern Ireland Secretary, John Reid, rubbed shoulders with the area's businessmen.

The events would have gone unnoticed were it not for the fact that, six days after the third dinner in 2002, one of those who attended was shot dead in a drugs war. Following the murder of twenty-eight-year-old Justin McAlroy, it emerged that he and his father Tommy, a co-owner of the country club, had been spotted in Estonia meeting two Scottish heroin smugglers who were under SCDEA surveillance. One of McAlroy Snr's firms won £9.3 million of work from Labour-controlled North Lanarkshire Council. His building firm had been a financial supporter of the local Labour party.

Pearson declines to discuss specific events or personalities but warns:

> If we are complacent it will overcome us. This isn't the business of cops and robbers any more – the stakes are [very] different. What drives so many of the high-level criminals is not so much wealth – that's almost a by-product – it is power, influence and stature. In Colombia, the drug barons don't just want to be drug barons, they want to run the country. In Italy, with the Mafia, it's exactly the same. US crime gangs wanted to own City Hall and, in fact, did corrupt police forces. We would be so naive to think it's going to be different in Scotland.

Why do criminals want to sit with politicians? In days gone by, why would a licensing official attend an event with Arthur Thompson? Were his jokes that good? You often just need to look at someone who has paid £2,000 for a football strip in a charity auction to get an idea of what they are.

These businesses need planning permission – they need licences. In days past, the gangsters controlled their own local environment for status, power and control. They're now taking it to a new level.

Asked if corruption had taken deep root in Scotland, Pearson is unable to answer, saying, 'I don't know is the true answer. I'd like to think there is very little. I think it's parochial enough that we'd get to know about it.'

Pearson believes the financial isolation of organised criminals is the key to putting them out of business. He said:

They need these advisers to help them to clean their money – they can't do it themselves. We need to break into a couple of these. I'd like to create a sea around an island of organised crime. They might have £1 million but they can't spend it and then we come and take it from them.

The international contacts built by Stevenson stretched across the world and Pearson believes some of the challenges faced by the Folklore team will become commonplace because of the globalisation of crime. He commented:

It was surprising how efficient his international contacts were and how easily they were made. You have to remember that they operate at an advantage. They can just get up, buy a bucket seat for £20 and, three hours later, they're in mainland Europe, hiring a car, driving to another country and doing their business.

It's not just getting officers on the plane, driving after them, tracking their phones. It's quickly getting to the people in foreign jurisdictions who can authorise that and supply assistance if required. These guys don't have to phone ahead to get authorisation to go to a country and commit crime. They jump on a plane and take off . . .

Folklore touched three continents – the Americas, Europe and Africa – but it can take weeks, even months, to find a way into another criminal jurisdiction. The problem is getting law enforcement agencies to co-operate with each other. Historically, we have always viewed ourselves as nation states with distinct borders but that is not how these guys see the world. They do not see a map with boundaries and borders. They see the world as a bus route and they get on and off the bus where they like. They get off, do business and get back on.

International crime groups commit crime in Scotland but we're not really on the beaten track for that. Places like Scotland become interesting if we make it easy. Organised crime will weigh up the risks in doing business here and, when they see that we seize assets and jail them and do so quickly, that should put them off coming here.

Increasingly it will become a world community. We're going to find it very difficult to see each other in the tribal ways that we did. Criminals gangs are co-operating a great deal more in pursuit of their interests. We want to make life very difficult so they think, 'To hell with this – we'd better go somewhere else. It's time to get on the bus and go elsewhere.'

I think Scotland has got a reasonable reputation in that regard. Certainly some of the English criminal gangs find us pretty draconian in policing and in sentencing from the courts. Some Liverpool criminals up here got fifteen-year sentences when they would have got three or four years at home. They were wondering what kind of country this was. That's the message we want to send out. We're here to look after the Scottish community and the Scottish economy.

Pearson has explored various legal methods that could be adopted to make life more uncomfortable for high-level criminals. In recent years, businesses like law firms, estate agents and car dealers have been obliged by law to disclose suspicious cash transactions. Any such transaction 'with a kilt' – or Scottish angle – now passes through the SCDEA for analysis. The thousands of little jigsaw pieces of information can create a vivid picture.

Lifetime financial reports are soon to be introduced, compelling the targets to disclose details of their financial affairs for many years. Pearson also believes that the tag of 'career criminal' could be given to those suspected of involvement in organised crime. He said:

I would like to see people characterised as serious and organised criminals. We could then put pressure on every one. Every time they are involved in an alleged offence, no matter how minor, we would treat it seriously because it is a serious criminal involved. A breach of the peace at a nightclub is the kind of thing that these men often walk away from. Perhaps officers think there is little point in pursuing serious criminals for something so minor. Perhaps the case drags on and a year later witnesses are unavailable or do not remember. Whatever the reason, they walk away and that adds to this image of them as somehow untouchable. That would change. As soon as one of these criminals is involved in something, however mundane, detectives would be there taking statements, getting witnesses, getting forensics and fingerprints. The case would be flagged to the Crown and fast-tracked into court with a far greater likelihood of these guys being put in the dock and getting convicted of something. That will send a message.

They believe they can behave how they want and get away with it. That's why you get people like Stevenson being convicted of serious organised crime yet he has no previous convictions. How does that happen?

Pearson also believes that the fortunes paid out in Legal Aid to suspects later convicted of serious crime should be clawed back and he hails the introduction of Organised Crime Prevention Orders intended to curb criminals' travel. However, he believes Operation Folklore has only underlined the increasing focus on the dirty millions being stashed and laundered as the authorities open a new front in the war against serious and organised crime.

Pearson stepped down from the SCDEA amid speculation that he fears the expanding role of the recently formed Police Services Authority will undermine the fight against serious and organised crime. However, he believes his old agency's priority must remain the disruption, if not detention, of Scotland's most successful criminals. He said:

The landscape has changed and people need to understand that. Money laundering is going to be key. It's a question of following the money. Operation Folklore defines what we are about as an agency. Ultimately, it is up to the people of Scotland to debate and decide if what we are doing here is worthwhile – if we should be doing more Folklores.

50
Down but Out?

It took four years for Operation Folklore to put Stevenson behind bars but, with good behaviour, he may not spend that much longer in jail. There is nothing to suggest he will not be a model prisoner. In Shotts jail, where he joined Scotland's most serious criminals in May 2007 after being held on remand at Edinburgh's Saughton Prison, he is vocal in his determination to do his time and get out to his wife, family and fortune as soon as possible. He is applying to the Open University Business School. He says he is going straight.

Stevenson has shrugged off reports that his old enemies in Springburn might still have a thirst for revenge now that he is a captive target. One ally who has spoken to him about an alleged McGovern plot to have him killed in jail for a £50,000 bounty said:

> He's laughing about it. He thinks they're dafties. His biggest regret is not taking care of them all when he had the chance.
>
> Robert O'Hara, who threw the can of Coke at Stevenson, was meant to be an ally of the McGoverns but he now seems as thick as thieves with Jamie. They were meant to be deadly enemies and people thought O'Hara might have a go at Stevenson but they wander around the exercise yard talking with each other.
>
> Shotts is like most jails – if you've got money, it's a lot

easier. Guys like Stevenson can lay their hands on pretty much anything they want.

Stevenson might be inside but he's got so many formidable guys still loyal to him on the outside. I don't think he's bothered at the moment but, if he has to take care of the McGoverns or anyone else by remote control, then he will. It's not his priority though.

The main concern is for his wife. The friend said:

He's worried about Caroline – about how she's coping on her own. The authorities are still all over his money so she was having a wee cash-flow problem after he got jailed. He's tasked some guys to chase up debts that are owed. There's four guys in particular who owe him a fair bit of money – amounts like £300,000. I would imagine his people will be fairly effective in collecting once they find them.

One of Stevenson's associates is twenty-eight-year-old Barry Hughes, a millionaire boxing promoter. The former lightweight fighter, nicknamed 'Braveheart' in the ring, made money from car sales and property deals. Another ally said:

Stevenson knows Hughes well and received a couple of visits from him while at Saughton. Hughes has been asked to ensure that Caroline is all right for cash in the meantime.

The business Stevenson is in, jail is an occupational hazard. You can run your end of things like clockwork but you're at the mercy of events, of other people doing their job. You've no insurance if you get banged up. Your pals outside are your insurance – what you've managed to amass and stash away is your insurance.

He says he's going legitimate – that he's had enough. But it's in his blood. I don't think he'll do anything to rock the boat unless he can't avoid it. He's determined to do his sentence and get out as quickly and painlessly as possible.

Stevenson's high-powered legal team are currently preparing an appeal against the length of his sentence but, even if they are unsuccessful in having it reduced – or, Stevenson's worst-case scenario, it is lengthened – he is likely to serve a maximum of eight years behind bars. One lawyer, with knowledge of the case, said the decision to drop the drugs-smuggling charges could signal a sea change in future prosecutions. He said:

> If the drugs [charges] had stayed, Stevenson would have been looking at twenty-five, thirty years – easily. He might never have got out. Instead of which, he'll be out training for freedom in six years or so. He'll be on home visits doing his Christmas shopping in Sauchiehall Street in 2013. He's a white-collar criminal – no drugs, no violence, good behaviour inside. He got twelve years and nine months. Take off his remand time, he's down to twelve and could be out after half. That is not a long time. Not when you fully appreciate the time, energy and money that went into Folklore.
>
> Of course, the evidence is the biggest factor in what happens with these plea deals but you'd be naive to think it is the only thing that matters. The Crown are under so much pressure that tying up a court for four, five, six months is a huge consideration. The trial would easily have cost £5 million, probably more, without any certainty of getting the right verdict at the end of it. That's a lot to commit to when you're being offered the chance to jail the bad guys right now for free.
>
> Stevenson's stepson Carbin got concurrent sentences so basically he ended up with little more than five years or so. It's the same sentence as some drunk going into a

corner shop with a water pistol and demanding a bottle of Buckfast. He's helped import tonnes and tonnes of drugs, made millions and he'll be walking out the gates in a couple of years beside the bam with the water gun.

The legal source highlighted the case of Gordon McLeod, fifty-one, who was jailed for nine years in August 2005 after heroin worth £10 million was found at his home in Uddingston, Lanarkshire. Detectives believe the consignment was one of Stevenson's but could never prove it. The experienced defence lawyer said:

> It's hard not to compare that sentence to Stevenson's. McLeod was a minion, a foot soldier, but was getting the same stretch, give or take a few years, as the millionaire criminal running the show for years and years. I've no sympathy for McLeod but, if he deserves nine years, then Stevenson should never see the light of day.
>
> I can understand why the police would be spitting nails about Stevenson and they must be asking if it's worth the candle. Is it worth all the man-hours, all the surveillance, to get to the drugs when they are only pleading to the money? Let's just go after the money.

Since April 2007, the SCDEA has been exempt from freedom of information laws which means that the full cost of Folklore is unlikely to ever be made public. One detective, who worked on surveillance during Folklore, agrees that the operation is one of the most expensive ever pursued in Scotland but insists the investment was justified.

> It would have been cheaper to have gone to Stevenson and said, 'Look, here's a million quid, now piss off.' But you can't put a price on the message his conviction has sent out to men like him. We get accused of only getting to the

small fish, the guys near the bottom of the pile. Well, you don't get any bigger than Stevenson.

He thought he was untouchable – so far up the chain that we couldn't get to him even if we tried. Well, putting him away shows we can get anyone and that is going to alarm the others like him.

They know we're not kidding.

Stevenson and Carbin were back side by side in the dock eight weeks after being sentenced as the Crown launched an offensive against their hidden fortunes. The hearing in June 2007 was intended to strip Scotland's biggest criminal of the millions of pounds made from his international drugs-trafficking business. It was adjourned until later in the summer, but the legal process was still grinding on nine months later, when Stevenson had still to lose a single penny to the Crown's official asset-strippers.

Then they were targeting £2 million of criminal assets, but Stevenson's counsel Jane Farquharson told the High Court in Edinburgh that the Scottish Legal Aid Board had drawn the line at funding a forensic accountant to test the Crown's assessment of his fortune. After protracted haggling, the publicly-funded SLAB had finally agreed to pay the accountant's fee. As the men were being brought upstairs from the cells, Carbin briefly burst into song, his voice clearly heard in the court above. Stevenson just laughed.